THE NEW WORLD
OF THE CHILDREN

THE NEW
WORLD OF THE CHILDREN

VOLUME TWO

New Caxton Library Service Limited

LONDON

Printed and Bound in Great Britain by
Hazell Watson & Viney Limited
Aylesbury, Bucks, and
Cymmer, Glamorgan

CONTENTS

This edition is intended for infants and up to a 13 year age group, it also includes a guide to parents. It is complete in itself, references to other pages and volumes can be ignored.

VOLUME TWO

v

SECTION EIGHT
THE FINE ARTS

SECTION NINE

PAST, PRESENT AND FUTURE

Section Six

TWENTIETH-CENTURY SCIENCE

Section Six: Twentieth-Century Science

Chapter 1

INTRODUCTION

Towards the end of the nineteenth century scientists became dissatisfied with the space and time concepts of Euclid, Newton and other intellectual giants of the past. Fresh discoveries in the domain of physics and astronomy were proving inconsistent with natural law as defined by classic formulæ. The disturbance to preconceived ideas was profound, and for a while science suffered something of a set-back in public esteem. In the middle of the nineteenth century the scientists had been convinced that they were on the brink of discovering the ultimate secrets of the universe. A few had been rather boastful. Now, at the turn of the century, all their calculations, so recently assumed to be final and correct, were being upset by alarming anomalies in experimental determinations. It was not a single instance of " the result that would not come right"; it was an ever-growing host of quite inexplicable deviations. Worst of all was the negative result of an important experiment by Michelson and Morley to determine the velocity of drift of the all-pervading ether that was then confidently imagined to fill all space and be the means of transmitting heat, light and other radiations. The experiment seemed to deny that this ether was any more than a figment of the imagination.

A few bold spirits began to examine matters that had been treated as axiomatic. They worked at these things mathematically in order to find out what alteration in preconceived ideas would be needed to give new formulæ that agreed with the whole range of scientific observations, recent as well as ancient. Boldest of these spirits was the late Albert Einstein. He managed to write all the known observational determinations of astronomy and physics in a mutually consistent set of equations, and although these new equations did not supersede the classic equations for everyday practical purposes they did require people to believe some very extraordinary new things about the universe. For one thing, they upset the idea that matter was indestructible and uncreatable—that the sum total of matter in the universe always remained the same. Einstein asserted that matter could be converted into energy and vice versa. He said that such transformation escaped notice where the amounts of energy involved were small—as in chemical changes—but became noticeable in certain new experiments, particularly those concerned with radio-activity.

Einstein asserted also that in certain circumstances light travelled in curves and not in straight lines; therefore the assumed straightness observed by optical methods was sometimes fallacious. He asserted many other things, and it all added up to a new and by no means easily comprehensible view of the universe. His work has given us the so-called " Theory of Relativity," which is generally agreed to be rather more than a mere untested theory to-day. According to Einstein, there is no need to postulate an all-pervading ether in space. The presence of massive bodies leads to a curvature of adjacent space; consequently neighbouring bodies are obliged to move in curves instead of in straight lines. This curved motion could give rise to inertia effects like those we attribute to gravitation under the possibly mistaken impression that there is a mutual attraction between massive bodies acting across empty space.

So great is the revolution in ideas caused by Einstein and his fellow mathematicians that scientists no longer believe our universe to be of a kind we can readily envisage in the mind's eye; it can now be described only in mathematical terms, not visual ones. Mathematics can easily deal with things outside our comprehension, and a very simple instance of its doing so can be given here. An equation relating two variable quantities (say x and y) together can be shown to represent a line drawn on a flat surface (a graph). An equation relating three variables (x, y and z) represents a surface—for instance a cone, a sphere, a cylinder or simply a plane. Thus any equation admits of a geometrical (two- or three-dimensional) interpretation so long as it connects not more than three variables. But it is just as easy to write an equation connecting four, five, six or indeed any number of variables, and not one of these can possibly define a picture in the mind. This is only one of many instances where algebra easily outruns geometry, and hence the powers of the human imagination.

Einstein's equations suggest that the universe is really a four-dimensional affair in which we must reckon not only with the usual three dimensions of space (length, breadth and depth) but with some fourth dimension as well. The dimension in question is TIME, and the concepts of Relativity require us to believe that the mass and physical dimensions of material objects are affected by movements of these objects. Thus, a rod moving lengthwise becomes shorter; and if its speed of movement approaches the speed of light then it becomes very short indeed.

It will now be apparent that the science of the twentieth century differs from the science of preceding centuries in failing to give us readily acceptable visual images of what goes on in nature. It is satisfied to defy and even outrage common sense and give a mathematical account with little or no relation to everyday human experience. It goes forward in blind faith, like an aviator trusting to his instruments in a fog.

But although the thinking of scientists has left all of us behind, and destroyed our once clear picture of the universe without substituting another, it still yields positive results. Without cease it has gone on giving us new marvels of invention and discovery. Some of these marvels are difficult to describe—electronic calculating machines, for instance—but others lend themselves to description in their more elementary forms. The purpose of this section is to describe some of these practical scientific developments of the twentieth century, grouping them roughly under the two heads of electronics and nuclear physics.

Radio, television and radar come under the head of electronics. On the border-line between the two is the phenomenon of X-rays. Nuclear physics has given us the heat-producing pile for electricity generation, the fission (uranium or plutonium) bomb and the fusion (hydrogen) bomb; also activated materials for use in medical and other branches of research. Finally, nuclear physics has given us the answer to some very puzzling questions, chief among which is the question of how our sun manages to pour out light and heat endlessly for millions of years without appearing to suffer any diminution in size or brightness.

What is the place given to twentieth-century science in our schools and colleges? The answer must be hardly any place at all, because its principles are to be mastered only by going through a course in orthodox science to begin with—the sort of science dealt with in Volume III of this work. Very few young people graduate in orthodox science and mathematics well enough to pursue their studies to the level where they can comprehend the work of the latter-day physicists and mathematicians. Our more brilliant students must proceed to an honours degree course in physics at a first-rate university if they wish to meet professors who are capable of giving them up-to-the-minute instruction in the most modern developments.

The man-in-the-street must accept such explanation of modern marvels as he can be made to grasp, and the same applies to children. In the chapters which follow, no further attempt has been made to explain what scientists are thinking, but only to describe what they are doing in practical fields, such as engineering, medicine and so forth. Everyone should possess some rudimentary knowledge of what is going on in science because their lives are already being touched by the new science at many points. Some of its accomplishments might seem like sorcery or witchcraft to anyone who had not been adequately initiated. However, the marvels of one generation readily become the commonplaces of the next, and less than thirty years hence there may be popular acceptance not only of the new aids to living that twentieth-century science is giving us, but also of the novel and difficult concepts that seem to be in defiance of ordinary human common sense. That "things are not what they seem" in our universe is now past all doubting, and the time to begin acquainting children with this truth is here and now. They do not have, as yet, the illusions that pre-twentieth-century experience has foisted upon us; they are not hampered by any traditional view of things. Therefore, if early opportunity is given them to witness what is new or comparatively new in scientific achievement they may more easily follow the new thought than we are able to do and never have to suffer the shocks of incredulity and revolt that have been the first effects of the new science upon ourselves.

Chapter 2

ELECTRONICS

ELECTRONICS is a special branch of electrical engineering that has to do with the discrete or subdivided nature of electricity. In ordinary engineering we are content to treat an electric current as a fluid flow of a continuous kind, but in electronics we have to envisage the flow as being a stream of separate particles called electrons. An electron is the smallest imaginable amount of electricity and it is negative in character. The flow of electrons is towards the positive or high-potential point in the circuit; so, in electronics, we have to get used to thinking of current flow as being in the direction opposite to the usually accepted view, which shows it passing from + to −.

Scientists were obliged to reject the idea of a fluid-like flow when they discovered that electricity could travel from one electrode to another in a glass tube containing nothing but rarefied gas. The well-known neon light is an instance of this. Now, everyone knows that gases are extremely poor conductors of electricity, and the more dense they are the less capable they are of conducting. In fact, it is usual to regard a gas as an insulator. How, then, can quite an appreciable electric current traverse a tube with nothing inside it but a rarefied gas? The fact of the matter is that when the voltage across the electrodes is sufficiently large the gas molecules are broken into two pieces and the separate pieces, called "ions," are oppositely

7

charged, half being positive and the other half negative. The negative ions drift towards the positive electrode (called the anode) and the positive ions drift towards the negative electrode (called the cathode). These ions carry charges, which add up to form a current.

How are the molecules disrupted? Mere electrostatic attraction of the electrodes for opposite charges will account for the movement of the ions in opposite directions but not for the initial break-up of the molecules. This calls for an intense local force, and scientists have proof that the result is brought about by *bombardment*. The molecules are struck violently by high-speed particles with enough force to smash them in two. The bombarding particles are found to be infinitesimal negative charges of electricity (electrons) shot off by the cathode. The shock of rupture produces vibrations in the structure of the ionised molecules, and it is these vibrations that send out visible light. The colour of the light depends on the particular gas being ionised; neon gas gives us a beautiful rosy-red light.

Why must the gas in the tube be rarefied in order to become ionised and hence a conducting path for electricity? The answer is that there is too much jostling between ions and molecules in a tube that is overcrowded with molecules to begin with. Imagine two people trying to communicate with one another across a wide-open space by sending messengers carrying letters. If the space is empty of all but a few hundred messengers on similar errands the exchange will be quite possible, but if the space is crowded with thousands of idle people all trying to go different ways at once, then useful traffic across the space will be slowed almost to a standstill.

If the gas inside the tube is reduced to nothing, then the flow of electricity almost ceases, but not quite, because electrons from the cathode, instead of being stopped by collision with molecules, manage to get across to the anode. When the cathode is made hot, the rate at which electrons are shot off from the cathode is vastly increased; hundreds become thousands or millions or even billions. The first thermionic valve was only an electric glow-lamp with an extra plate or electrode placed above the hot filament (see page 29).

Electrons passing in an empty tube from a hot cathode to a cool anode do so invisibly, though the effect of their hitting the anode (called the " shot " effect) can be made to sound like a hailstorm on a tin roof. In very sensitive valve apparatus feeding a loud-speaker you will often be able to hear the electronic bombardment occurring in the first valve as a persistent hiss, almost like the hand-clapping of a far-away concert audience. Also, if the anode is painted with certain chemicals it will glow with a strange phosphorescent light whenever and wherever an electron strikes it. A steady bombardment produces a continuous light of considerable brightness. The colour of the light depends on the nature of the chemicals used.

The two-electrode thermionic valve, called a " diode," has many practical uses, but this usefulness is vastly increased by the addition of a wire-mesh grid between cathode and anode. The improved valve is called a " triode," and it was the invention of Dr. Lee De Forest, an American scientist. The electron flow between hot cathode and cool anode can be varied by applying a varying electric potential to the grid. Making the grid positive accelerates the flow, whereas making it negative may suppress it altogether. An almost imperceptible electric effect applied at the grid of a triode can control a relatively powerful anode current. This is the so-called principle of " amplification." In one well-known application, tiny electric impulses from a gramophone pick-up are made to control the current through a valve amplifier feeding a loud-speaker. In another, minute electric resonance effects occasioned by radiations from a distant broadcast station are caused to give magnified effects in local circuits so that the programme is not only detected but re-created in full vigour and made to work, once again, a loud-speaker.

Bringing music into the home is by no means the only application of thermionic valves. A valve will amplify the tiny electric effects produced in certain substances by light; consequently it can be used to switch on street lamps at dusk, when daylight fails, and to turn them out again at dawn. Objects travelling on a conveyor belt can be made to interrupt a light beam from a lamp; consequently a combination of photo-cell and valve can be used to operate a counter like a cyclometer, pushing it on by one for every object that goes by. Similar combinations of detecting devices (operated by light or sound or touch) and thermionic valves can be made to control automatically a variety of factory machines and processes. The time has arrived when an entire factory might be operated by a species of electronic robot. We read of this happening on a limited scale in America and elsewhere, and the principle is called "automation." The same principle can be applied to the direction of gunfire against a target in wartime or to the flying of civilian aircraft without the intervention of the pilot. The electronic control is given its flying directions by electronic navigation aids.

The cathode-ray tube is a large thermionic valve in which the electron stream is focused to a fine beam and made to impinge on a screen that gives a visible glow at the spot where it is bombarded. In television some wanted picture is impressed on an electric vibration at the transmitting end, and when this vibration is picked up at the receiving end a cathode-ray tube, with the help of some other valves, is able to re-create the picture. In radar the vibration pattern is compared with its echo on a cathode-ray tube so that an observer can determine his whereabouts in the densest of fogs or the blackest of nights.

The thermionic valve is being superseded today by a new device called the transistor, of germanium, silicon or other substance that can be made to conduct more readily in one direction than the other. The conducting characteristic is varied by the electric potential given to a third electrode so that transistors are taking the place of the triode valve in many applications. In a hearing-aid for deaf people the transistor saves weight, eliminates one of the batteries and enables the instrument to be made small enough to go in a cigarette-case. The same device enables signal relays in long-distance submarine telegraph cables to be made cheaper, more compact and more enduring. Thanks to the transistor television sets and radios are already being made much neater and cheaper than formerly. The wiring in such sets can be replaced by a circuit diagram printed in electrically conducting " ink." Transistors and other components are stuck on at appropriate places on the diagram. Already most manufacturers utilise the printed-circuit technique in radio construction. Even inductances and capacitors can be printed on a flat surface provided the values are of the minute order usual in radio-frequency circuits. The " ink " is in reality thin copper foil.

It is not possible to enlarge further on this general picture of electronics except to say that assemblages of valves or transistors can even be used to perform lengthy and abstruse mathematical calculations rapidly enough to compress a thousand years of work with logarithms or slide-rule into a matter of a few minutes. The larger university colleges and technical schools already possess electronic computers to assist students whose research work confronts them with too many long sums.

The electronic computer is a very complicated piece of equipment so I have not attempted to describe it, but, in the next two chapters, I have described the use of the valve, the cathode-ray tube and the transistor in "communications", that is to say in the science of conveying information by radio, television, etc.

TRANSISTORS

Before closing this chapter I would like to sound a warning. Transistors are readily available for experimental and constructional purposes but they are easy to damage or destroy. They are usually tiny cylindrical things with three bare wires sticking out at one end. The main electric current (conventionally regarded) usually flows from the "emitter" (+) to "collector" (−), which means from one outer wire to the other, and the collector is distinguished by a spot or line marked nearby in red or black. The middle wire goes to the "base," or control electrode. Never must the battery polarity be reversed, because if the collector is made + and the emitter − the transistor will be ruined. A few special-purpose transistors are, how- ever, made to work the other way, with the collector +, so you must learn to distinguish the common (or p-n-p) type from the less usual (n-p-n) type.

If no spot can be found to distinguish the collector from the emitter you must look for that outer wire which emerges farthest from the middle one: this will be the collector.

Another warning relates to soldering. Do not cut the wires shorter than 3/4 inch and never apply the soldering iron for more than a second or two, because excess heat running up the wires can destroy a transistor. A useful safety tip is to fasten a crocodile clip to the wire being soldered, to intercept the heat before it can enter the transistor.

Chapter 3

RADIO

From long before the beginning of history, men have needed to send messages to one another over a great distance—a greater distance than they could make themselves heard by shouting.

Credit for first using electricity to send messages over a wire is usually given to the American inventor, Finley Breese Morse, who was born in Charlestown, Massachusetts, in the year 1791. The idea of the electric telegraph came to him in 1832 and in 1844 he managed to send messages from Washington D.C. to Baltimore and receive replies.

Electricity can be made to give the signal in several different ways. It can ring a bell, buzz a buzzer, light a lamp or cause a magnetised needle to waggle one side or the other of its neutral position. When Peter and his daddy decided to make an electric telegraph for themselves, they chose to use flashing lamps because they did not have bells or buzzers or magnetic needles. You can use lamps too.

HOME-MADE ELECTRIC TELEGRAPH

Spare bulbs for flash lamps are cheap to buy and you need two of them; also a couple of little lamp holders with terminal screws for the wires. You need two batteries with screw terminals, and each battery should contain 1, 2 or 3 cells, depending on the voltage figure stamped on your bulbs. A bulb for 1·5 to 2 volts will need 1 cell; a bulb for 3 or 3·5 volts will need 2 cells, and a bulb for 4·5 volts will need 3 cells.

To make the lights flash on and off, you will need some kind of switch, and telegraphists always use tapping keys, so I suggest you do the same. You can make a couple of tapping keys for yourself quite easily by copying the one in the accompanying sketch.

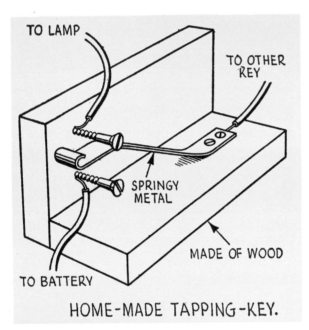

TO LAMP

TO OTHER KEY

SPRINGY METAL

MADE OF WOOD

TO BATTERY

HOME-MADE TAPPING-KEY.

When you are working it, you keep tapping it against the bottom screw — short taps for short lamp flashes, longer contacts for longer flashes.

My next sketch shows you how to connect the lamps, batteries and tapping keys. We will call the station on the left "Peter's" station, and the one on the right "Daddy's" station. Between them is a length of two-wire flex, or two separate wires. Along these two wires Peter can send messages to Daddy and Daddy can send messages back to Peter. (See next page.)

Shall we see how it works? When Peter presses down his key, electric current flows from the "+" terminal of Peter's battery along the top wire through the top contact of Daddy's key to Daddy's lamp and back along the bottom wire to the " − " terminal of Peter's

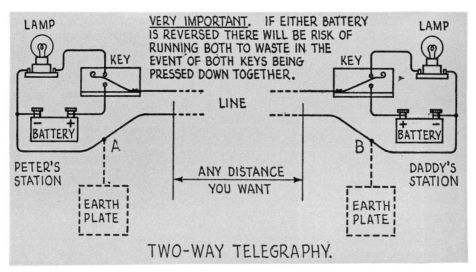

LAMP · KEY · VERY IMPORTANT. IF EITHER BATTERY IS REVERSED THERE WILL BE RISK OF RUNNING BOTH TO WASTE IN THE EVENT OF BOTH KEYS BEING PRESSED DOWN TOGETHER. · LAMP · KEY · LINE · BATTERY · A · BATTERY · B · PETER'S STATION · ANY DISTANCE YOU WANT · DADDY'S STATION · EARTH PLATE · EARTH PLATE

TWO-WAY TELEGRAPHY.

battery. In this way, Daddy's lamp is lighted by Peter's battery. Peter makes quick taps for quick flashes and presses more slowly to make long flashes. Daddy must not touch his own key while Peter's message is coming through, or he will interrupt the circuit.

When Peter has finished flashing his message to Daddy he lets go his key so that it presses up against the top screw. Now it is Daddy's turn to talk back.

When Morse invented the electric telegraph, he invented a code for flashes or buzzings as well. In the Morse Code, letters are made of signals called dots and dashes, a dot being a short flash, or a short buzz, and a dash being a long flash or a long buzz. The letter " A " is a dot followed by a dash; it can be written •– as you see here. The letter " B " is a dash followed by three dots, thus –•••, and " C " is –•–•, and all the other letters of the alphabet are made up in this way of dots and dashes. On the next page is the complete code for all the letters and for the full stop at the end of your message.

I have given you the code for a question mark as well; it is ••––••, and you can use it as a reply when you want your friend to repeat his message. Until you have had plenty of practice, you will not easily translate into letters and words the stream of dots and dashes sent out by your friend.

To make your message clear, be sure to send each letter smartly with no long pauses between dots and dashes or between dots or

MORSE CODE			
A •—	H ••••	O ———	V •••—
B —•••	I ••	P •——•	W •——
C —•—•	J •———	Q ——•—	X —••—
D —••	K —•—	R •—•	Y —•——
E •	L •—••	S •••	Z ——••
F ••—•	M ——	T —	END OF MESSAGE (•) •• •• •• WHAT DID YOU SAY ? •• •— — ••
G ——•	N —•	U ••—	

dashes. The pauses must be between whole letters and not in the middle of the letters. Between words you can put still longer pauses.

The sketch on page 15 shows two dotted squares each labelled EARTH PLATE. By burying a large copper plate underground at each end, you could manage to send your messages using only *one* wire (the top one) because the earth would serve for the second conductor between A and B. I do not advise you to try this, because you would need to use plates about 3 feet square, buried 2 or 3 feet below the surface; this would be expensive and difficult to arrange. In real long-distance telegraphy, it is often a saving to use earth plates and only one wire.

RADIO TELEGRAPHY (EARLY DAYS)

I expect you already know about magnets from being given one to play with at some time or another. A mariner's compass is a magnet and it is pivoted so that it can turn any way it likes. It points North with one end and South with the opposite end, every magnet is like this; it has a North-seeking or "North" pole and a South-seeking or "South" pole. Your toy magnet may be in the form of a horseshoe, or it may be a straight bar, but whatever its shape it will have a "N" pole and a "S" pole.

Any iron bar can be made into a magnet by winding a coil of covered wire round it and then connecting the coil to a powerful battery. The magnetism appears when the current flows, but it usually disappears again when the current is stopped. Some kinds of steel will retain the magnetism indefinitely, thus becoming permanent magnets, but ordinary iron loses its magnetism when the current is interrupted. Here is a sketch to show you two permanent magnets of special steel and two temporary magnets of ordinary

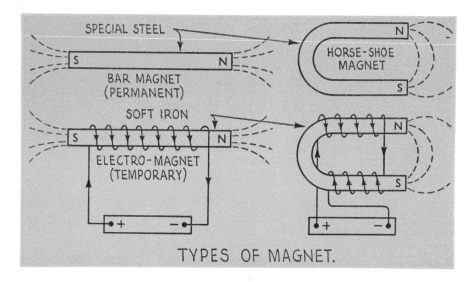

TYPES OF MAGNET.

iron. The temporary magnets produced by electric currents are called electro-magnets.

Now I am drawing for you a rather strange electro-magnet. Its core is not one bar of soft iron, but a bundle of iron wires, and it has round it not one coil of wire, but two. One coil is made of fairly

thick wire and there are not many turns; the other coil has a great
many turns and it is usually made of very thin wire to enable hundreds or even thousands of turns to be packed into a small space.

The funny thing about a double-wound electro-magnet is this.

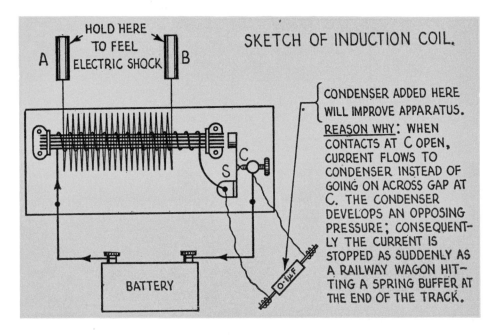

SKETCH OF INDUCTION COIL.

HOLD HERE TO FEEL ELECTRIC SHOCK

A   B

CONDENSER ADDED HERE WILL IMPROVE APPARATUS. REASON WHY: WHEN CONTACTS AT C OPEN, CURRENT FLOWS TO CONDENSER INSTEAD OF GOING ON ACROSS GAP AT C. THE CONDENSER DEVELOPS AN OPPOSING PRESSURE; CONSEQUENT-LY THE CURRENT IS STOPPED AS SUDDENLY AS A RAILWAY WAGON HIT-TING A SPRING BUFFER AT THE END OF THE TRACK.

BATTERY

You can get a current out of the second winding by starting or
stopping a current in the first winding.

In my sketch, the winding of thick wire is connected to a battery,
but the current has to pass up a spring S to a screw contact C to get
back to the battery. At the end of the spring is a piece of iron and
when the current makes the bundle of iron wires into a magnet, the
spring S is pulled away from the contact C, because the iron at its
end is attracted by the temporary magnet. In this way the current
is interrupted. The iron wires at once lose their magnetism so the
spring flies back, only to complete the circuit again. The spring S
is alternately attracted and let go, so it buzzes away merrily. You
could fix a bell clapper on the spring and make it tap a bell—then

you would have an ordinary electric bell. (See Volume III, page 18.)

Just now we do not want a bell, but we are interested in the constant interruption of the current causing the iron wires to gain and lose their magnetism many times in every second. This gaining and losing of magnetism, going on inside the second coil of wire of many turns, causes electricity to be produced in this second coil. If you catch hold of the two ends of the coil, and I have shown metal handles A and B for you to take in your two hands, you will feel a very disagreeable electric shock, although the battery by itself could not possibly give you all this discomfort. It may be an innocent flashlight battery producing only a few volts of electric pressure.

If you put A and B very close together, you may see tiny electric sparks jump between them. You will make the spark much fiercer (or the electric shock much worse) if you connect a small radio condenser at the points shown.

Now this arrangement for magnifying small voltages is called an induction coil, and some very powerful ones have been made, giving electric pressures high enough to make sparks 12 inches long and even more.

What has all this to do with radio telegraphy? I will tell you.

A powerful electric spark in the open air sets up a wave-like

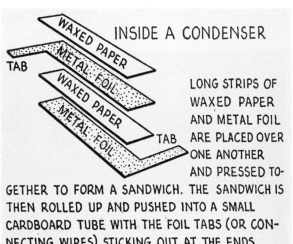

INSIDE A CONDENSER

LONG STRIPS OF WAXED PAPER AND METAL FOIL ARE PLACED OVER ONE ANOTHER AND PRESSED TOGETHER TO FORM A SANDWICH. THE SANDWICH IS THEN ROLLED UP AND PUSHED INTO A SMALL CARDBOARD TUBE WITH THE FOIL TABS (OR CONNECTING WIRES) STICKING OUT AT THE ENDS. THERE IS NO ELECTRICAL CONTACT BETWEEN THE TWO STRIPS OF FOIL, BUT THE ARRANGEMENT SERVES TO STORE SMALL CHARGES OF ELECTRICITY.

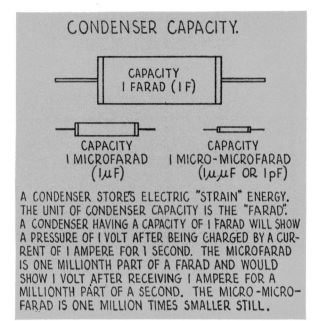

CONDENSER CAPACITY.

CAPACITY
1 FARAD (1 F)

CAPACITY
1 MICROFARAD
(1μF)

CAPACITY
1 MICRO-MICROFARAD
(1μμF OR 1pF)

A CONDENSER STORES ELECTRIC "STRAIN" ENERGY. THE UNIT OF CONDENSER CAPACITY IS THE "FARAD". A CONDENSER HAVING A CAPACITY OF 1 FARAD WILL SHOW A PRESSURE OF 1 VOLT AFTER BEING CHARGED BY A CURRENT OF 1 AMPERE FOR 1 SECOND. THE MICROFARAD IS ONE MILLIONTH PART OF A FARAD AND WOULD SHOW 1 VOLT AFTER RECEIVING 1 AMPERE FOR A MILLIONTH PART OF A SECOND. THE MICRO-MICROFARAD IS ONE MILLION TIMES SMALLER STILL.

disturbance in space, which spreads in all directions at the furious speed of 186,000 miles a second, and this can be detected by sensitive listening apparatus many miles away. The first radio messages ever to be sent out by Marconi in the early years of the present century were sent out with the help of a spark-generating induction coil resembling the one I have sketched for you below.

The spark is not able to create a very powerful disturbance unless the coil ends are connected to some kind of radiating aerial or antenna. In my sketch you can see an induction coil with a

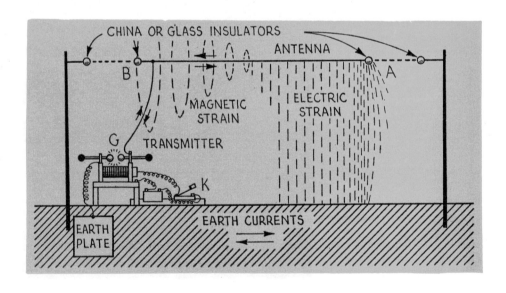

CHINA OR GLASS INSULATORS
ANTENNA
B
MAGNETIC STRAIN
ELECTRIC STRAIN
A
G TRANSMITTER
K
EARTH PLATE
EARTH CURRENTS

battery and a tapping key. Sparks crackle across the gap G whenever the key K is pressed down. A short stream of sparks makes a dot and a long stream of sparks makes a dash. The knobs where the sparks jump across are connected to antenna and earth. Between these two there is an enormous electric strain indicated by dotted lines. When a spark occurs, there is a flow of current from A towards B and this current generates magnetism in the space around the connections. I have represented this magnetism by rings round the end of the antenna near B. The flow of current causes the electric strain to be reduced. However, the current overshoots itself because it cannot suddenly stop at the exact moment when the strain becomes nothing. It goes on flowing and causes a reverse strain to be set up. This helps to stop the current, but then it starts to flow the opposite way. The reversed current overshoots itself like the original one, and soon the original strain is back at nearly its old strength. Thus electricity goes surging backwards and forwards several times as a result of each spark discharge.

The antenna wire and the earth really serve as a small store, like a condenser, and the induction coil keeps on filling up this store and then emptying it again. The instant before the spark flashes across the gap at G the store is full. Then the pressure becomes too much to be endured by the air between the knobs at G and so the spark flashes across and the store of electricity is partly used in making it and partly used in creating the to-and-fro surge I have described. The space surrounding the antenna experiences ever-changing electric and magnetic strains and the pattern of this change is spread in great waves all over the face of the earth. To detect these waves, we shall need a radio receiver and this receiver must be able to translate their message into an intelligible signal.

Most important part of the receiver is an antenna similar to the transmitting antenna, only smaller; this antenna is connected to the receiving apparatus, part of which is shown in the accompanying

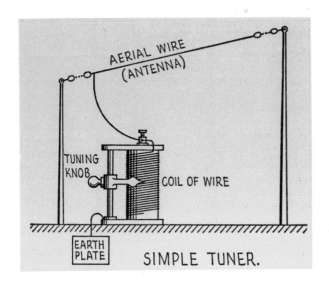

SIMPLE TUNER.

sketch. The receiving apparatus is connected to an earth plate also. Between the antenna connection and the earth plate connection is a coil of wire that can be " tuned " to give the strongest indication of the passing waves. A sliding contact enables the number of turns of the coil between antenna and earth plate to be carefully selected.

How does "tuning" work?

Imagine you live in a place where the earth quakes ever so slightly from time to time and you want to make a simple device for showing you when this happens. Imagine that the quaking is quite regular and that you happen to know the earth waves pass you by at the rate of one wave in every second. From a bracket in your house, you would hang up a heavy weight on a strong spring and you would adjust the size of the weight (by adding or taking away smaller weights) until the arrangement bobbed up and down at a natural rate of exactly *once* in every second. To make such a system oscillate for ever, you would only have to tap the weight with your finger very gently once in every second.

Guess what happens when the earth waves go by at a rate of one in every second? Why, simply this. The bracket holding up the spring would give a gentle tug once in every second, and this would be enough to start the weight bobbing up and down. Because the spring and weight are *in tune* with the earth waves, receiving a tug in time with their natural time of oscillation, the oscillations would soon increase to so great a degree that you would be able to *see* them. Consequently, this simple arrangement would make invisible and imperceptible earth waves clearly visible to you; you could call it a "detector" or "receiver" of earth waves.

Our simple earth wave detector would not work unless there was agreement between the natural time of oscillation of the weight on the spring and the time between successive earth waves. It is the same with radio waves in space and the antenna we put up to receive and detect them.

Our antenna must be *tuned*, and it is the purpose of the coil between antenna and earth to *tune* the antenna. We cannot know at once how many turns our coil will need and so we must make a sliding contact to regulate their number.

As you know already, radio waves pass by at a speed of 186,000 miles a second, so, if the interval between waves is one second the waves must have an interval between them of 186,000 miles. No radio waves are as long as this or as infrequent as one per second. In the early days a usual length for the waves was about 1 mile, and so the receiving antenna had to be tuned by its coil to oscillate at a rate of 186,000 times a second.

One complete electric oscillation is called a cycle; 1,000 cycles are referred to as a kilocycle and 1,000,000 cycles are referred to as a megacycle. A receiver taking waves at a rate of 186,000 per second is "tuned to a frequency of 186 kilocycles." A receiver taking waves at a rate of 1,500,000 per second is "tuned to a frequency of $1\frac{1}{2}$ megacycles." The wavelength in this last instance is 186,000 miles divided by 1,500,000, or rather more than a tenth part of a mile.

Radio engineers to-day prefer to use metres as a measure of wave-length. A metre is the French unit of length—it is rather more than one yard, about 39 inches in fact. The distance of 186,000 miles is 300 million metres and we must remember this figure if we wish to convert wavelengths to kilocycles or megacycles back to wavelengths. The conversion is quite easy to do mentally in many instances. Thus, 1 megacycle corresponds to a wavelength of 300 metres; 2 megacycles corresponds to a wavelength of 300/2=150 metres, 3 megacycles to 300/3=100 metres, and so on. Suppose you want to know the kilocycle or megacycle figure for a wavelength of 20 metres. You perform the calculation in your head like this. I know 300 metres is the same as 1 megacycle; 20 metres is 15 times shorter than 300 metres and so the frequency must be 15 times faster, namely 15 megacycles. Now let us do the calculation the other way round. A television receiver is working on 50 megacycles; what wavelength is this? One megacycle is the same as 300 metres and so 50 megacycles must be for a wave 50 times shorter, namely, 6 metres.

Our business now is with waves having lengths between 100 metres and 2,000 metres. These longer waves will spread in all directions and reach everybody everywhere. That is why they are so useful for broadcast entertainment. They are useful at sea as well, especially for sending out urgent messages such as "Save our Souls" (S.O.S., meaning we are sinking, come to our aid. In Morse, S.O.S. is ••• −−− •••).

We must go back now to consider our simple receiver, sketched on page 22. It is not finished yet and we could not get a murmur from it. We know that the transmitter is sparking away and send-ing out a bunch of waves with every spark. These waves I am drawing for you now (at (*a*) in the diagram on this page). They have their own natural frequency or wavelength because the transmitter antenna is tuned to ensure this, but they are not waves of equal strength. Following each spark, energy surges to and fro, but the

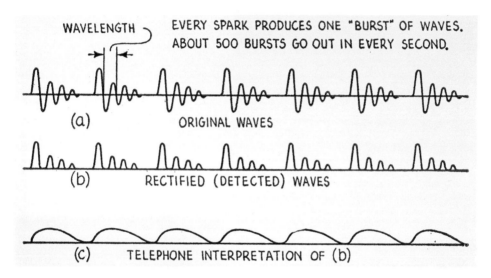

WAVELENGTH EVERY SPARK PRODUCES ONE "BURST" OF WAVES. ABOUT 500 BURSTS GO OUT IN EVERY SECOND.

(a) ORIGINAL WAVES

(b) RECTIFIED (DETECTED) WAVES

(c) TELEPHONE INTERPRETATION OF (b)

extent of this surge gets less and less and the oscillation is what is called a *damped* oscillation. Although the sparks occur at frequent intervals (one at every make-and-break of the interrupter described on page 18), there is time in between sparks for a bunch of ever decreasing waves to go out into space. They decrease in strength (or amplitude as it is called), but not in wavelength. These waves reaching our receiving antenna and sympathetic oscillations are produced in the tuning coil of our receiver. A few wave bunches arrive for each dot, and for each dash a longer collection of wave bunches arrives. Could we not hear short and long buzzings if we connected a telephone

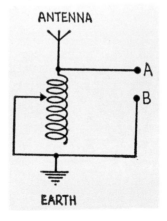

ANTENNA

A

B

EARTH

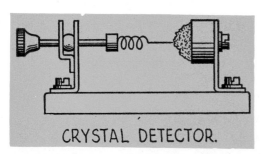

CRYSTAL DETECTOR.

receiver between A and B (page 25)? The answer is "no." The waves would try to make our telephone detector vibrate with their own frequency of something like 186 kilocycles in short bursts lasting about a five-hundredth part of a second each. No telephone diaphragm could possibly follow such a rapid oscillation, and even if it could manage to do so, we should not be able to hear it. Our ears will respond to a vibration as high in pitch as 10 or even 20 kilocycles, but not to 186 kilocycles! We must make use of another device, and this is a sort of valve allowing electric current to go one way, but not the other. We could use a thermionic valve, and many receivers employ valves, but in the early days of radio, people did not have valves, so they had to use something else. Let us use what they used. Their "valve" took the form shown in my sketch above, and it was called a crystal detector. In a little metal cup sat a piece of some natural crystalline substance, and prodding it in the centre was a springy piece of wire called a "catswhisker." The astonishing thing about this arrangement is that it will pass current one way but not the other.

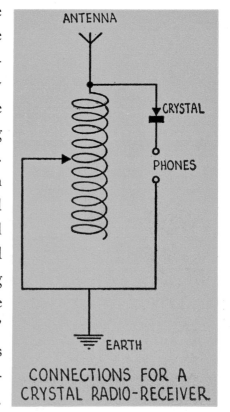

CONNECTIONS FOR A
CRYSTAL RADIO-RECEIVER.

Thus, if it is put in series with our telephone, it will not allow the whole of the waves, as shown at (*a*) on page 25, to pass through, but only half of them, as shown at (*b*). The telephone diaphragm still gets kicks that are too fast for it to follow, but they all go the same way. While any one wave-bunch is passing the diaphragm receives a series of pulls (or pushes) in the same direction and it can answer to these by making one movement out and back again, as shown at (*c*).

Right now we shall be able to hear something. The diaphragm moves out and back at about 500 times a second under the influence of the "rectified" waves and we shall hear a musical buzzing just like the buzzing of the interrupter belonging to the induction coil at the transmitting end—short buzzing for a dot, long buzzing for a dash.

How does the telephone part of our receiver work? For a description of this, please turn to page 455, Volume III.

A crystal radio receiver is well worth making, because it will pick up entertainment programmes in speech and music as well as Morse. Radio transmitters to-day do not send out damped waves in bunches, as indicated on page 25. They are able to send out a continuous wave called a "carrier" wave, as shown at (*a*) in the diagram on page 28. The "message" is impressed on this wave by "modulating" it and modulation usually means a variation in the strength or "amplitude" of the wave. At (*b*) you see a modulated wave. When this is "rectified" by your crystal, it will appear as at (*c*). Your telephone will treat it as being a wave like (*d*), and so it will repeat in your ear the pattern according to which the carrier was modulated originally; in other words, you will hear the speech or music that was impressed on it at the transmitting end.

If you wish to make a crystal receiver for yourself, you should

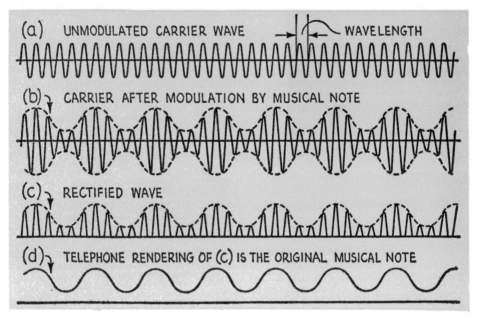

make your tuning coil 3 inches in diameter and it should have about 350 turns of enamel-covered wires not thinner than 30 gauge, wound on a cardboard tube.   When used with an antenna 50 or more feet long this will receive either long-wave or medium-wave radio programmes.   The enamel must be scraped off the wire where the tuning slider rubs up and down.

For hearing the programmes you need to have a pair of earphones on a headband, like the army signal engineers use.   You can probably buy a cheap pair from a store dealing in obsolete army equipment.   There are two kinds of headphone—the low resistance kind (these are useless) and the high-resistance kind (which you need).   See that the resistance (about 4,000 ohms the pair or 2,000 ohms each) is stamped on them somewhere, or else have the salesman test them in front of you.

Having bought suitable phones, you will need to buy a crystal detector.   This will be a crystal in a cup, with a catswhisker to tickle it, or it may have two crystals, large and small, pressed together.

The crystal has sensitive and insensitive spots and you need to poke about delicately with the catswhisker (or the movable crystal) in order to get the best results. If you wish you can buy a germanium diode in which crystal and whisker are sealed into a glass bubble ready for instant use without any need to search for the best spot.

The antenna for a crystal receiver needs to be good because you do not use any power from a battery or from the household electric supply. *The whole of the power needed to buzz the headphones in your ears must be picked up from space by the antenna. It will not pick up enough power unless it is at least 50 feet long and as high as you can make it, also it must be free from all contact with other things.*

With headphones over your ears, adjust the catswhisker so that it prods the crystal. Now move your slider slowly up and down. Maybe you hear nothing. Try making a fresh contact on the crystal and then move the slider again. Repeat until you hear a faint signal. When you have got a signal to work on, leave the slider alone and keep prodding the crystal with the catswhisker to get the best result. Now hold the base securely so that you can make a final adjustment to the slider without shaking the crystal and spoiling its action.

THERMIONIC VALVES

More than 60 years ago, Thomas Alva Edison fitted up one of his electric glow lamps with an extra electrode in the shape of a plate above the filament. These early glow lamps were made with the glass bulb exhausted of air; this vacuum was essential because any air left inside the bulb would help the glowing filament to burn away and destroy itself. Edison noticed that in his modified vacuum lamp a rather mysterious electric current appeared to get across from the plate to the filament without there being any connection between them. This current passed only when the filament was glowing hot, and it always passed only the same way.

In 1904, the British scientist J. A. Fleming found that the Edison lamp with its extra plate would make an excellent detector of radio waves. The one-way current was increased whenever the passing wave made the plate more positive ("+") and it was decreased, or even stopped altogether, when the plate was made more negative. If you had one of these Edison lamps, you could build it into your

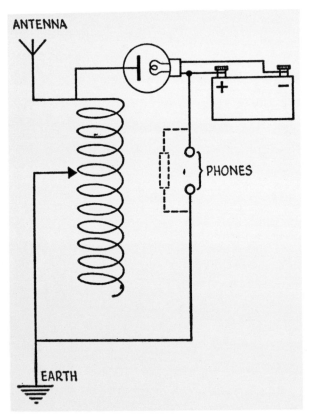

radio receiver to take the place of the crystal detector, as shown in the accompanying sketch. The battery is needed to keep the filament glowing, but that is its sole purpose. The lamp would not be able to strengthen your received signal in any way, only it would make a more reliable detector and it would not need a delicately adjusted catswhisker contact. It would go on working even when

vibrated or bumped about. Used in this way, the Edison lamp was called the Fleming "valve." To-day, we should call it a "diode" to distinguish it from all the more complicated valves now in use.

The filament and plate are called electrodes (cathode and anode respectively); to-day, there are many valves with additional electrodes (wire mesh screens) in between the cathode and anode. A valve with *one* electrode extra (close to the cathode) is called a " triode "—" tri " being the prefix meaning three. A valve with yet another electrode (it goes between the anode and the third electrode of a triode) is called a screen-grid valve. This four-electrode valve, or " tetrode," with a fifth electrode put near to the anode, is called a " pentode "—" pent " being the prefix meaning five.

All these improvements and adaptations of the simple Fleming valve, or diode, were started off by the American inventor Dr. Lee de Forest, when, in 1907, he invented the triode with its extra electrode. This electrode, made like a wire strainer, he called the " grid " and it bears the same name to-day. The triode is a huge improvement over the diode for our purpose because it can be made to amplify (which means magnify) a radio signal after detecting it.

Go back to the sketch on page 30 and study it carefully. I do not want you to make this outfit, because you are going on now to make something much better. But I want you to believe me when

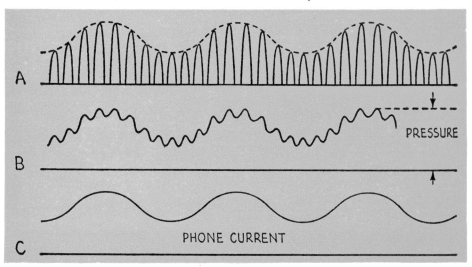

I tell you that it would probably work much better if you put a little condenser across the phone terminals, as shown by the dotted line. I will explain why.

In the diagram on page 31, you see, at A, the little bursts of current passed by the tube—perhaps 186,000 in a second or even more. These will try to pass through the telephones, but the resistance of

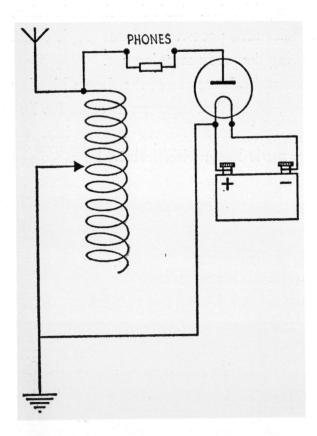

the phones to such a rapidly varying current is very great and the condenser serves the purpose of storing little bursts of current and allowing the energy to pass through the phones in smoother fashion. At B you can see how the pressure in the condenser will build up. This pressure will be effective in sending through the phones a current like that shown at C and, as a result, you will hear a musical note. The condenser must not be too big or it will flatten the slower pulses you want as well as the very quick radio pulses. One marked 0·0003 μF or 300 pF will do nicely and it will only cost about sixpence. My next sketch (on this page) shows the same circuit altered a little. With some further changes, it forms part of the circuit using a triode.

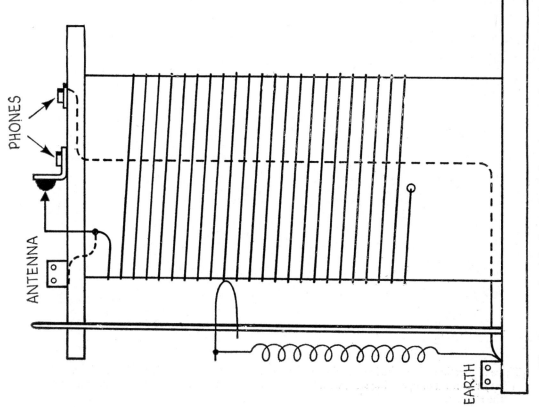

The picture on the right shows a crystal receiver completed and ready for use.   The diagram on the left shows the wiring connections.

These illustrations show the front and rear views of a home-made one-valve radio receiver. (*Top*) The front or operating side, with the coarse tuner on the left and the fine tuner on the right. (*Bottom*) The back of the receiver showing the various wire connections.

Look now at the simplest triode receiver shown in the next sketch. So far as the grid and filament connections go, the circuit is exactly the same as the one given in the last sketch, except that between A and B there are not any phones. Instead of using phones to complete the circuit, we use a resistance of many ohms. We could use a resistance having a value of only 4,000 ohms, the same as the phones, but we shall get much better results if we employ one of about 1,000,000 (a million) ohms. The condenser will be 0·0003 μF as before, and now this condenser will not be *optional* but *essential*.

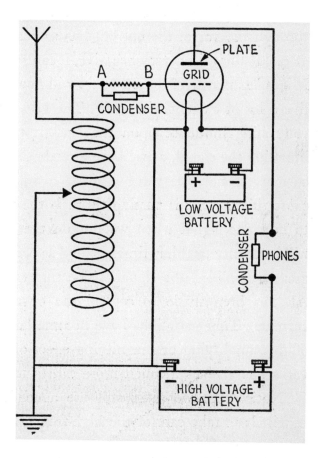

The grid of the valve acts like the plate or anode of the diode we described above. When the coil is tuned to an incoming signal, the waves are rectified, the terminal B, and hence the grid of the valve, experiences the varying electric pressure indicated on page 31 by diagram B. This pressure is a faithful reflection of the speech or music being received except that on top of the speech- or music-making wave, there is still a small ripple due to the carrier wave.

We must think now about the plate of our valve. Going from

here, we have a wire to the phones, and from the phones there is a connection to the "+" terminal of a high-voltage (High Tension or H.T.) battery. The other terminal of this battery (the "−" terminal) goes to "earth" and also to the cathode or filament of the valve. The plate of the valve receives the current flowing through the vacuum when the filament starts to glow, and this current is greatly increased by the use of the high-voltage battery. But in passing through the valve, the current has to pass through the wire mesh grid. If this grid is very negative, it can *stop* the current altogether. If it is *less* negative, some current will flow, and if it is slightly positive a lot of current will flow. The grid clearly has an important controlling influence upon the current passing. But the grid is imitating the signal, as we have already seen, and consequently, the current through the valve is made to imitate the signal too. Because this current is passing through the phones, we shall be able to hear the signal when we put on the phones. What we hear will be twenty or thirty times as loud as before, because the valve has greatly amplified the signal. The tiny current through resistance AB has been made to control the enormously greater "plate" current. Tiny variations have become large variations on account of this amplifying or magnifying effect of the valve. These large variations give us a much more satisfactory result in our phones.

Notice that we must still use a condenser across the phone terminals to take care of the high-frequency ripple in the signal.

A PRACTICAL ONE-VALVE RECEIVER

If you make a receiver to the description given above, following the diagram on page 33, you would be delighted with the volume of sound it would give you, but it would still have some of the faults of the crystal receiver. In particular, it might mix the programmes

from two or more stations, because it is not selective enough to cut
out unwanted signals and leave you with only the one you are trying
to tune in.

You can make the one-valve receiver much better by adding two
refinements, as shown in the accompanying circuit diagram. Firstly,
you can add a "fine-
tuning" control. Your
slider control jumps a
whole turn of your coil
at a time and, conse-
quently, *accurate* tun-
ing is not possible. By
adding the variable
condenser C, you can
regulate the strength of
signal until it really is
as strong as possible.
The condenser C does
not use a foil and paper

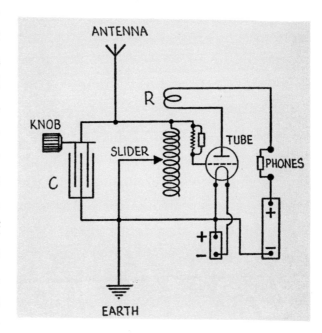

sandwich: instead it is made with thin aluminium plates, and the
separating medium is air instead of paper. This form of construction
enables you to pull the plates apart, so altering the condenser's
storage capacity. When the plates are apart, the condenser has no
effect at all, but when they are meshed together, the storage capacity
of the antenna system is increased and it is as though you used a
more easily stretched spring in the earthquake-detecting arrangement described on page 22. The spring would absorb more energy
than the one it replaced, for it would stretch further under a given
weight, and the frequency of oscillations would be reduced. An
electric condenser added to the circuit, as shown, has the effect of

lowering the response frequency of your tuned coil.   In other words,
you get the same signal with fewer turns of your coil in use.

The way to tune the receiver is as follows.   You put the condenser in its mid-position—half in and half out—then you move
your slider until you hear a programme at its best.   You then leave
the slider alone and turn the knob of the condenser; this may further
increase the clarity of reception when you turn it one way; it will
reduce the sound when you turn it the other way.   You will, of
course, turn it to give you the best obtainable results.

Refinement number 2 is the coil shown on page 35 at R.   This
gives you an effect known as "reaction."   Coil R is so near to the
tuning coil that their magnetic effects intermingle.   What happens
in coils thus "coupled" together is the Coil R, carrying the strong
amplified signal from the tube, "feeds back" some of the energy
into the tuning coil.   The original, rather feeble oscillations in this
coil are helped to become stronger and so the grid of the tube gets a
better input signal to work on.   This better input signal gives a
further increase in the amplified signal through R and, consequently,
the amount of "feed back" is increased, leading to a new increase in
the input signal to the grid, a new increase in the amplified signal,
a new increase in the feed-back effect, and so on.   You can see that
this circle of events might go on for ever until there was enough noise
in your phones to blast your head off.   Usually, the effect stops short
of this result, because the increased oscillations encounter increased
resistances and eventually these are enough to prevent the system
from "running away" out of control.   However, it is very easy to
have too close a coupling between the coil R and the tuning coil and
then running away *does* occur.   The tube and the connected coils
and condensers develop an oscillation of their own and no signal is
needed to keep it going once it starts.   Besides making programme

listening impossible, such over-exaggerated reaction causes weird whistles and howls to be heard in receivers belonging to neighbours.

The oscillating tuning coil of the antenna has now become a transmitter, and it sends out a carrier wave having the frequency of the oscillations. If you make a receiver to the design shown on page 35, and allow oscillation to occur, you will be *breaking the law* and you will be annoying a lot of people. Reaction is desirable in a simple one-valve receiver, but I must warn you that the effect needs to be strictly limited and kept well under control. The reaction coil R has to be made movable so that the amount of magnetic "coupling" can be varied from almost nothing to an amount that will prove excessive. You must be on guard to prevent any excess at any and all times. If you become careless habitually, your sins will find you out because the annoyance can be traced to its source by Authority without much difficulty, and you would be made to pay a fine. You might even have your receiver taken away from you!

Triode valves are still obtainable for old battery portable receivers. When you buy one, ask if the filament needs a 2-volt supply (from an accumulator) or a 1·4-volt supply (from a dry cell). If the reaction coil does not increase the signal when moved nearer to the tuning coil, interchange the end connections, because it may be causing *negative* instead of *positive* feedback.

RADIO TRANSMISSION

A radio transmitter resembles your home-made receiver, with its reaction coil set to generate oscillations, plus some way of varying the strength of those oscillations to give them the required modulation. One way of providing modulation is to inject a varying voltage in the high-tension circuit so that the valve gets more or less plate voltage. The modulating voltage can be derived originally from a microphone or a gramophone pick-up. It will have to be amplified to make it sufficiently effective.

TRANSISTORISED RADIO RECEIVER

Because they need two batteries, valve receivers are clumsy and heavy. If tied to an outside aerial they are not portable either. Transistors give the same results as valves but with much less battery power: a relatively light 4½ to 9 volt battery suffices. When five or six transistors are used to step up the signal amplification the aerial can become part of the receiver, because a small coil of wire round a six-inch rod of magnetic material called "ferrite" will suffice to pick up all the signal required. Making one of these sophisticated multi-transistor portables calls for experience so that the beginner is advised to start with a single-transistor circuit on the lines of the single-valve receiver already described. Closely equivalent to it, and using a Mullard OC 44 transistor, is Circuit No. 19, illustrated and described (with all construction particulars) in *Modern Transistor Circuits for Beginners* by Clive Sinclair (Bernard's Radio Manuals No. 177), obtainable from most good radio constructor shops.

Chapter 4

TELEVISION AND RADAR

THE waves received by a tuned antenna can be made visible by a large valve of the kind used in television receivers. I must tell you about these large valves, so look now at the diagram on this page.

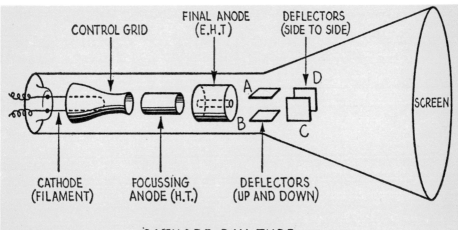

CONTROL GRID
FINAL ANODE (E.H.T)
DEFLECTORS (SIDE TO SIDE)

A
D
B
C
SCREEN

CATHODE (FILAMENT)
FOCUSSING ANODE (H.T.)
DEFLECTORS (UP AND DOWN)

CATHODE RAY TUBE.

ALL ELEMENTS NEED SUPPORTS AND CONNECTIONS TO BASE BUT THESE ARE OMITTED TO MAKE SKETCH MORE CLEAR. THE FOCUSSING ANODE NEEDS A FEW HUNDRED VOLTS, THE FINAL ANODE NEEDS FROM 1000 TO 10,000 VOLTS DEPENDING ON SIZE OF TUBE.

It shows you a valve of the kind used in older television receivers. The same kind of valve is still used in oscilloscopes.

An oscilloscope is a wonderful invention for making radio waves and sound waves visible.

The valve is like your triode, except that the "plate" is now a hollow cylinder. The flow of current from the filament towards the plate occurs at a very high speed and is in the nature of a stream of particles. These particles are called "electrons" and their flow is concentrated into a narrow beam, or ray, by a focusing electrode. This ray, coming from the filament or cathode, is called a "cathode ray" and the valve is often called a "cathode-ray tube." The electron stream (or cathode ray) approaches the "plate" at great speed and shoots right through it and across the wide part of the tube to hit the screen at the far end. On this screen some special paint is used: it glows with a bright light under the impact of the cathode ray. A sharply focused ray causes a very bright dot to appear on the screen.

The cathode (or filament), together with the cylindrical plate and other electrodes, is called a "gun," because the sole purpose of this part of the tube is to fire off electrons in an endless stream at the screen. The energy or strength of this stream is governed by the control grid. The bright spot on the screen can be dimmed by making the control grid negative: it can be made brighter if the control grid is made positive.

The position of the bright spot on the screen can be altered if the stream of electrons (the cathode ray) is deflected aside from its straight path. Beyond the final anode, we see deflector plates. One pair, A and B, can be used to move the spot up or down; the other pair, C and D, can be used to move the spot from side to side. The cathode ray consists of electrons, as already described, and these are small negative charges of electricity. If plate A is made positive and plate B is made negative, the ray will be bent upwards because the positive plate A *attracts* the negative electrons, whereas the negative plate B repels them. Sideways bending can be caused in the same way by making plate C positive, while plate D is made negative.

Clearly, the cathode-ray tube is a wonderful device for making electricity write its own signature!

If we have an oscilloscope, we shall find that it consists of a cathode-ray tube in which the spot of light is made to travel from side to side so fast that it draws a straight line across the screen. The mechanism for making it do this is designed so that the spot travels at a definite speed from left to right, like the hand of a man writing. When it reaches the end of the line it flies back in a millionth of a second or so.

When we want to look at a radio wave, we connect our antenna and earth to plates A and B of the tube and then tune our receiver to get the wave we want. At once the plates A and B cause the spot of light to rise and fall in step with the wave. The spot is moving to the right at the same time and so it will trace a wavy line on the screen exactly like the wave at (*a*) on page 28. If the wave is modulated, we shall obtain on our screen a picture like the one at (*b*).

A real oscilloscope may not be quite so simple as the one described here. To make it more sensitive to feeble waves, there will probably be an *amplifier* to strengthen the wave before it is applied to plates A and B. But you will understand the principle now. This is television in its earliest form and you will agree that it has entertainment value only for a scientist like yourself.

Television for enjoyment requires us to use the cathode-ray tube in a different manner. The spot of light has to make a picture covering the whole screen. Plates C and D are still used to make the spot move from left to right at a good fast writing speed and then flash back to the start of the line again.   Plates A and B are used to make the lines go lower and lower down the screen like the lines of printing on this page.   If you examine a television picture very closely, you will see that it is made up of hundreds of fine lines going across the screen from left to right.   The spot "writes" a whole page in about a fiftieth part of a second.   While it is writing lines in this way, its intensity or brightness is varying.   It goes dark to make dark parts of the picture and gets brighter when making a bright part of the picture.   This varying brightness is caused by applying the signal to the control grid.

The signal sent out by the studio is a modulated carrier wave, but the modulation is quite complicated.   There is the picture signal which strengthens and weakens the light spot in sympathy with what the camera sees as it scans the scene before it, line by line.   On top of this there are the synchronising pulses.   The line scanner in your television receiver gets an order to flash back at the end of every line. In the same way the frame scanner, causing the lines to appear one below the other all the way down the screen, is triggered by a synchronising pulse after the correct number of lines has been drawn. These synchronising pulses occur at the ends of the lines and at the finish of the last line, so they do not produce any visible effects on the picture.   The tuned receiver is able to take in the whole signal and pass on the synchronising pulses to the scanning units.   The control grid of the cathode-ray tube gets its orders from the tuned receiver too.   A nearly positive voltage is given to the control grid when the spot is tracing a bright part of the picture, but a strongly negative voltage is applied when the spot needs to be "blacked out." Intermediate control grid voltages give intermediate shades between light and dark.

The television camera at the studio is a wonderful "eye," which views the subject to be televised line by line from top to bottom. It converts variations of light and shade into a varying electric signal, and this signal, imposed on a carrier wave, is radiated into space for your receiving antenna to pick up and feed to a cathode-ray tube. The scanning units in the camera provide signals too—at the end of each line and at the end of each line group forming a "frame." These "synchronising" signals are radiated on a carrier along with the picture signal. The valves in your receiver can sort out this three-part signal and deliver its component parts to the right departments. Speech and music accompanying the picture must be transmitted on a different carrier wave, and so every television receiver needs a second tuned receiver to operate the loudspeaker. In present-day television receivers the picture tube lacks the deflectors A, B, C, D: it has instead coils of wire round the outside of the glass to provide magnetic deflecting forces. For many years the television programme authorities have provided pictures consisting of 405 lines, but foreign authorities use a 625-line system and Britain also has a programme using this system. The lines are scanned in the order 1, 3, 5, 7, etc. and then in the order 2, 4, 6, 8, etc., so that two scans of interlaced lines are needed to provide each 405 or 625-line picture. Twenty-five such double scans occur in every second.

In coloured television, the picture tube has three "guns" and they shoot the electrons through fine holes in an otherwise opaque screen placed close to the picture end of the tube, the glass face of which is coated with dots of three different kinds of fluorescent paint, to provide three distinct colours of luminosity, combinations of which (in various degrees) will produce all colours of the spectrum. Each gun is responsible for illuminating the dots of a particular colour— the perforated screen ensures this—and the resultant picture, made up of the differently coloured dots, shining with various (and varying) brightnesses, is akin to the coloured picture in a book or a magazine. Examined under a strong magnifying glass, magazine pictures are seen to consist similarly of dots of 3 or 4 colours.

RADAR

When radio waves are very short indeed, say less than 1 metre, corresponding to a frequency of 300 megacycles, they behave more like sound waves or light waves. These very short waves are reflected by obstacles in their path and it is possible to detect echoes. An aircraft in flight is a sufficiently large obstacle to send back an echo, and in World War II enemy aircraft were successfully detected on their way to an attack by radio echoes while they were still 100 miles away. This gave the defenders a chance to get ready for them.

The use of radio wave echoes to locate aircraft, or to guide ships among rocks or icebergs at night, or in fog, is called Radar.

In the most modern Radar apparatus, the waves used may be as short as an inch or two, corresponding to a frequency of some 10,000 to 15,000 megacycles. The antenna for such tiny waves is itself tiny, being about as large as one of your fingers. If put inside a sort of hood or reflector, the transmitting antenna will send out a powerful beam of waves like a car headlamp sending out a beam of light. If these waves hit against an aircraft, some part of them will be reflected back again and the same antenna can be used to receive them. In practice the waves are sent out in very short bursts or pulses. The echo comes back in similar, but more feeble pulses. The receiving unit is able to tell us how long the signal has taken to reach its target and come back as an echo: it needs to be very quick in its action, because an echo would be received back from a target ninety-three miles away in a thousandth part of a second!

The searching antenna, high up on the deck of a ship, turns

round and round, pointing to all parts of the horizon in turn. When an echo is received, the sailors know there is some other ship, or a rock, or an iceberg in the direction towards which the antenna points at the instant the echo arrives. The distance is calculated on the basis of 93,000 miles for every second between the transmission of a pulse and the receiving of its echo. Needless to say, the operator does not have to measure this time himself: the apparatus does it for him. Again, the wonderful cathode-ray tube is used. Plates C and D are used as before to make the spot of light trace a line across the screen. Maybe it does this in a thousandth part of a second. The line is very faint except when the control grid is fed with extra positive electricity. The outgoing pulse is made to send along this positive electricity at the start of a line. The returning echo will send along positive electricity too, and consequently, the line has two bright spots in it. If these occur half the length of the line distant from one another, then the time interval must be half of a thousandth of a second and so the reflecting object must be forty-six and a half miles distant from the ship. Against the screen of the tube, a scale in miles can be placed so that the distance can be read off at once. If the tube is made to turn round in step with the scanning antenna, the line traced by the spot will actually point to the direction in which the danger lies. In modern Radar the tube itself remains still but the spot trace is caused to revolve by electronic means, and instead of going right across the tube screen it goes only from the centre to the edge. This radial line swings round in time with the scanning antenna. Usually the screen is painted with a special material that goes on glowing for a little while after the electrons have lighted it up, so the whole map-like picture created by echoes is left impressed on the screen after each rotation of the scan line.

Chapter 5

X-RAYS AND OTHER SPACE WAVES

WE have seen that in radio-communication we can use electro-magnetic space waves ranging from a few thousand metres in wavelength down to an inch or two. Specialised services like television and radar call for the shorter waves. Can waves be made even shorter than one inch? Truly they can, but right here scientists are near the end of their resources. Waves less than 1 centimetre are difficult to produce and have only a very limited application.

When I say less than 1 centimetre, I mean $\frac{1}{2}$ centimetre or $\frac{1}{4}$ centimetre. If we are thinking of waves very much shorter still—say a ten-thousandth part of a centimetre or less—then there is much less difficulty about producing them. Nature herself produces such waves because they are radiated by any substance that is made hot. When we draw near to a hot fire, we feel the impact of such radiation on our skins. Radiant heat is an electro-magnetic space wave generated by the internal vibrations of hot objects and the wavelength ranges from about a thousandth of a centimetre to a ten-thousandth. This means that from one to ten thousand heat waves are squeezed into a space of less than half an inch. As they fly past at the rate of 186,000 miles a second, I leave you to imagine what the frequency of vibration must be! But in Nature, this vibration is by no means fast. When speeded up to give about 20,000 waves per centimetre,

46

the vibration makes a hot object visible—it is then *red* hot. An object like the sun, which is of dazzling white heat, or even an electric lamp, gives out visible radiations of many different wavelengths corresponding to red light, orange light, green light, blue light and violet light, with innumerable intermediate shades. The waves of violet light pack more than $2\frac{1}{2}$ million into a centimetre. Shorter waves than this, going down to 25 million to the centimetre, are very visible to the camera, but not to the human eye—they are called "ultra-violet" radiations.

Have we reached the limit of shortness in wavelength? Certainly not. In 1895, Dr. Wilhelm Röntgen, in Germany, was experimenting with a primitive cathode-ray tube and he received from this an extraordinary radiation that would pass through solid opaque objects to affect photographic plates or a fluorescent screen placed on the other side. Soon he was able to make shadow photographs of the bones in his hand or foot by means of these invisible radiations. At first the radiation was a complete mystery —it was named the X-ray, X being the unknown quantity in algebraic calculations. Before long, however, the X-ray was found to be merely an electro-magnetic radiation of exceedingly short wavelength. To-day, X-rays are utilised at frequencies anywhere between 100 million and 10,000 million waves to the centimetre. These extremely small waves are produced partly by man and partly by Nature. We might say that man provides the opportunity for Nature to make them. This opportunity is afforded by a tube of the kind shown in the sketch on the next page. Between the electrodes marked "+" and "−", an extremely high voltage is applied.

The bowl-shaped cathode sends out a stream of electrons at high speed, and these strike the anode or "target" electrode, setting up vibrations within the atoms of which it is composed. The vibrating

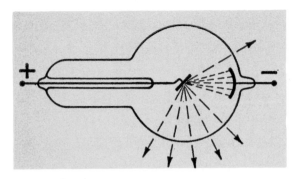

atoms send out the short-wave radiation we call the X-ray, and I have indicated the direction of this radiation by arrows. The radiation will penetrate human flesh, but its intensity is diminished by bones and so, if you stand in front of an X-ray tube, it will cast a shadow of your skeleton on any surface placed behind you. You cannot see this shadow unless it happens to fall on a screen of special material that *glows* with visible light under the impact of X-rays, but a photographic plate will receive the image and record it for you. In the X-ray department of a hospital, you are made to lie on an envelope of black paper holding photographic film or plate, and an X-ray tube showers its radiation on you from above. In that way the doctor obtains a shadow picture of the bones and other more solid parts of your inside. The modern X-ray tube is more like a radio valve. It utilises a heated filament or cathode to give a stronger and more easily controlled X-ray, but the anode or target-electrode still requires a high voltage. The invention of the present-day type of X-ray tube is attributed to William David Coolidge, an American physicist, who was born in 1873.

Waves even shorter than X-rays, called gamma rays, are emitted by radioactive materials and especially in an atom-bomb explosion. These very short waves are very destructive to animal or human life, and even the X-ray can be dangerous if it is allowed to play on a person's body for too long. The ray can be stopped from spreading in directions where it might do mischief by a thick screen of lead, or by a sturdy wall made of concrete, and it can be allowed to pass out through a small window in the direction where it is needed.

Chapter 6

THE ATOMIC THEORY

WHEN we look around us we see that our universe is made up of two things—matter and emptiness. Both are puzzling, and from very early times—long before the beginning of history, as recorded in our books—men wondered about matter and emptiness. The emptiness they felt they could understand because it seemed to them that nothing was simply nothing. Matter was altogether different, and the puzzling thing about it was its changeableness. The air that was clear one moment became filled with clouds in the next, and then, out of an apparently dry sky, down fell quantities of rain—or perhaps it was snow that fell, or hail. The field that lay bare all the winter began to sprout with greenery directly the warmth of the spring sun fell upon it. A patch of heath, dried by a long warm summer, only needed the spark from two flints clashed together to set it ablaze with the terrible self-destroying life called fire, which could destroy other things too. In a matter of minutes a great forest might become reduced to so many dead black stumps. Much of the matter comprising the forest had gone up in flames and clouds of smoke; where was it afterwards? A puddle of water, even a puddle in a water-tight dish, was spirited away in a few hours; what became of it?

It seemed to our forefathers that matter must be of several

different kinds which, by mixing together, could produce other kinds. For a while they believed that there were four simple kinds of matter—namely fire, earth, air and water. Thus the wood of trees was supposed to consist of earth and water. If fire entered into wood it became air—or at any rate most of it did because it vanished.

Some kinds of matter were pretty and therefore desirable. Gold was one of these desirable substances and men supposed that, like other substances, it consisted of fire, earth, air and water. They had the idea that gold ought to be easy to make out of other substances merely by altering in it the proportions of the four elements, fire, earth, air and water. The business of turning one kind of matter into another was called "alchemy" after a Greek word meaning "change," and the early experts in this business were called "alchemists." We get our words "chemistry" and "chemist" from this source.

I am afraid the alchemists never managed to achieve their object of turning other substances into gold. Neither did they fulfil any of their other hopes. But they spent a life-time doing experiments, and so they did learn a great deal about the changes it is really possible to perform, and we owe much of our present-day knowledge to the alchemists of long ago. They discovered things that seemed of little value at the time but are known now to have been useful in opening men's minds to the real truths of the universe. One of these truths is that the elementary substances comprising matter are more than four in number—many more.

None of the so-called elements of the alchemists are regarded as elements to-day. Earth is a complicated mixture of complicated compounds; air is a mixture of different gases; fire is not matter at all but only an effect produced by rapid changes in matter; and water is compounded of two invisible gases. These truths were not uncovered in a day nor yet in a thousand days. Many centuries of experiment and much pondering on the results by thoughtful men have gone into the science of chemistry as we now know it.

In the last 300 years or so the idea has persisted that all matter could be reduced to elementary substances of one kind or another. Under normal conditions some of these substances were seen to be solid, others were liquid and others again were gaseous. Some solids and some gases could be mixed with the liquids by being dissolved. Most liquids could be mixed. The mixing sometimes produced unexpected effects such as heat or cold or fire or explosion. Liquid substances could generally be turned by heat into the gaseous condition; on being chilled they again became liquid. Solid substances melted and became liquid if sufficiently heated, but they solidified again later, after a period of cooling.

For a while, many compound substances were regarded as elementary because nobody had ever got other substances out of them, and because nobody had ever made them from other substances. Thus the idea that water was an elementary substance persisted until relatively modern times. Eventually it was noticed that water appeared in the combustion products of certain fires. Thus, you can get water out of a candle flame if you let this flame play on a cold surface. You get soot too, and it is the dampness of the soot that proves the creation of water. You could imagine the water to have been mixed with the tallow of the candle in the first place, but the same result is obtained even when perfectly dry tallow is burned.

When an acid is poured on a metal much fizzling and bubbling occurs. The chemists found that this commotion was caused by the creation of a gaseous substance, usually the one that came to be called hydrogen. Mixed with air, this hydrogen gas would burn, and

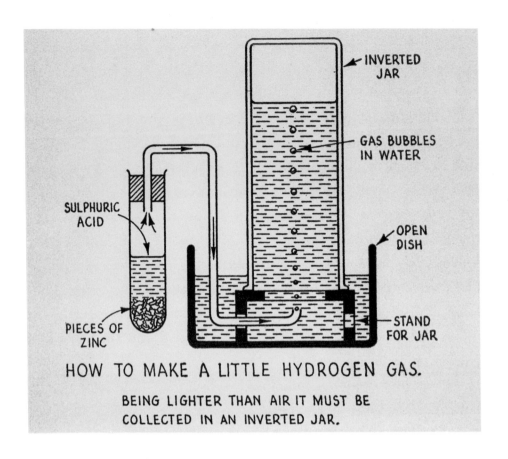

HOW TO MAKE A LITTLE HYDROGEN GAS.

BEING LIGHTER THAN AIR IT MUST BE
COLLECTED IN AN INVERTED JAR.

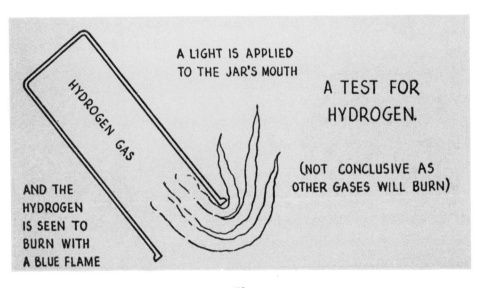

A LIGHT IS APPLIED
TO THE JAR'S MOUTH

A TEST FOR
HYDROGEN.

(NOT CONCLUSIVE AS
OTHER GASES WILL BURN)

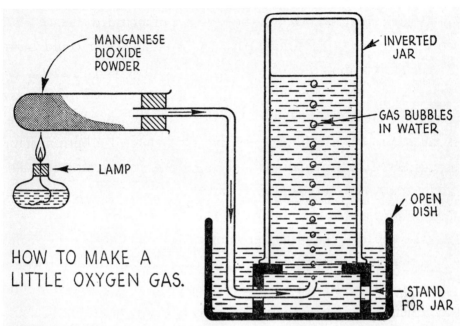

MANGANESE
DIOXIDE
POWDER

INVERTED
JAR

GAS BUBBLES
IN WATER

LAMP

OPEN
DISH

HOW TO MAKE A
LITTLE OXYGEN GAS.

STAND
FOR JAR

THOUGH SLIGHTLY HEAVIER THAN AIR IT IS BEST COLLECTED
IN AN INVERTED JAR. WHEN THE JAR IS FILLED A GLASS SLIDE
IS SLIPPED OVER MOUTH AS THE JAR IS STOOD UPRIGHT.

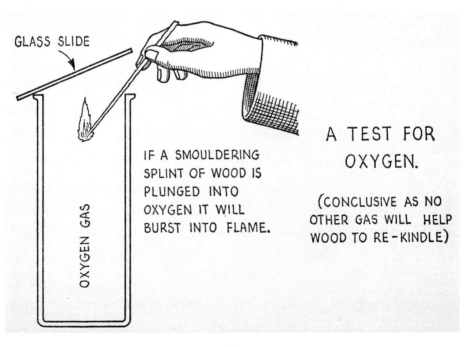

GLASS SLIDE

A TEST FOR
OXYGEN.

IF A SMOULDERING
SPLINT OF WOOD IS
PLUNGED INTO
OXYGEN IT WILL
BURST INTO FLAME.

(CONCLUSIVE AS NO
OTHER GAS WILL HELP
WOOD TO RE-KINDLE)

OXYGEN GAS

when the burning occurred in the presence of a chilled surface beads of water appeared. It seemed likely then that water could be regarded as a combination of hydrogen gas and some part of the air. Careful experiment showed that not all the air entered into the formation of water: the burning robbed the air of rather less than half its volume to leave behind a gas that extinguished a burning taper and suffocated any small animal attempting to breathe it. This residue is the gas that came to be called nitrogen. The gas blending with hydrogen to form water was called oxygen.

Naturally the chemists were not completely satisfied even now that water consisted of hydrogen and oxygen. It was never wise to believe in the results of only one experiment. They needed another experiment to convince them. Most convincing of all would be the experiment of breaking water up again to see whether it yielded hydrogen and oxygen, and nothing else. Eventually a way was found to split water up into its component elements. If the wires from a strong electric battery are dipped into water much bubbling occurs at each wire and if the bubbles are collected they are found to consist of hydrogen on the one hand and oxygen on the other. This process is known as the electrolysis of water (see opposite).

When all the water has been used up in this experiment nothing remains except hydrogen and oxygen—two volumes of hydrogen for every volume of oxygen. By burning the hydrogen and oxygen together and collecting the result we can get back our water again.

Chemistry is made up of discoveries like this, and we know now that all matter can be resolved into elementary substances fewer than 100 in number. Some of these elementary substances, or "elements," are very common and very well known to us, though it is not always possible to see them by themselves. In their natural state they are usually combined with something else. Iron, for in-

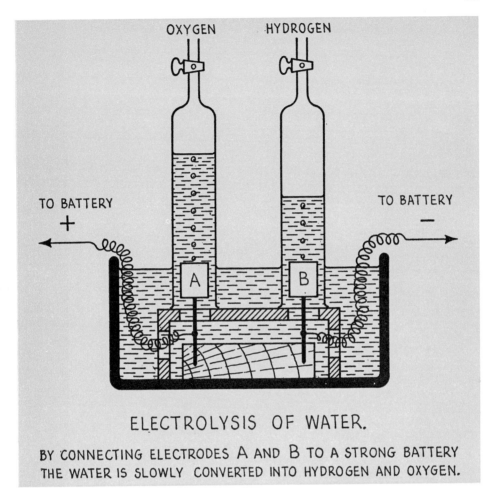

ELECTROLYSIS OF WATER.

BY CONNECTING ELECTRODES A AND B TO A STRONG BATTERY
THE WATER IS SLOWLY CONVERTED INTO HYDROGEN AND OXYGEN.

stance, cannot exist for long in the natural state: it rusts away and becomes a brown powder. Iron is found in nature only in this impure state, as a rock or a stone, and it tries to return to its natural state whenever water allows it to rust. The fact is that iron has a strong affinity for oxygen so that it will rob water of its oxygen and set the hydrogen free. A small amount of acid in the water hastens the process.

Sulphur is another element rather hard to find by itself, but great deposits of it do exist in volcanic regions where it is one of the extraordinary consequences of natural thermal activity. We can buy sulphur as a fine yellow powder, or as a browny-yellow stick. It burns with a blue flame giving off a suffocating smell. The smell is a property of the gas which is given off when sulphur combines with atmospheric oxygen in the process of burning.

I have mentioned carbon already. This is the soot or lamp-black you see when a candle flame is played against cold glass. There is much carbon in coal, tallow, paraffin and petrol—in all fuels in fact. Carbon burns readily, combining with atmospheric oxygen to form an invisible gas. When a candle flame is played on cold glass the carbon in the flame is chilled below the point where it can burn, so it stays on the glass. When a coal fire is denied the air it needs much of the carbon passes unburnt up the chimney as black smoke. Some of it is burned to combine with only half of the oxygen it really needs. The result of this incomplete burning is still an invisible gas, but now it is an inflammable and poisonous gas—the one chemists call carbon monoxide.

Will any amount of hydrogen and oxygen do for making a quantity of water? The answer is no. Will any amount of iron and oxygen do for making yellowish-brown rust? The answer again is no. The chemists of long ago, and particularly John Dalton, who lived from 1766 to 1844, noticed that when the elementary substances combined to form some new substance they did so in definite proportions. Thus, hydrogen always needed half its own volume of oxygen to form water; carbon always needed oxygen amounting to $2\frac{2}{3}$ times its own weight in order to form carbon dioxide. Sometimes substances could be induced to combine in some other proportion to form a different compound, but again the proportion was definite and invariable. Thus, when carbon takes to itself oxygen to form the poisonous carbon monoxide gas the proportion by weight is always 1 of carbon to $1\frac{1}{3}$ of oxygen, never anything else.

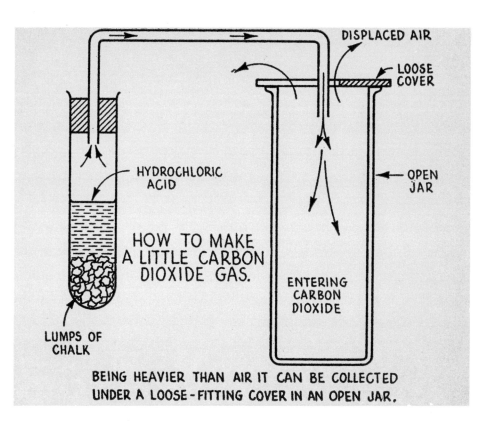

DISPLACED AIR

LOOSE COVER

HYDROCHLORIC ACID

OPEN JAR

HOW TO MAKE A LITTLE CARBON DIOXIDE GAS.

ENTERING CARBON DIOXIDE

LUMPS OF CHALK

BEING HEAVIER THAN AIR IT CAN BE COLLECTED UNDER A LOOSE-FITTING COVER IN AN OPEN JAR.

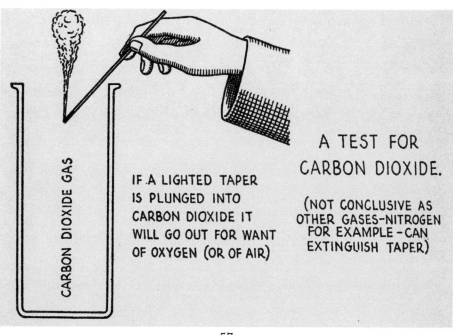

CARBON DIOXIDE GAS

IF A LIGHTED TAPER IS PLUNGED INTO CARBON DIOXIDE IT WILL GO OUT FOR WANT OF OXYGEN (OR OF AIR)

A TEST FOR CARBON DIOXIDE.

(NOT CONCLUSIVE AS OTHER GASES-NITROGEN FOR EXAMPLE - CAN EXTINGUISH TAPER)

Dalton prepared tables of combining weights and discovered that for a given substance—oxygen, for instance—the weights taken up were always whole-number weights of a certain unit. Thus the amounts taken up by carbon were $1\frac{1}{3}$ or $2\frac{2}{3}$ times its own weight. Here it is clear that carbon will take up either of two quantities, but one quantity is always *exactly* twice the other—never $1\frac{1}{2}$ or $1\frac{3}{4}$ or any other ratio but exactly twice. In other combinations the same rule was found to apply.

Now in cookery, as any girl knows, it is possible to vary the proportions of flour, butter and sugar in a cake mix. Chemistry brings us face to face with something different. We get substances coming together in invariable proportions decided by nature and not by the "cook." They form new substances that are often totally different from either of the ingredients. What resemblance is there between water and the invisible gases hydrogen and oxygen? None! What resemblance is there between iron rust and metallic iron or gaseous oxygen? None again!

Dalton pondered over the figures for the combining weights of different elements in all sorts of compounds, and he came to the conclusion that all material substances must be made up of tiny indivisible bricks or particles all exactly the same for any given substance and all weighing the same amount. The bricks of hydrogen were of very light weight; those of oxygen were heavier and those of iron heavier still. When elementary substances combined to form compounds they made new bricks having the combined weight of the several bricks joining together. In a carbon dioxide brick there would be a brick of carbon and two of oxygen: in a carbon monoxide brick there would be a brick of carbon and only one of oxygen.

This idea of Dalton's was not completely new. More than 2,500 years before, the Greek philosophers had talked of the divisible nature of matter and decided that substances were made up of countless millions of tiny atoms. To-day the atom is imagined to be the smallest possible particle of any given elementary substance. If an atom is split it ceases to be an atom of that particular substance and becomes two atoms of other and dissimilar elementary substances. When atoms of different substances join together to form a compound substance the little family of atoms newly formed is called a molecule. Thus, a molecule is the smallest imaginable particle of a compound substance. If a molecule is split in two it ceases to be a molecule of that particular compound and it becomes two molecules or atoms of other substances.

We can see that the idea of atoms and molecules will explain the mystery of Dalton's definite and invariable combining weights. Wherever an atom of carbon appears, its weight counts as 12 if, at the same time, the weights assigned to oxygen and hydrogen are 16 and 1 respectively. The weights we must allow to be true of the atoms of the other substances we have mentioned are 32 for sulphur and 56 for iron. The following table gives a few more " atomic weights " together with those already mentioned.

TABLE OF ATOMIC WEIGHTS

Element	Atomic Weight (in commonest form)	Element	Atomic Weight (in commonest form)
Hydrogen	1	Copper	63
Carbon	12	Silver	108
Nitrogen	14	Gold	197
Oxygen	16	Mercury	200
Aluminium	27	Lead	207
Sulphur	32	Radium	226
Iron	56	Uranium	238

These weights are only relative, but nevertheless they are very useful for purposes of calculation. Using them we are able to find the relative weights of molecules of compounds. Thus, for water, the molecular weight is $2+16=18$ because there are two atoms of hydrogen and one of oxygen in a molecule of water. The molecular weight of carbon dioxide is $12+32=44$, of carbon monoxide gas $12+16=28$ and of sulphur dioxide (the gas resulting from the burning of sulphur) $32+32=64$.

We can say that a molecule of sulphur dioxide is more than twice as heavy as one of carbon monoxide, although for the moment we do not know the actual weight of either. It is, for the purpose of comparison, enough to be sure of the *relative* weights.

Chemists have had a good knowledge of the relative weights of atoms and molecules for more than 100 years now, but it is only in the present century that they have been able to get down to the business of actually weighing and measuring individual atoms.

After Dalton's work the next great discoveries concerning the nature of matter came towards the end of the nineteenth century. By this time scientists were faced with the need to explain electricity. Also the newly invented light-sensitive photographic plate was showing an ability to register mysterious effects through the light-tight box that was supposed to keep it safe and unaffected. Mystery was piling up on mystery faster than anyone could find reasons to account for them. Before the new century had dawned, men (and now, in deference to the late Madame Curie, we must include women too) were beginning to doubt whether atoms were indeed the smallest imaginable particles of matter. Experimental evidence suggested that atoms could break up into something even tinier. The new idea sprang up that the atoms of the elementary substances—atoms of nearly 100 different kinds—could all be resolved into simpler particles of only three or four different kinds and that the various atoms of the elementary substances differed only in the number and arrangement of these simpler and smaller particles.

Chapter 7

INSIDE THE ATOM

THE great scientist and mathematician, Sir Isaac Newton, who lived from 1642 to 1727, was more concerned with the emptiness we call space than with the fullness we call matter.

"What held the earth on its course round the sun? A pull of some sort, surely, but how could the sun pull the earth to itself when no rope or chain stretched between the two?"

It is easy to give a learned name to some observed effect and then regard it as being explained. Newton gave the name of "Gravitation" to the mysterious attraction of the sun for the earth and of the earth for the moon, but he never ceased to wonder at it. The name does not explain it away.

When Newton came to study the behaviour of light he was again puzzled. "How was the light of the sun able to reach us on the earth, more than 90,000,000 miles away?"

Gravitation was a force appearing to act across empty space between one body and another, but Newton thought there was no need to make a similar mystery of light. He imagined that light consisted of tiny particles (he called them "corpuscles") which shot out from the luminous body to strike the observer in the eye, thus creating the sensation of vision. Such particles could be supposed to shoot across space from the sun to the earth.

Various optical experiments made it rather difficult to believe in the corpuscular theory of light and so the scientists of a later day found it more reasonable to suppose that light came to us by a wave motion in space—a sort of ripple generated by the luminous body which spread in ever-widening circles or spheres.

Waves are to be regarded as a periodic or regular disturbance in some medium such as air or water, but no medium had been proved to exist between the earth and the sun. It had been supposed by Newton that outer space was empty of all matter. The wave theory of light required scientists to believe that space was filled with some imponderable (weightless) medium. This imaginary medium was called the "luminiferous ether."

Watching the movements of the satellites of Jupiter through a telescope, astronomers were able to calculate the speed at which light travelled through this ether. Events (such as eclipses) viewed when the earth is nearest to Jupiter are seen to happen about sixteen minutes late when the earth is farthest away, at the opposite side of its orbit. This suggests that light travels across the earth's orbit (a distance of about 186,000,000 miles) in sixteen minutes. The speed works out to about 186,000 miles a second, and there are other experiments which verify this result (see Vol. III, page 219).

In 1887 two American scientists, Michelson and Morley, conducted an experiment to find out how fast the earth was travelling through the ether. They sent out beams of light in two directions, one along the earth's path and one across it. Measuring the light's speed of travel in both directions they ought to have discovered a difference, because any man who can row a boat knows that it is quicker to row there and back a distance of ten miles across a current than in the direction of the current. What one gains when the current helps is more than offset by what one loses when rowing against the current. Michelson and Morley were disturbed to find that there was no difference at all in the light velocities they measured. It was just as though the ether moved with the earth.

Their experiment was so upsetting to preconceived ideas that it was repeated again and again by other scientists, but always with the same negative result. Either the luminiferous ether did not exist at all or else it belonged to the earth and moved with the earth. The second explanation seemed too ridiculous to accept and scientists, accepting Einstein's theory of relativity, are now trying to explain everything without the help of any ether at all. They are inclined to go back to Newton's corpuscular theory of light but with some variation to allow for increased knowledge.

The idea of tiny particles shooting about in all directions was adopted in the nineteenth century to explain some quite different happenings. A gas is able to exert a pressure on the walls of any vessel containing it. There was reason to believe that this pressure was the result of a terrific bombardment by millions of tiny molecules in a state of perpetual motion. Clerk Maxwell, a famous Cambridge scientist (see also page 495, Volume III), was convinced that heat gave motion to molecules and that the hotness (or temperature) of a body was directly related to the motion of the molecules—the hotter the faster, in fact.

In a cold, solid body molecular motion was supposed to be relatively slow and over a short average distance. Heating the body made the molecules move faster—so fast that they tended to bang each other apart and lose their grip on one another. At this stage the solid body became a liquid. Further heating caused the molecular motion to become so energetic that molecules could leap clear of all the rest and become lost in space. At this stage the liquid evaporated and became lost. If the heating of the liquid took place in an otherwise empty vessel enclosed on all sides, then the liquid became a gas and exerted a great pressure on the inside of the vessel. This pressure could only be explained by imagining a continuous bombardment of the surface by massive little molecules—millions of them going very fast.

This idea of the agitated molecular nature of liquids and gases did not please everyone—it seemed a little absurd to some. However, an English botanist, Robert Brown, in the first half of the nineteenth century had observed a very curious happening which seemed to support the idea of the molecular nature of matter. He was watching tiny grains of pollen in water through his microscope and he saw them darting about in a most curious manner. He soon confirmed that tiny grains of non-living matter behaved in exactly the same way as pollen grains. Each grain behaved as though it were being buffeted hither and thither in a crowd of invisible but very impatient grains of a different nature. This mysterious movement, called the Brownian movement, can easily be observed by anyone with a suitable microscope and a collection of sufficiently fine particles. The easiest explanation is the one supposing water molecules to be in a state of perpetual movement. The pollen grain gets pushed all ways at once but on account of its tiny size the pushes do not always average out to be the same all ways at once, as happens if the particle is larger. The push one way is greater than in other ways, so the grain is forced to stagger that way. In a moment it is staggering elsewhere under the effect of another unbalanced molecular bombardment. We do not experience this rough treatment ourselves because we are so large in comparison with molecules, but microbes must have definite impressions on the subject.

The twentieth-century scientist is now quite satisfied that molecules and atoms exist in a state of perpetual agitation and that the

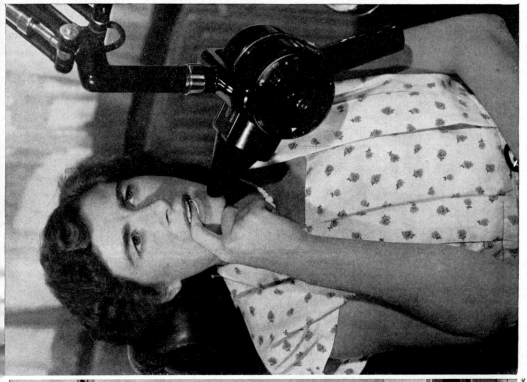

X-ray of elbow being taken by shockproof apparatus.

The smallest X-ray unit in the world. The film is held behind the teeth by the fore-finger.

Photo by Wakefields, Ltd., Chiswick

(*Both reproduced by courtesy of Philips Electrical Ltd., whose appartus is shown and by whom photos were supplied.*)

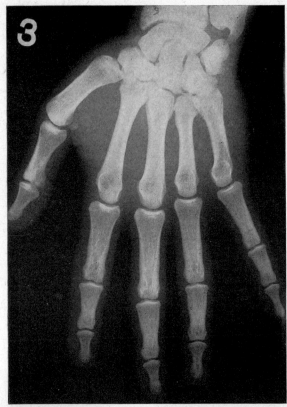

These radiographs of human bones show (*left*) a view of a hand, and (*below*) two views of an elbow joint.

By courtesy of Philips Electrical Ltd.

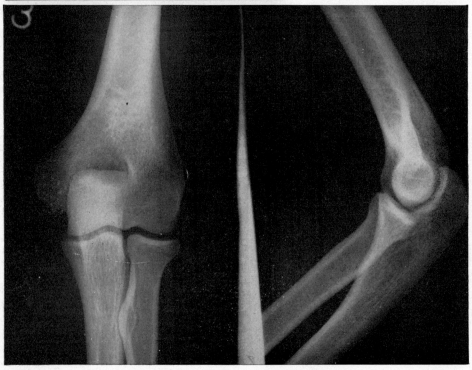

hotness of a body, as measured by a thermometer, is related to the average speed of motion of the molecules of which the body is made.

In 1896, shortly after the discovery of X-rays by the German physicist Röntgen, a French scientist, Henri Antoine Becquerel, noticed that boxed and sealed photographic plates had been fogged and spoilt by being allowed to come near a chemical compound containing the heavy metallic element uranium. It seemed to Becquerel that the effect must have been caused by spontaneously generated X-rays.

Many other scientists, including the famous husband and wife, Monsieur and Madame Curie, began to study the emanations of uranium and other natural compounds, and Madame Curie succeeded in isolating the particularly active element called radium. She gave the name radioactivity to the ray-like emanations of radium, uranium, thorium and kindred substances showing such effects. Eventually it was proved that the radiations were of three distinct kinds and that a particular radioactive substance might exhibit all three in greater or lesser degree. The three radiations were termed α-radiation (α is the Greek letter alpha), β-radiation (β is the Greek letter beta) and γ-radiation (γ is the Greek letter gamma).

Alpha radiation consists in a throwing off of electrically charged helium atoms at sufficient speed to give them a moderate penetrating power. Beta radiation consists in a scattering of high-speed electrons, the electron being a particle of practically no weight at all but with a negative electric charge. About 8,000 electrons are needed to equal the weight of a single alpha particle. The penetrating power of the beta radiation is much greater than that of alpha radiation.

Gamma radiation is a wave-like effect similar to X-rays but with a very much shorter wavelength.   It is very penetrating, like X-rays.

Alpha particles may move with sufficient speed to smash the atoms of any substance getting in their way and the English scientist Rutherford used such particles in his experiments to break up atoms. When an atom of some heavy substance such as uranium is broken up it releases a great deal of energy, usually in the form of an

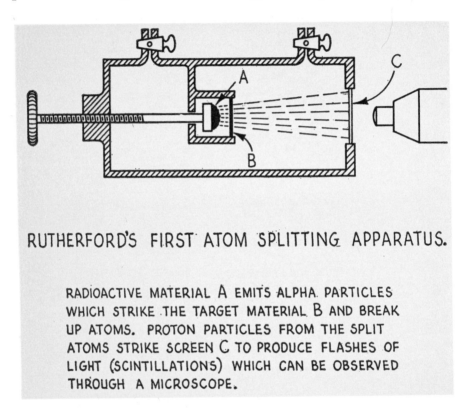

RUTHERFORD'S FIRST ATOM SPLITTING APPARATUS.

RADIOACTIVE MATERIAL A EMITS ALPHA PARTICLES WHICH STRIKE THE TARGET MATERIAL B AND BREAK UP ATOMS. PROTON PARTICLES FROM THE SPLIT ATOMS STRIKE SCREEN C TO PRODUCE FLASHES OF LIGHT (SCINTILLATIONS) WHICH CAN BE OBSERVED THROUGH A MICROSCOPE.

energetic dispersal of the component parts.   Experiments show that the atoms comprising even the most solid and compact of bodies are relatively far apart so that the bombarding alpha particles are more likely to pass between them than strike them.   They may pass right through the substance without striking a target, or they may lose their energy in collisions of a glancing nature that are not effective in breaking up any atoms.   Only at rare intervals can the experimenter hope to achieve a direct hit and so smash an atom.

Every atom appears to consist of a small massive centre or nucleus surrounded by a cloud of electrons. The nucleus carries a positive charge of electricity and this is what constrains the negatively charged electrons to remain in the vicinity. When a positively charged alpha particle approaches an atom it may be thrown aside

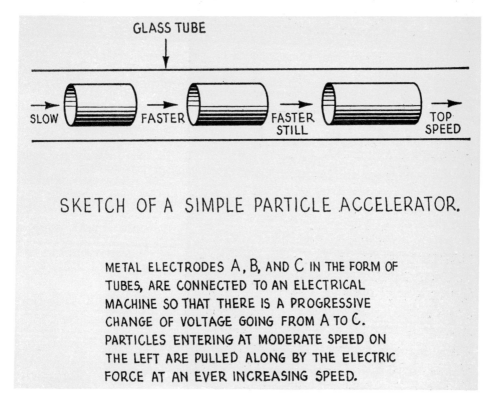

GLASS TUBE

SLOW   FASTER   FASTER   TOP
                          STILL   SPEED

SKETCH OF A SIMPLE PARTICLE ACCELERATOR.

METAL ELECTRODES A, B, AND C IN THE FORM OF
TUBES, ARE CONNECTED TO AN ELECTRICAL
MACHINE SO THAT THERE IS A PROGRESSIVE
CHANGE OF VOLTAGE GOING FROM A TO C.
PARTICLES ENTERING AT MODERATE SPEED ON
THE LEFT ARE PULLED ALONG BY THE ELECTRIC
FORCE AT AN EVER INCREASING SPEED.

by the electric force set up by the similar charge within the atom. To ensure that alpha particles might possess sufficient speed to burst through the electrons and strike the nucleus Rutherford used a machine called a "particle accelerator" for hastening their natural rate of travel. In a particle accelerator an electric field is brought to bear on the electrically charged alpha particles so that they are forced to go at an ever increasing pace. Many millions of volts

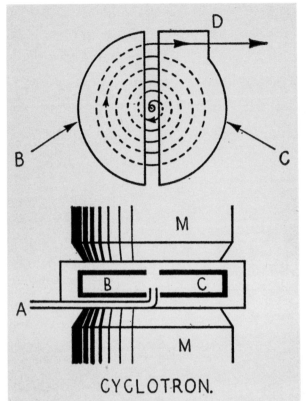

CYCLOTRON.

PARTICLES ARE ADMITTED TO THE SPACE BE-
TWEEN THE DEE-SHAPED ELECTRODES B AND
C, WHERE THEY ARE SHUTTLED TO AND FRO
BY AN ALTERNATING VOLTAGE. POLES OF THE
MAGNET M PROVIDE AN ADDITIONAL FORCE
CAUSING THE RESULTANT MOTION OF THE
PARTICLES TO BE A SPIRAL. THEY EMERGE AT
HIGH VELOCITY FROM THE WINDOW AT D.

were employed in the early kinds of particle accelerator, though in more modern ones, such as the cyclotron, the particles are made by a magnetic force to go round and round in a spiral path so as to experience the same accelerating voltage over and over again. A more moderate voltage repeatedly applied is as good as an extremely high voltage having only one chance to act.

The beta radiation is very penetrating because the electrons have a speed approaching that of light (186,000 miles a second) and so they are not easily deflected from their path. Moreover, when a light-weight particle strikes more massive ones it bounces off with hardly any loss of speed. Heavy particles such as alpha particles are obliged to share their energy with target particles (atoms) of comparable weight and so they are soon slowed down. Not so the beta particles, which are high-speed electrons about 8,000 times smaller. Beta particles slow down eventually and then they are captured by atoms that are in need of further electrons. Such atoms exist everywhere, for every flow of electric current represents a bandying of electrons from atom to atom along the line of flow. The hold of the atomic nucleus upon the outer electrons in its cloud is rather feeble and so both matter and space are relatively full of free electrons at all times.

Radioactivity is dangerous to human life because, in its more penetrating forms, it can destroy living tissue. Alpha, beta and gamma rays must be prevented from reaching the human body and consequently all experiments with radioactive materials must be performed behind thick protective screens of lead or concrete.

Radioactivity can be present without our being aware of it. That is why it constitutes such a deadly peril. Fortunately there are some simple ways of detecting its presence. Any very powerful stream of electrons or other particles will cause certain chemicals to glow with strange phosphorescent light. X-rays and gamma rays produce a similar effect. The glow from our television screen is a consequence of cleverly controlled electron bombardment. The old name for an electron stream is the "cathode ray" because the electrons spring from the hot cathode of the tube. They are attracted to the screen by an electric particle accelerator forming part of the tube, and you must be careful not to poke about inside a television set because the voltage used in the tube may run into five figures—usually it is 8,000 to 12,000 volts, and quite enough to kill.

On their way through the air harmful radiations may scatter electrons belonging to atoms of oxygen or nitrogen, so causing these molecules to appear electrically positive. Alpha particles eventually pick up stray electrons and become electrically neutral. They lose their speed and after capturing electrons they take their place in

nature as quiescent helium atoms.   Minute amounts of helium gas
are present in the earth's atmosphere everywhere, chiefly as a result
of the radioactivity going on in the earth's crust.

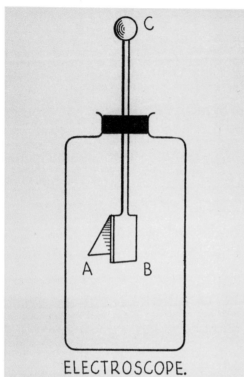

ELECTROSCOPE.

IN A SIMPLE ELECTROSCOPE A THIN
PIECE OF METAL FOIL (OFTEN GOLD LEAF)
IS HINGED ALONG ITS UPPER EDGE TO A
RIGID METAL PLATE B. WHEN AN ELECT-
RIC CHARGE IS GIVEN TO THE APPAR-
ATUS, THROUGH KNOB C, THE FOIL
MOVES AWAY FROM B AS FAR AS
POSSIBLE. IT FALLS BACK AGAIN
SLOWLY AS THE CHARGE IS LOST.

The original alpha particle leaves behind it a trail of positively charged atoms of atmospheric gases and if there is an intensive radiation of alpha particles much of the air in the vicinity becomes electrically charged or "ionised" as a scientist would say.   Now ionised air differs from ordinary air in being able to conduct electricity, so we can detect the presence of radioactivity by noticing whether the air is still an electrical insulator or not. If we hang up two balls of pith side by side and give each of them a small electric charge they will fly apart and they will stay that way in ordinary air for a long time.   In ionised air, however, they will quickly lose their charges and so fall together again.   The simplest radiation detector or "monitor" is called an "electroscope" and it depends on this principle of the loss of an electric charge whenever and wherever danger from radioactivity is encountered.

Another detector is the Geiger counter. This is a glass tube having electrodes like a valve but containing a gas that is ionised and so made electrically conducting whenever a charged particle shoots through it from outside. The electrodes are part of a circuit including a battery and a relay so that current flows through the

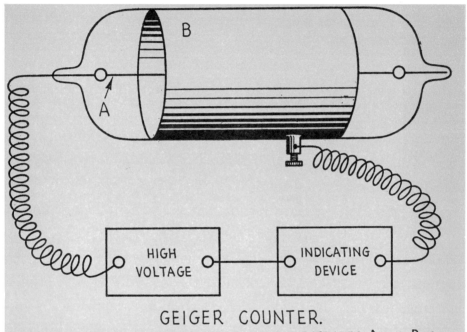

GEIGER COUNTER.

A THIN-WALLED GAS CONTAINER HAVING TWO ELECTRODES A AND B IS CONNECTED THROUGH AN INDICATING DEVICE TO A HIGH-VOLTAGE SOURCE. THE GAS IN THE TUBE IS IONISED (AND MADE ELECTRICALLY CONDUCTING) BY THE ENTRY OF α, β OR γ RADIATION AND SMALL AMOUNTS CAN THUS BE DETECTED.

relay whenever a particle passes through the tube. The closing of the relay by the current is only momentary, and it operates a counter or makes a clicking noise. In the presence of dangerous radio-activity the Geiger counter clicks quite frantically. Even the emanations from the dial of a luminous wrist-watch are sufficient to set it clicking. So too are the particles ever present in our atmosphere as a consequence of the mysterious cosmic rays reaching us from outer space.

Since particular heavy substances are always throwing off alpha particles and electrons, their atoms must be made up of such particles in the first place. The loss of alpha particles represents a loss of mass. In fact the atoms of some radioactive substances become measurably lighter. They become transformed or transmuted into atoms of other and less heavy elements. It is a case of the alchemists' dream coming true, only the end product is not gold but lead. Radioactive elements turn atom by atom into something else. The new element may be radioactive too, and so the process of transformation continues. Stage by stage the elementary transformation goes on, and after a period of years—it may be millions of years— only lead remains.

The rate of transformation of a pure element like radium is rapid at first but it gradually tails off. After a certain interval (1,620 years for radium) only half of the original element remains. In another interval of the same length the quantity of the original substance will be halved again. Yet a third interval will see a third halving. In theory the original substance can never vanish completely but the amount of it grows ever smaller. The interval during which the amount of the substance is halved is called its "half life." For uranium it is 45,000,000,000 years. By measuring the amount of uranium left in a natural mineral that must have consisted wholly of uranium at the time when the earth was first created, scientists are able to estimate the present age of the earth— it comes out to some thousands of millions of years.

Rutherford and other scientists engaged in splitting atoms were always longing to discover a particle that would be more effective than the alpha particle. Owing to its electric charge, an alpha particle was always liable to be thrown off its course by an electric force. Since every atomic nucleus is surrounded by an electric force this meant that the alpha particle made an unreliable missile. The real need was for a particle with the mass of an alpha particle, or something comparable, but no electric charge.

In 1930 some German scientists exposed beryllium to alpha rays from polonium and obtained a new kind of radiation that was first mistaken for supremely powerful gamma rays. In 1932 the English scientist Chadwick said that the effects of this radiation could be explained only by supposing that it consisted of particles comparable in weight with alpha particles but without electric charge. These newly discovered particles, called neutrons because of their electric neutrality, were the dream particles of Rutherford. Given sufficient speed they would go straight to their target and smash it. The problem was to give them the necessary speed, since an electrically neutral particle could not be influenced by an electric particle accelerator. Fortunately the speed of those neutrons which could be induced to appear naturally was, if anything, too high for most practical purposes rather than too low, and it was always possible to slow them down by mechanical means.

Neutrons were soon found to occur in the vicinity of natural uranium. They had not been noticed before because the most common ways of observing the flight of particles did not show up the neutron. They all depended on the ionisation effect produced by electrically charged particles. This was true not only of the Geiger counter (first introduced in 1908), but also of the "cloud chamber" invented by the English scientist C. T. R. Wilson in 1911. The working principle of the cloud chamber must now be described.

Air saturated with moisture is expanded in a glass vessel that

c. 11—3*

can be enlarged suddenly by having one of its walls retracted. A mist forms as a result of the sudden cooling and the moisture, as always, chooses to condense on particular particles of dust or other nuclei present in the space occupied. Wilson observed that ionised molecules of atmospheric gases would serve as nuclei for condensation. He filled his chamber with air that had been made free of all dust and he expanded it after he had reason to think the space had been traversed by alpha or beta particles. After the expansion he saw thin white lines of mist crossing the chamber from side to side, showing where a particle had gone along ionising molecules in its path. If a particle had actually struck a molecule and bounced off at an angle, then the cloud track showed a sudden change of direction at that point. The cloud chamber was a marvellous new device for keeping track of alpha and beta particles, but it failed to show the passage of neutrons because neutrons did not ionise the air through which they passed. Neutrons escaped observation until the Germans produced an unexpected effect in 1930 as already explained. Not even the Geiger counter

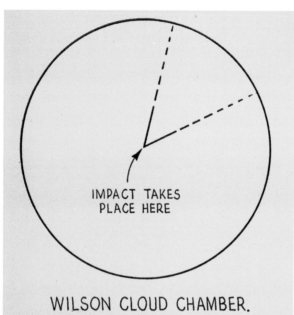

IMPACT TAKES
PLACE HERE

WILSON CLOUD CHAMBER.

A NEUTRON CANNOT IONISE THE AIR SO IT CANNOT LEAVE A CLOUD TRACK. IF HOWEVER, A NEUTRON STRIKES AN ATOM IT MAY SEPARATE THE NUCLEUS FROM THE ELECTRONS AND THE SCATTERED PORTIONS ARE ABLE TO LEAVE TRAILS AS SHOWN.

can detect neutrons because this device too depends on ionisation.

After the identification of the neutron in 1932 it became evident that an atom of any particular substance might consist of particles of three distinct kinds. The nucleus could consist of neutral particles called neutrons together with similar but positively charged particles called protons. Surrounding the whole was the usual cloud of electrons, their number being equal to the number of protons in the nucleus. The charges on electrons and protons were equal but of opposite sign, the electrons being negative.

According to this view of the atom (and I am afraid it is a simplified view that most scientists to-day would regard as misleading) the hydrogen atom (lightest in all Nature) consists of one proton and one electron. Its weight is counted as 1. The helium atom contains two protons, two neutrons and two electrons. Its weight is counted as 4. As we get to heavier elements we may have a nucleus containing more neutrons than protons. The weight is to be taken as the number of neutrons and protons added together because a neutron weighs the same as a proton for all practical purposes. The

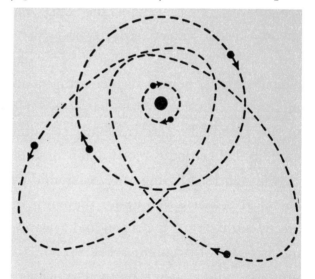

A CARBON ATOM AS IMAGINED BY RUTHERFORD AND BOHR.

SIX ELECTRONS TRAVEL ROUND THE MASSIVE NUCLEUS, WHICH HAS SIX POSITIVE ELECTRIC CHARGES TO BALANCE. ATOMS ARE BOUND TOGETHER TO FORM MOLECULES BY THE INTERLINKING OF THEIR ELECTRON PATHS.

electrons in attendance on a nucleus are equal in number to the protons in that nucleus. If there is any difference the atom as a whole shows an electric charge and is called an ion. For many purposes the weight of the electrons can be ignored.

The nature of an element is determined not by its atomic weight but by the number of protons in its nucleus. This is called the atomic number. It is now known that a particular substance— chlorine, for instance—can have two or more atomic weights, the difference being due to the fact that some chlorine atoms contain more neutrons than others. Hydrogen consists normally of a proton and an electron per atom, but there is a heavy hydrogen, called deuterium, in which every atom comprises a proton and a neutron for nucleus together with the usual electron for attendant. So called "heavy water" is water in which heavy hydrogen occupies the place of ordinary hydrogen. It is dangerous stuff to drink and it appears after a time in increasing quantities in the electrolyte of motor-car and other storage batteries. Heavy water is very valuable to the scientist because it is slow and difficult to make in any great quantity. It costs £20,000 a ton or more.

Substances differing only in atomic weight but having the same chemical properties go under the name of "isotopes." Thus there are two isotopes of hydrogen and several of uranium. The interesting isotopes of uranium are U235 and U238. The former has 92 protons and 143 neutrons in its nucleus whereas the latter has 92 protons and 146 neutrons in its nucleus. Uranium as found in nature is a mixture of the isotopes and the proportion of U235 is very small. Nevertheless U235 is of particular interest to the scientist because its atoms can be split by neutron bombardment and there is a great release of energy.

A splitting U235 atom releases further neutrons with the requisite velocity (after being slowed down somewhat) to split other atoms of U235. Thus a lump of U235, if large enough to prevent the escape of an unduly large number of fast neutrons, will spontaneously disintegrate, atom after atom splitting in progressively increasing numbers until there is a catastrophic explosion.

The first of the atom bombs used in World War II consisted of

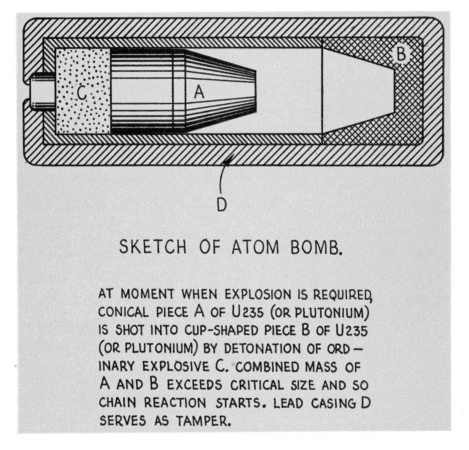

SKETCH OF ATOM BOMB.

AT MOMENT WHEN EXPLOSION IS REQUIRED, CONICAL PIECE A OF U235 (OR PLUTONIUM) IS SHOT INTO CUP-SHAPED PIECE B OF U235 (OR PLUTONIUM) BY DETONATION OF ORD— INARY EXPLOSIVE C. COMBINED MASS OF A AND B EXCEEDS CRITICAL SIZE AND SO CHAIN REACTION STARTS. LEAD CASING D SERVES AS TAMPER.

two pieces of uranium 235 each too small to start the necessary chain reaction. At the moment the bomb was required to explode, the two pieces were brought together to form a single lump larger than the critical size. Surrounding the uranium and forming a container was a vessel of some massive substance, such as lead, the purpose of which was to hold everything together as long as possible and thus give the chain reaction time to get well under way before scattering of the uranium occurred. For this purpose you might think a strong steel container would have been needed but, actually, a soft easily ruptured lead one was better. The strength of the strongest steel would offer little resistance to the expansion of the uranium, but the inertia of the massive lead can offer a resistance which is great in proportion to the rapidity of the uranium's attempt to expand. Used in this way to confine an explosion in its earliest stages, a massive surrounding body of material is called the "tamper."

Before a bomb of $U235$ could be made the scientists needed to separate a substantial amount of $U235$ from its other isotope $U238$. This separation could not be achieved chemically because any chemical showing an affinity for one isotope is equally affected by the other. It was necessary to pick out the $U235$ atom by atom, as though by hand. One appliance for sorting into separate places the atoms of different weights is the "mass spectrograph," an appliance developed in 1919 by the English scientist Aston. A stream of gaseous molecules, ionised beforehand, is made to pass through a strong electric or electro-magnetic field. The molecules are all deflected in their path by the interaction between their charges and the electric field. They behave like the electrons forming the cathode ray in a television picture tube. However, the electrons in a picture tube all keep together, being of equal mass, whereas the molecules of a gas may tend to fan out into two or more separate beams. This happens if the gas is one with isotopes of separate atomic or molecular weights. Natural uranium can be combined with other substances to form a gaseous compound. The molecules made with $U238$ atoms are more massive than those made with $U235$ atoms, consequently they will take a straighter course through the mass spectrograph. The relatively lighter molecules containing U235 atoms will be more easily deflected. At the far end of the instrument, therefore, we can collect separate lots of gas—one lot contain-

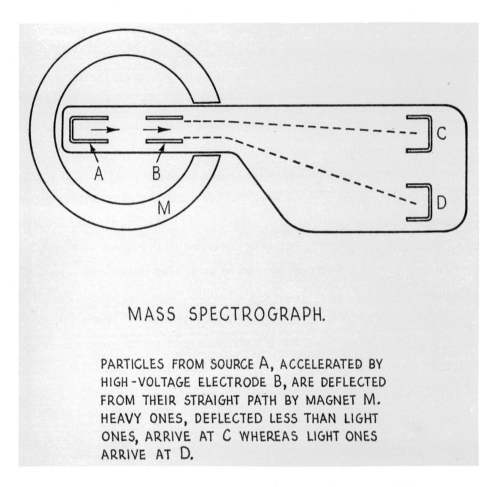

MASS SPECTROGRAPH.

PARTICLES FROM SOURCE A, ACCELERATED BY HIGH-VOLTAGE ELECTRODE B, ARE DEFLECTED FROM THEIR STRAIGHT PATH BY MAGNET M. HEAVY ONES, DEFLECTED LESS THAN LIGHT ONES, ARRIVE AT C WHEREAS LIGHT ONES ARRIVE AT D.

ing U238 and the other (and much smaller lot) containing U235. By chemical means it is possible to recover pure U238 from the first lot of gas and pure U235 from the second.

The process is painfully slow, many years being needed to obtain as little as one ounce of U235 by this means. To obtain worthwhile quantities of U235 the Americans set in motion many thousands of identical mass spectrographs. Simultaneously, however, they evolved and brought into use another method of separation. Here too the natural uranium was combined with other substances to form a gas. This gas was put into a chamber with a porous wall through which it could percolate. Now, light-weight molecules have a higher average speed than heavy-weight ones at any given temperature (see page 64) and therefore they get through a porous barrier rather more readily than heavy-weight ones. Taking the gas from the far side of the porous barrier you would find the proportion of U235 in it had been increased relative to what it had been originally. This enriched gas was passed through another porous barrier and yet another, the process continuing until practically all the molecules contained U235, almost all the molecules bearing U238 having been left behind. Once again the process was slow, and to make it effective the Americans were obliged to make a plant covering many acres of ground.

During the last years of World War II the American scientists were able to collect enough U235 to make an atom bomb and this bomb was exploded over the city of Hiroshima in Japan.

A material which can have its atoms split in two to form other and dissimilar substances is said to be "fissionable," and the process of splitting is called "fission."

Chapter 8

PEACEFUL USES OF ATOMIC ENERGY

In the last chapter you learnt how, in a slow and difficult way, the isotopes of uranium can be separated one from another, a necessary preliminary to the construction of a bomb or any other appliance requiring pure atomic "fuel."

A much better idea for the manufacture of atomic fuel occurred to some French scientists shortly before World War II. Their idea was taken up by the University of Chicago and put into practical effect during the war. According to this idea lumps of natural uranium, consisting mainly of U238, are embedded in a large mass of some substance called a "moderator" and left to work their own miracle of change. What happens is that neutrons projected from the U235 at great speed are slowed down by the moderator until there is a greater probability of their striking and splitting other U235 atoms than of being absorbed or "captured" by U238 atoms. Fast neutrons are more likely to be captured by U238 atoms, and when this happens a new isotope of uranium, U239, is formed. This is radioactive and has a half life of only 23 minutes. It gives off beta particles during its decay, and it turns into an element not present in nature called neptunium. This in turn decays very fast, becoming, as a result of beta radiation, yet another element called plutonium. The half life of neptunium is 2·3 days, which explains why you will never find any of it lying about. Plutonium has a larger half life, for one isotope at least it is 24,000 years. It re-

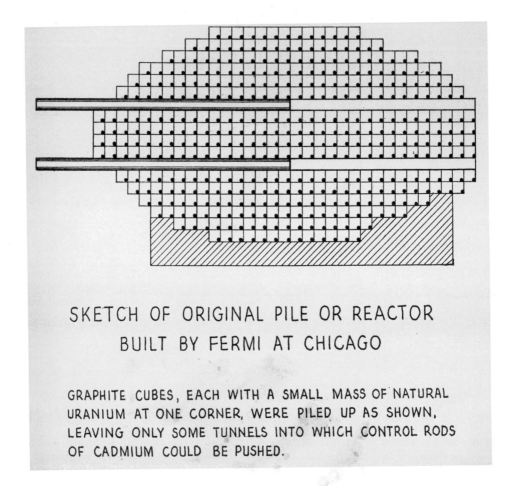

SKETCH OF ORIGINAL PILE OR REACTOR
BUILT BY FERMI AT CHICAGO

GRAPHITE CUBES, EACH WITH A SMALL MASS OF NATURAL
URANIUM AT ONE CORNER, WERE PILED UP AS SHOWN,
LEAVING ONLY SOME TUNNELS INTO WHICH CONTROL RODS
OF CADMIUM COULD BE PUSHED.

sembles U235 in being fissionable and therefore suitable for bomb manufacture.

The "plum-pudding" arrangement of natural uranium in a moderator is called a "reactor" or "pile." It is kept going by the splitting of U235 atoms, and it produces a quantity of heat as well as converting U238 into plutonium. The pile has to be made very large so that the escape of neutrons near the edges can be tolerated. Obviously the neutrons emitted in the pile must be enough to allow for losses to the outside world and losses by capture. If the splitting of a U235 atom did not produce enough neutrons to split another, despite neutron losses, the reaction would come to a full stop.

Is there in a reactor any danger of U235 atoms being split at an ever-increasing rate, causing the reaction to get out of control and lead to an explosion? Yes, indeed, there is this danger in a simple pile, but control can be exercised by having rods of cadmium running through holes in the moderator. These rods will capture neutrons to any desired extent if they are pushed into the pile far enough. The man responsible for controlling the pile can adjust the position of the rods until a thermometer shows that the reaction is neither too fast nor too slow.

The original idea was to use heavy water as a moderator, and this is why, during World War II, so much great trouble was taken to destroy German installations in Norway and elsewhere for the manufacture of heavy water.

The purpose of the moderator is to slow down the pace of neutrons shot off by U235 until their speed is about the same as that of molecules in an ordinary gas. The motion of ordinary molecules is what gives a substance its temperature, and neutrons slowed to about the same speed are referred to as "thermal" neutrons on account of the similarity.

You might think a heavy substance would make the best moderator, but it is not so. If a large object is struck by a small one the small one rebounds with hardly any loss of speed. If a small object is struck, however, the energy is shared and the original traveller rebounds with a much diminished speed. The ideal moderator for neutrons therefore is one which has light-weight molecules. Unfortunately, the lightest substances are able to capture neutrons, and so they would completely stop the chain reaction. Ordinary water could capture neutrons because the hydrogen in it would seize them in order to become deuterium. Heavy water has had its appetite for neutrons fully satisfied already and so it will serve very well as a moderator. A better substance still, however, being a solid and not a liquid, is pure graphite (a form of carbon), and this is the substance used nowadays.

The heat from a properly constructed pile can be used to generate steam and so operate an electricity-generating plant. Not long after the war of 1939–45, small-scale pilot plants were set up in France, the United States and Soviet Russia, the most powerful providing about 7,000 horse-power. Of more practical proportions was the Calder Hall power station in Cumberland, England. Opened in 1956 it was one of several that were destined in the future to supply Britain's need for electricity by utilising atomic energy. The boiler utilises a reactor instead of a coal-burning furnace. The beauty of the arrangement is that although $U235$ is consumed in relatively small amounts the vastly more plentiful and vastly less useful $U238$ is turned into plutonium at a rate exceeding the consumption of $U235$. So the engineers will be able to do better than eat their cake and have it. They will eat their cake and have one a good deal larger!

A reactor of sufficient size to provide the power needed in a generating station is a large and heavy affair. Some of this great weight is occasioned by the need for screening the human operatives from harmful radiation. Neutron radiation is particularly dangerous. The question may be asked whether it will ever be possible to make a small reactor of sufficient power to propel a train or a motor-car or an aircraft. The United States Navy already has in service a number of submarines powered by reactors and ships of this type are in use by Britain and other naval powers. There is the likelihood that a railway locomotive could be constructed to work on similar principles, but for motor-cars and aircraft the bulk and weight of the necessary equipment are likely to be prohibitive. Some new ideas will have to arise from a study of the problem before there can be any atomic motor-cars or atomic aircraft.

Although atomic energy promises to become an alternative to coal as a means of providing energy in power stations and in heavy pro-pulsion units such as ships and locomotives, it is not likely in the near future to decrease Man's dependence on petroleum on the road and in the air. It would be easy to exaggerate the future prospects of atomic energy, and as Sir Francis Simon, of Oxford University, said on the radio (January 15th, 1956), "Too many people have con-veniently developed a childlike belief in the miraculous powers of atomic energy; they regard it as a good fairy who will give all, even the naughtiest children, what they ask for."

On the whole, the peaceful uses envisaged for atomic energy, though important, are not spectacular. Small reactors are used for making ordinary non-radioactive materials into short-lived radio-active ones. Phosphorus and iodine can be given the property of mild radioactivity for a brief period of hours or days and, thus affected, they can be of great use in biological or medical research. Either can be fed to a sick person or animal and then its journey into the body can be followed very closely with a Geiger counter. By this use of so-called "tracer elements" scientists can discover just what happens to anything that is taken into the body.

Tracer elements have their uses in complex chemical or indus-trial processes too, and no doubt the crime-detection experts at Scotland Yard find them useful for marking things that are likely to go astray and then be normally hard to trace. No need to search a person having radioactive objects on him, or to open his luggage! A Geiger counter will give the game away at once!

In medicine and biology the functioning of normal healthy organisms can be studied and compared with the functioning of diseased ones, and here again the radioactive tracers are of enormous assistance. The reactor at Harwell, England, supplies tracers to all who have a genuine need for them, and a special express delivery service has been set up to deal with those tracers whose useful life is limited to minutes or hours. Unfortunately a number of the most important chemical elements can be made radioactive only for a fraction of the time we would like to have them under observation. This is a limitation of the method, and there may not be any way of overcoming it.

Although radioactivity in large doses is very harmful to living things, medical evidence seems to show that small doses can be experienced without injurious effects again and again. There is no adding-up or cumulative poisoning effect. If the second dose is given after an interval long enough to allow the effect of the first dose to wear off, then no harm is done. This is only to be expected, as we are all of us subjected all the time to natural radioactivity in minute degree. For a while the Russians and the Americans continually tested new kinds of atomic bomb and these tests caused the atmosphere to be laden with radioactive dust, particles of which drifted many thousands of miles to become harmful as " fall out " in other countries all over the world. When China exploded her first atomic device in 1964, the fall-out was detected in Britain in less than 3 weeks. Some of the chemicals broadcast as fall-out, particularly Strontium 90, may cause an increase in the natural level of radiation lasting for hundreds or even thousands of years so the testing of bombs has now been stopped by most of the great powers.

Chapter 9

RADIOACTIVITY IN NATURE AND SPACE TRAVEL

IT is becoming fashionable with some people to grumble at scientists and treat them as though they invented radioactivity and brought the curse of the hydrogen bomb upon the human race. Of course, it is not altogether true. Radioactivity has always been with us. Scientists now believe that the internal heat of the earth is generated by radioactive minerals beneath the surface. The whole earth is in effect like a great pile or reactor, as described in Chapter 8.

Heat percolates through layer upon layer of rock to reach the surface at last. In some places this emergence of heat is very noticeable, as there are hot springs, geysers and volcanoes to mark the spot. Among the older theories about the birth of our earth are several which begin with the supposition that the planets once formed part of the sun. Modern physicists are now of a different opinion because they say that the heavy elements, and especially the radioactive ones, could never have been created in the relatively mild heat of the sun. Vastly higher temperatures were required— temperatures attainable only in stars of the white-dwarf variety. Be this as it may the moment of creation certainly left our earth with substances of an atomic complexity not paralleled by anything observable in the sun, where the chief elements seem to be hydrogen and helium—simplest of all the elements. This legacy of the past includes elements such as uranium, thorium and radium, which have never accepted their lot in the universe. Their atoms are unstable in the sense that sooner or later they must fall apart. Radium atoms are disintegrating at such a rate that in every 1,620 years the amount of radium in the world would be halved were there no process of replacement. A similar process of disappearance is overtaking all the other radioactive materials.

These large unstable atoms give off a great deal of energy in the process of their decay. If an atom of any one of them is shattered by the impact of a neutron or an alpha particle the release of energy is sudden and spectacular. When many such atoms are split in a second of time or less the result is a catastrophic explosion. However, there is a similar release of energy at the other end of the atomic scale when light-weight atoms fuse together to form heavier atoms. The uranium bomb is an example of energy from the *fission* or splitting of atoms, but in the sun and in the hydrogen bomb we see energy resulting from the rushing together or *fusion* of pairs of hydrogen atoms to form helium atoms.

In 1939 H. A. Bethe of the United States and C. F. Von Weizsäcker of Germany predicted that in the presence of oxygen and carbon it should be possible to bring about the fusion of hydrogen atoms to form helium atoms and that the result would be an immense liberation of energy. In practice the reaction could not be obtained experimentally because it required the generation of a sun-hot temperature to set it going. Bethe and Weizsäcker suggested that the reaction might actually be taking place in the sun and that, if so, it would explain what had long been a profound mystery, namely how the sun, after some thousands of millions of years, was still able to go on pouring out heat on a scale quite inexplicable by the ordinary laws of physics or chemistry.

The atom bomb developed temperatures comparable with those occurring in the sun, and so scientists foresaw the possibility that they could test out the theory of Bethe and Weizsäcker. Using the heat generated in an atom bomb to start the reaction going they actually succeeded in combining hydrogen atoms to form helium according to the process foreseen as possible. We now know our sun for what it really is, and we can predict how long it will last with a fair degree of accuracy. It is good for many millions of years yet. At the same time this triumph of science has left us with ideas for a new and even more terrible instrument of destruction, because the conversion of hydrogen to helium, as in the sun, is a principle that can be embodied in a bomb many thousands of times more powerful than the ordinary bomb of fissionable material.

But we ought not to complain that a new situation has been created as the problem of right usage of scientific instruments has always been with us. A hammer developed for banging nails into wood, or a knife, friends of many uses, can both be weapons in the hands of a foe. Motor-cars, aircraft and all the other implements of common and beneficial usage have their harmful possibilities. The hydrogen to helium conversion is usable in bad ways too, but scientists are hopeful that one day they may be able to regulate the process at will, so deriving useful heat and power from it. A beginning was attempted at Harwell, England, in a piece of equipment called Zeta. The solar process is too complicated for imitation in a machine but in Zeta some atoms of heavy hydrogen, or deuterium, were thought to have been fused together at a temperature of five million degrees centigrade. The useful output of heat was scarcely measurable but, if the temperature could have been raised to about 500 million degrees, the heat output might have become great enough to realise men's hopes of extracting power from sea water, which contains enough deuterium to make it, bulk for bulk, as valuable as petrol. The greatest difficulty is to achieve such an enormously high temperature in the face of heat's natural tendency to escape by radiation, and melt anything in its way.

One other aspect of radioactivity needs to be mentioned because of people's growing interest in space travel. By means of the Geiger counter and in other ways we are made aware of a ceaseless bombardment of the earth from outer space by particles of enormous energy content. The so-called cosmic rays can be detected even at the bottom of a deep mine or at the bed of the ocean. Scientists do not believe that the effects we observe at or near the earth's surface are caused by the original particles from outer space; in their opinion the original particles from outer space are stopped by our atmosphere but only because their energy is used up in creating and setting in motion secondary particles. It may be a case of particle A bumping particle B, thus causing B to bump C which bumps D and so on. The cosmic ray as we experience it may be an ordinary terrestrial particle that has obtained its enormous energy indirectly from a cosmic particle. The only thing we can be sure of is that outer space is shot through and through with powerful and in some cases mysterious radiations as well as with ordinary meteors. The question naturally arises whether human beings, beyond the protective shield of the earth's atmosphere, can make themselves safe against what lies beyond.

Man has always dreamed of being able to venture into outer space on a journey towards the moon or one of the other heavenly bodies. Aircraft require an atmosphere to sustain them and assist in the combustion process that provides the propulsive effort. But in World War II the Germans perfected a self-contained rocket—

the dreaded V2—that could shoot up so high into space as to enable it to cross over from the Continent of Europe and land with a bang in the heart of London. Since the end of the war, experimenters, employed by their governments, have evolved rockets powerful enough to project capsules weighing pounds, hundredweights and even tons, into space with such speed as to escape from the earth altogether. These rockets are in several parts or stages and the heaviest is only to give the remainder a good start. When its fuel is spent it breaks away, leaving the second stage rocket to push on upwards. In the final stage the jet of the rocket operates in virtually empty space and its flame is maintained with no help from atmospheric oxygen as the rocket carries its own supply.

The capsule may be directed outwards to intercept the moon or some other planet. Alternatively it may be sent into orbit round the earth so as to circle round and round like a little moon. Used in this way it is called an artificial satellite.

The Russians and Americans have both put capsules full of scientific instruments into orbit round the earth, but the Russians were first with their Sputnik I, launched on October 4th, 1957, and weighing 184 lb. The instruments in a Sputnik are for measuring temperature, cosmic radiation and other effects and for sending coded reports back to earth by radio. Electric power for the instruments may come from dry batteries, but if prolonged service is needed then solar batteries can be provided. These are in principle like the tiny element in a photographic exposure or light meter but much more powerful.

On November 3rd, 1957, the Russians put into orbit Sputnik II, which weighed half a ton and carried the dog Laika. Both Sputniks remained circling the earth at a rate of one circuit in approximately 90 minutes for several months, but the dog Laika was a sacrifice to science as no arrangements were made for getting her back alive. The problem of recovering passengers alive by means of auxiliary power rockets and parachutes was not solved until August 19th, 1960, when the Russians brought back alive and well the dogs Strelka and Belka, after an orbital flight of 18 earth circuits in a space-ship weighing 4½ tons. Belka has since had six healthy puppies, which suggests that she suffered no harm from her experience. On April 12th, 1961, Major Yuri Gagarin completed the first manned space flight, orbiting the earth at 18,000 miles an hour. In August 1961, Major Gherman Titov circled the earth 17 times. In the same year the Americans successfully transported first Commander Shephard and then Captain Grissom by rocket over a distance of several hundreds of miles. Colonel Glenn was the first American to orbit the earth in February 1962, and in May 1962 Commander Carpenter, another American, orbited the earth 3 times, both landed safely.

In September 1959 the Russians hit the moon with a rocket weighing about a ton and a half, and on October 4 in the same year a Russian rocket circumnavigated the moon and sent back by television some photos made of its remote face—never before seen by humans. In February 1961 a space probe of about 1500 lb. was sent towards the planet Venus on a journey of over 54 million miles. This was to be the first of several " probes " equipped to find out about the planets. In 1969 a " probe" confirmed that Mars seemed to be as dry and lifeless as the moon. The Americans made three successful manned moon flights and landings, two in 1969 and a third in 1971, on each occasion astronauts walked on the moon's surface and returned to earth safely bringing with them samples of lunar rock and dust, television pictures were relayed to earth during flight and from the moon's surface.

Chapter 10

MORE GREAT NAMES

AT the end of Volume III you were able to read about some of the scientists whose names are enshrined in such everyday electrical terms as Volt, Ampere, Watt and so on. In this chapter you will be able to read a little about the people whose experiments and discoveries prepared the way for the two great twentieth-century developments of electronics and nuclear (or atomic) physics.

Both developments may fairly be said to have originated in the efforts of scientists to determine the nature of light. During the first half of the nineteenth century there was the conviction that light consisted of waves, but nobody could say what kind of waves. Waves in water and waves in the air were tangible things, and their existence could be demonstrated in so many ways as to leave their nature in no doubt. Light waves, however, occurred in empty space and were non-material. Such waves were very hard to imagine, and proofs of their existence were mathematical rather than physical or experimental.

Now empty space was known to transmit magnetic and electric strains as well as light. Gravitation too was an influence exerted across empty space. It was natural for scientists to think, sooner or later, that there might be some connection or similarity between light and the forces of electricity, magnetism and gravitation.

93

It is believed that William Thomson was the first scientist to have this idea.

Thomson was born in Belfast in 1824, and he was to become famous as Lord Kelvin. At the age of 21 he achieved distinction in mathematics at Cambridge, and one year later he became Professor of Natural Science at Glasgow University. He held this office for 53 years. Besides adding enormously to the scientific understanding of heat and electricity, Thomson achieved many successes in the practical field of engineering. The success of the first telegraph cable to be laid across the Atlantic Ocean must be attributed to him, for without his mathematical planning beforehand nobody would have managed to receive an intelligible signal at the far end of so long a wire. Careful preliminary design was needed to avoid losses and distortions on the way.

When Thomson suggested that light waves might be of electromagnetic nature the idea was taken up by James Clerk Maxwell, another mathematical genius.

Maxwell was born in Edinburgh in 1831. He became a Fellow of Trinity College, Cambridge, in 1855, and in 1871 he became the professor of experimental physics there. He investigated Thomson's theory concerning the nature of light waves, and in 1864 he gave to the world his famous but very difficult mathematical account of the whole matter. From this work it was quite clear that electromagnetic waves might be of any length and not be confined merely to the spectrum of visible light. On the one hand they could be even shorter than light waves (and measurable only in millionths of a millimetre); on the other hand they could have a length measurable in whole millimetres, centimetres, metres or even kilometres. Maxwell could not know anything about waves far outside the visible spectrum because the methods for generating or detecting such waves did not exist in 1864, but his equations showed clearly that such longer or shorter waves were within the bounds of possibility.

The longer varieties of invisible electro-magnetic wave were the first to be generated and detected in practice. Heinrich Rudolf Hertz, who was born in Hamburg and lived from 1857 to 1894, constructed apparatus which amounted to a crude short-wave radio transmitter and a tuned receiver, or detector. He was able to produce electro-magnetic waves of a few metres in wavelength and detect them over a space of several yards. Had his detecting device been more sensitive he might have obtained results over much greater distances. He published the results of his experiments in 1890, but it does not appear that he envisaged the possibility of using these waves as a basis for telegraphy without wires—or " wireless telegraphy " as the idea became called when, at a later date, Marconi developed it and made it successful.

What are " wireless " waves? They are, according to the Maxwell theory, a longer variety of the waves that produce light or radiant heat. Any movement of an electric charge produces a magnetic effect in surrounding space. A periodic movement produces a pulsating magnetic effect. When an electric current surges to-and-fro in a coil of wire the surrounding space is filled with lines of both electric and magnetic force. The two forces, electric and magnetic, are at right angles to one another in space: also they are out of step, one being a maximum when the other is nothing and vice versa. This state of affairs in the space round a coil is contagious, just like the displacement of one end of a long stretched rope. The disturbance at the coil is transmitted to a distance like the wave in a rope, only it spreads in more directions than one. It spreads at an equal rate in all directions at once over a spherical front, and the rate at which the electro-magnetic ripple travels is equal to the speed of light—about 186,000 miles a second.

Light waves are not generated by electric surges in a coil of wire but by some vibration inside the atoms of very hot objects. Clearly the vibration must involve the rapid to-and-fro movement of electricity because it is the movement of electricity that generates space waves. The idea of the electrical content of the atom dates from Maxwell's proof of the identity of light with electro-magnetic waves.

Who was the first person ever to generate waves shorter than light waves? The answer to this question must be in two parts. Waves only a little shorter than light waves are generated in nature by all hotly luminous bodies, and they are called " ultra-violet rays " because they are like light of the shortest wavelength (violet light) only shorter still and they cannot be seen except with the aid of a photographic plate or a fluorescent screen. Such a screen is a piece of glass or other substance covered with a chemical that becomes luminous when rays of very short wavelength impinge on it. Actually our teeth and finger-nails have this property of fluorescence, so that if you were to meet a friend in a pitch-dark room flooded with ultra-violet rays from a special " dark " lamp all you would see of him would be a ghastly grin and glistening talons.

Waves shorter even than those of ultra-violet " light " were first generated by Wilhelm Konrad Röntgen, of Prussia, who lived from 1845 to 1923. He was director of the Physical Institute at the University of Würzburg, and he was experimenting with a cathode-ray tube when he saw a fluorescent screen mysteriously glowing, although it was a long way from his tube. It continued to glow even when he covered the tube with thick paper. He soon proved this new ray to be of a very penetrating nature, able to go through his own flesh and throw on the screen a shadow of his bones. Because of its unknown nature he called the newly discovered ray the X-ray. It still retains this name although its nature is now well understood—it is an electro-magnetic wave still shorter in wavelength than ultra-violet "light." Röntgen's discovery was made known in 1895.

When radioactivity was discovered, only a few months later, part of the effect, called the "gamma ray," was found to be an electro-magnetic wave even shorter in wavelength than the X-ray.

It is believed now that whereas light waves arise from vibrations among the inner electrons of atoms, X-rays and gamma rays arise from vibrations inside the atomic nucleus. A splitting atom emits a flash of gamma rays and, of course, an atom bomb releases a very dangerous dose of gamma radiation: enough to infect ordinary earth and bricks and mortar with radioactivity for days or weeks afterwards—enough also to penetrate to the marrow of people's bones and so prevent the renewal of the red corpuscles in their blood.

It is important to avoid too much exposure either to X-rays or gamma rays. Anyone can do himself an injury by playing about too long with one of those clever X-ray machines used in shoe-shops for testing the fit of new shoes. Before this danger was realised, many scientists who were following up the discovery of Röntgen exposed themselves to excessive doses of X-rays and thereby injured themselves. Nowadays all X-ray apparatus is properly screened (usually by a covering of lead) and the ray is allowed to emerge only in the direction where it is wanted and only for a few seconds at a time.

The discoverer of radioactivity was Antoine Henri Becquerel, professor of physics at the École Polytechnique in Paris. Becquerel lived from 1852 to 1908, and his discovery came a few months after

Röntgen's. He was investigating the nature of phosphorescence, which is the property some chemicals have of glowing in the dark with a queer greenish light for some minutes or hours after they have been exposed to a bright lamp. He tested the intensity of the phosphorescence by using photographic plates. Quite by accident he found that certain salts of uranium could darken photographic plates not only without previous exposure to light but even without the plates being taken from their light-tight box. Although this discovery was a pure accident, Becquerel was sufficiently well trained in science to probe the mystery intelligently, and he gave the world the first accurate account of radioactivity so, in 1903, he shared the Nobel Prize for Physics with Pierre and Marie Curie (see page 105). By this time it was understood that the emanation from uranium was something more than the intense kind of X-ray scientists had at first supposed it to be.

You will notice that none of the people so far mentioned, with the exception of the Curies, were twentieth-century scientists. Their main work was done in the nineteenth century. Nevertheless they provided effects and ideas which were to be the starting-point for twentieth-century science. Their work was aside from the main preoccupations of their time. Most scientists then were occupied with the more practical aspects of electricity and with steam or internal-combustion engines. The work done by the people I have described was not done with any practical purpose in view. Only in the twentieth century did its useful possibilities begin to show themselves.

First of the twentieth-century developments was that due to Guglielmo Marconi, an Italian who lived from 1874 to 1937. Marconi perceived the importance of the Hertz experiments. He foresaw that by sending wireless waves in long and short bursts it would be possible to make them convey signals or messages. By 1896 he had so far improved on the Hertz apparatus as to be able to send messages a distance of two miles. He offered his invention to the Italian Government, but as he did not receive any encouragement he brought his invention to England, where he patented it. In 1898 he was able to send signals across the English Channel, and in 1901, at St. John's in Newfoundland, he received signals coming all the way across the Atlantic Ocean from a transmitter in Cornwall, England.

An objection to wireless telegraphy (radio) often mentioned at that time was the supposed inability of the waves to follow the curvature of the earth. The waves, scientists said, would go in a straight line to the horizon and, afterwards, they would pass over the masts of ships at an ever-increasing altitude. By the time they reached the American continent they would be 300 miles above the ground and therefore quite unable to operate any detector or receiver.

By practical test Marconi proved the gloomy prophets to be wrong. Neither he nor anybody else at that time could explain why the waves hugged the earth's surface, but all were gratified to find that they did so.

From 1901 onwards it was clear to everybody that wireless telegraphy (radio) was a practical proposition full of extremely important possibilities. By 1902 an English scientist, Oliver Heaviside, explained that the probable reason why wireless waves followed the earth's curvature was some form of reflection in the upper atmosphere. By bouncing from earth to upper layer, back to earth again, up to the layer a second time, down again, and so on, the waves might go round the earth indefinitely. The imagined layer in the upper atmosphere where reflection was supposed to take place came to be called the " Heaviside Layer."

Not until 1924 was the existence of such a layer established beyond doubt. Another English scientist, E. V. Appleton, probed into the matter and made many experiments with reflected waves. The layer is known now to be a region where solar and cosmic radiations produce a varying degree of ionisation according to the time of day, the amount of sunspot activity and so on.

Marconi was soon equipping sea-going vessels with sending and receiving equipment, and the ill-fated liner *Titanic* was so equipped when, in May 1912, she set out on her first and final voyage across the Atlantic. If proper use had been made of the apparatus the ship might have been spared from disaster, but when the operator received a warning of "ice ahead" from a friendly vessel nearby he was unwise enough to reply (by wireless) that he was busy and wished his informant to "get off the air." He was, at the moment, trying to dispatch many personal messages from passengers to friends awaiting them in New York. Shortly afterwards the *Titanic* struck an iceberg and began to sink. The wireless operator then tried to attract the attention of the nearby vessel but by then the operator on this vessel had shut down his apparatus. After much delay the operator on the *Titanic* managed to attract the attention of another liner, the *Carpathia*, but this was 58 miles away. This ship steamed at full speed for the scene of the accident and she arrived in time to save many people, but well over 1,000 had already been drowned or killed in their lifejackets by the icy cold of the sea.

Marconi's early apparatus used ingenious detecting devices, but they were destined to be superseded by the much better thermionic valve, a device which was due in some part to Edison. Thomas Alva Edison, an American inventor, was born in Ohio in 1847. He owned more than 1,000 patents at one time or another, and when

he died in 1931 he was a wealthy man. He made little progress as
a boy at school, so his mother took him away and educated him
herself. His family was not poor, but young Thomas was ambitious,
so he went into business selling newspapers, sweets and tobacco on
railway stations and trains. In this way he came into contact with
railway officials and was shown something of the mysteries of the
railway telegraph. In the 1860s it was still somewhat crude and
Edison saw possibilities of improvement. In 1868 he became an
employee of the Western Union Telegraph Company at Boston. In
1870 he was on his own with some ideas that he was able to sell for
40,000 dollars. With this money he estabished a thriving business,
and when Graham Bell invented the telephone (see Vol. III, Section
9(f), Chapter 7) Edison followed it up with an improved form of
speech transmitter—the carbon microphone. In 1877 he invented
the gramophone—then called the "phonograph." In 1879 he
had discovered how to make a successful filament-type electric lamp.
An English inventor named Swan came upon the same idea at
about the same time. The basis of the idea was a filament made
of carbon.

In 1883 Edison fitted one of his lamps with an extra electrode
above the filament for some reason that does not seem to be known
now, and he discovered that it was possible to draw off a current
from this electrode although it was not connected to the filament
except externally. The effect became known as the "Edison Effect,"
but nobody saw any practical use for it at the time. More than
20 years later, in 1904, John Ambrose Fleming, an English electrical
engineer engaged by the Edison Electric Lighting Company to pro-
mote the use of electric lighting in Britain, invented a valve or one-
way current device that depended on the "Edison Effect" for its
action. We should call the Fleming valve a diode to-day because

it had only two electrodes. In its modern form it is useful as a rectifier for converting alternating current to direct current, and as a detector for converting radio-frequency signals to audio-frequency ones.

The next important advance in radio equipment was made by the American scientist Lee De Forest, who was born in Iowa in 1873 and took a degree in science at Yale. His first appointment was with the Western Electric Company of Chicago, where he worked on telephones. In 1900 he became interested in radio and in 1902 he established a company of his own for equipping ships with radio. In 1906 he made a valve of the Fleming type but with a wire mesh electrode between the other two, thus turning a diode into a triode. By varying the electric potential of this "grid" he was able to increase or decrease the current passed by the valve. The action was instantaneous and so it would follow potential changes of audio- or even radio-frequency.

In 1913 De Forest made his triode valve oscillate and so become a generator of continuous electric waves. Using these waves as "carrier" he was able to impress upon them the vibrations of the human voice. Hitherto radio had been able to transmit only Morse or similar crude signals: now it could transmit speech or music. In 1915 De Forest transmitted the human voice by radio from Arlington, Virginia, to the Eiffel Tower, Paris. In 1916 he started the world's first news broadcasting service. He is generally regarded as the "father of radio broadcasting." In 1923 De Forest invented a process for recording sound on film, so he can be said to have given the cinematograph its voice. Prior to this all films had been silent.

The story of radio would be incomplete without some reference to Edward Howard Armstrong, one-time professor of electrical engineering at Columbia University, New York. We owe to Armstrong the two greatest improvements of radio in recent years, namely the principles of the superheterodyne and frequency modulation.

In early radio receivers triode valves were used to amplify incoming signals again and again over many stages. Radio sets were complicated affairs with many independently tuned circuits, all of which had to be adjusted most carefully. At any moment the whole receiver was liable to burst into self-oscillation and emit fearful whistles and howls. Armstrong had the brilliant idea of converting the signal to one of a standard frequency before amplifying it. After conversion, the signal could be amplified in a number of fixed frequency stages that did not need tuning by the operator as they could be adjusted in advance and then sealed up in a box. To change the frequency of the received signal Armstrong used a valve oscillator to generate waves in the receiver. The frequency of these local oscillations could be varied to suit the frequency of the received signal waves, and by mixing the two in another valve a beat-frequency output could be obtained. This beat frequency was made to coincide with the natural frequency of the pre-adjusted amplifier stages. In practice a " superhet " receiver has only two circuits that require manual tuning and both of them can be tuned together by a single knob if the tuning condensers are " ganged " together. The two circuits in question are the aerial (or signal-receiving) circuit and the local oscillator circuit. All modern radio receivers work on the Armstrong superheterodyne principle.

Why the long name? The expression " to heterodyne " means to mix dissimilar waves and produce a new beat-frequency wave (see Vol. III, page 197, for a description of a similar effect in acoustics). " Super " means over or above, and it is used here to signify that the local oscillator usually generates a higher frequency than that of the incoming signal.

Ordinary broadcast radio transmitters send out a carrier wave that has its strength or "amplitude" varied by the speech or music or whatever else is being transmitted. A note of 200 cycles frequency will vary the amplitude of the carrier wave, making it increase and decrease 200 times in a second. The drawback to this system is that distant lightning or distant Morse transmitters or even the vacuum cleaner next door can put their own kicks into the received wave, with the result that we hear "interference."

Armstrong thought of the brilliant idea of varying not the amplitude but the pitch or frequency of the carrier wave at the transmitting end. The wave thus modulated must be received by a special receiver where it goes to a "discriminator" circuit which takes no account of amplitude changes but only of frequency changes. In this way the interference pulses picked up on the way are ignored. The discriminator converts a variable frequency effect into a variable amplitude one and, after this, the stages in the special receiver are the same as those in any ordinary use. When you listen to very high frequency, frequency modulated (VHF/FM) broadcasts from some special broadcasting station you will appreciate the difference between AM and FM for radio transmission. Background noise has been completely (or almost completely) eliminated.

The developments initiated by Hertz and Marconi have, within the span of a lifetime, proved extremely rewarding. Nobody could have foreseen 60 or 70 years ago how amazingly the human way of life would come to be affected by space waves of the Hertzian kind, but radio, radar and television have already exploited every imaginable possibility for waves lying between about 3 centimetres and some 3,000 metres.

Valve oscillators generating potential variations of a megacycle or so in frequency can be applied to the heating of things like plastics, glass, or even human tissue in places where no hot iron or soothing poultice can be applied. The alternating electric strain is enough to generate heat if it is sufficiently strong and sufficiently rapid. High-frequency heating, or " dielectric heating " as it is sometimes called, has many industrial and medical applications. Radio-type valves are used also in factories that run without any human hand to control them. A punched card of instructions is fed to a complicated transmitter rather like a radio, and this is able to operate every control as and when required.

The way to all these developments in electronics was opened up by discoveries made at the turn of the century—in the 1890s, or a few years earlier. In the same period Becquerel and Röntgen initiated the equally fruitful study of excessively short-wave radiations and radioactivity. After Becquerel the most important pioneers in the study of radioactivity were the Curies.

Madame Curie was a Pole by birth. She was born in Warsaw in 1867 and her maiden name was Marie Sklodowska. She was educated by her father and, for a time, she taught at a high school. In 1891 she went to Paris to study at the University, which is generally known as the Sorbonne. She obtained a degree in 1893 and in 1895 she married Pierre Curie, a French chemist. Together Pierre and Marie studied the discovery of Becquerel, repeating his experiments and making many others. In 1898 they announced the discovery of polonium and radium in a natural substance called " pitchblende." This pitchy black material is an ore of uranium. The pitchblende used by the Curies came from Joachimsthal in Czechoslovakia, but it is found also in Saxony, Rumania, Norway, Cornwall, East Africa, and on the North American continent. The other valuable ore of uranium, called carnotite, comes chiefly from the Belgian Congo and the Great Bear Lake region of Northern Canada.

After four more years of hard work the Curies were able to isolate radium in its pure form. Its intense radioactivity made it enormously valuable.

During all this time the Curies were so poor that Madame Curie was obliged to supplement the family income by giving physics lessons in a girls' school. In 1903, however, she was given an appointment at the Sorbonne as chief laboratory assistant in her husband's department of chemistry and physics.

In 1906 Pierre Curie was run over and killed by a dray in the street and then Madame Curie was appointed professor of physics in her husband's place. Madame Curie had shared the honour of receiving a Nobel Prize in 1903 jointly with her husband and Becquerel. In 1911 Madame Curie received the Nobel Prize for Chemistry, and this time she was not called on to share it with anybody.

The Curies had made no secret of their method of obtaining radium; they had given their discovery freely to the world for the benefit of everybody. For many years afterwards radium in minute quantities was employed for healing or ameliorating certain diseases in hospitals. It is still used in this way, and until recently it has been the only source of radioactivity available to doctors and surgeons.

In 1914 Madame Curie was put in charge of the experimental work of the newly formed Institute of Radium in Paris. She lived until 1934 and her daughter and son-in-law continued the good work in which, to the end of her life, she was still engaged.

In England the study of radioactivity was taken up by Ernest Rutherford. Born in 1871 at Nelson, New Zealand, Rutherford came to England to do research work at the Cavendish Laboratory, Cambridge. In 1898 he became professor of physics at McGill University, Montreal, Canada. In 1907 he returned to England as physics professor at Victoria University, Manchester. In 1919 he became the Cavendish Professor of Physics at Cambridge, and it was in this capacity that he did his famous work on splitting atoms with natural and accelerated particles. He received the Nobel Prize for Chemistry in 1908 and was knighted in 1914 and awarded the O.M. in 1925. In 1931 he was made a Baron.

Not himself an experimental physicist, but only a very interested and shrewd observer of ninetenth- and twentieth-century discovery, Albert Einstein began to reduce the findings of others to some sort of orderly mathematical system. His first publications appeared in the year 1905. He was of German nationality, born at Ulm in 1879. He received a scientific education at Zürich in Switzerland and from 1901 to 1909 he was an examiner of patents at Berne. His writings attracted much favourable attention so, in 1909, he was made physics professor at the University of Zürich. From there he moved to other universities, but his career in Europe ended when he resigned from an appointment in Berlin. Disliking the effect the Nazis were having on education in Germany he fled to America and there he became physics professor at the Institute for Advanced Studies at Princeton.

Einstein won the Nobel Prize for Physics in 1921, and up till the time of his death, in 1955, he was hopeful of establishing some sort of identity between the three space forces of electricity, magnetism and gravitation. He was working on what he called the " unified field theory." It is doubtful whether any branch of modern science could have prospered in so sensational a way in recent years if it had not been for the courage and imaginative genius of Einstein. Best

known among his findings, perhaps, is the convertibility of
matter (M) into energy (E) and *vice versa*, according to the much
quoted formula $E = Mc^2$, where c is the velocity of light. Prior to
Einstein's work both matter and energy were believed to be indestructible and, indeed, their amounts are seen to be "conserved," or
unaffected, throughout ordinary experiments in chemistry and
engineering (mechanical and electrical).

Science goes on from discovery to discovery in our own time.
Unmentioned so far has been the exploration of the universe by
radio telescopes of the kind used by Professor Ryle at Cambridge and
Professor Sir Bernard Lovell at Jodrell Bank. It was in 1932 that Karl
Jansky, experimenting with short wave radio reception by use of a
directional aerial, discovered that radio signals were coming from the
Milky Way. Following up Jansky's findings, other investigators
located definite (though invisible) celestial sources of radio waves.
The sun itself emits radio waves when there is intense sunspot activity.
So far radio astronomy is raising new questions faster than it answers
old ones, but eventually it must provide clues to much that remains
unexplained by optical observation. Incidentally the Jodrell Bank
dish aerial is much used for tracking artificial satellites by radar.

More can be learnt about radio astronomy and radio telescopes
from *Radio Astronomy*, by F. Graham Smith (Pelican Original A479).

Section Seven

HOME ENTERTAINMENTS

Chapter 1

TOYS MADE FROM PAPER

A GREAT number of useful, amusing and pretty things can be made with paper, mostly by folding, but, in some instances, by folding and tearing as well. If you learn how to make all the things described in the pages that follow, you will be able to entertain a group of friends for two or three hours, and it can all be done without any tools or appliances of any kind, though I prefer to have a paper knife and a pair of scissors handy. Folded paper is sometimes rather too hard for fingers to tear, and scissors make the work easier and neater.

When I have to make a long journey by train, I always put some sheets of white paper in my case, and get into a carriage where there are children. After a little while, the children usually get tired of sitting with nothing to do and then I speak to them, take the paper out of my case and make a few paper toys.

Doing this, I once had a great surprise. I was in a very crowded train, and, perched right on the edge of the seat, next to me, were two children, a boy and a girl. I started making toys for them in the usual way, when the boy jumped up suddenly and said, "Just a minute, sir, there are some more of us in the next compartment." He darted out and came back a few seconds later with two more girls and a baby boy. Then they all stood round, very excited, while I went on folding paper. The other grown-up passengers, who wanted to read and be quiet, were not very pleased at first. But eventually they became interested too, and when my supply of paper gave out, they offered me their newspapers.

Long before the train reached my station, I had made a great mountain of paper toys. In the middle of the fun, I saw a man peering through the window from the corridor outside. It was "Dad" come to see where all his children had got to. When he saw that they were happy he went away again, back to his own compartment.

Another day, making the same journey, but in the opposite direction, I met two little girls, who were travelling with their mother. They too ended their journey with a mountain of toys, and these they were loath to leave behind them in the train when the time came to get out. Their mother had a bright idea, however; she produced an enormous vacuum flask which, fortunately, was empty. We folded up the toys and crammed them into the flask.

Lewis Carroll, the writer of *Alice in Wonderland*, used to live at Oxford, and he too befriended children in trains, amusing them with puzzles, many of which, I am afraid, must have proved rather difficult for his little friends. You can read some more about Lewis Carroll on page 254. In the meantime, I want you to try your hand at making paper toys. It is an occupation that will delight you yourself now, and make you very popular with any other children you may happen to meet as you go your way through life.

Before leaving you, I ought, perhaps, to give you some good advice. When you have learnt how to make all the toys, and want to amuse a group of children whom you have never seen before, be sure you begin by making for them one of the hardest of the toys that they are not likely to have seen previously or, at any rate, one they are not likely to be able to do for themselves. If you begin by making one that everybody knows, your audience will look un-interested and look away, and you will have missed a chance of making them your friends. You should save up the easy toys till the end, when you do not know any more, and when your friends still keep pressing you to do another. You can then say. "Oh, well, one more, then; but I expect you all know it." Even if your friends do happen to know it, they will forgive you for doing it because, by this time, they will have been impressed by your earlier efforts.

When learning to make the toys you should go through the whole series, doing them in the same order as they appear in this book. If you just dodge about, picking out the ones you fancy, to do them first, you may find yourself in difficulties, as the harder ones are often only the easier ones carried several stages farther.

1. POINTED HAT

The easiest paper toy to make, and one that everybody knows, is the pointed hat. For this you need a piece of paper the size of one page of newspaper, but remember that newspaper tears rather easily, so that it is better to find something stronger. You will need a piece about 16 inches wide and 20 inches long. You fold it in half, as shown in (1), and then you fold it again, as shown in (2), to get a crease down the middle. You open the second fold, and then bend one of the bottom corners up to the crease, as shown in (3). You treat the other bottom corner in the same way, as shown in (4). Lastly, you fold down the narrow strips of paper that project above the two corner flaps. The top strip is folded forwards over the flaps, and the underneath strip is folded backwards. The folding of the two strips is as in (5), where the dotted line shows their

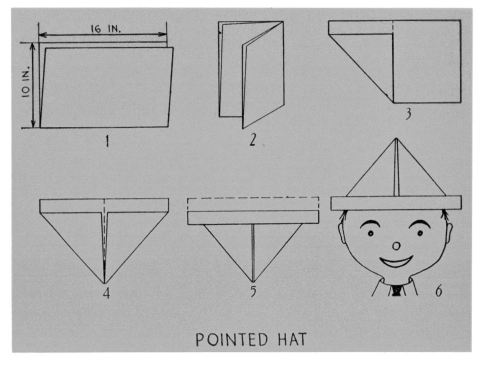

POINTED HAT

original position. The hat is worn as in (6), or it can be turned sideways with its points at the front and back of your head.

2. BOAT

After making a hat, the next thing to make is a boat. You begin by making a small hat, starting with a sheet of typing paper or notepaper about 8 inches wide by 10 inches long. You open out the hat as wide as it will go and then flatten it, so that it looks like (1). Next, you bring the two top corners down to the bottom corners, folding one over forwards, or towards you, and bending the other backwards, or away from you. When you have flattened it, you should have it looking like (2). You will find that what you have is a smaller hat. You must now open this as wide as it will go, and flatten it to appear as shown in (3). Once again, you bring the top corners down to the bottom corners, folding them towards

you and away from you, as before, and getting the object shown in
(4). If you turn this up the other way, with the three overlapping
points upwards, it will spring partly open and have the appearance
of (5). You now take hold of the paper and pull apart as indicated
by the arrows. You will find that you have made a boat as shown
in (6).

If made of good stiff paper, this boat will float in the bath,

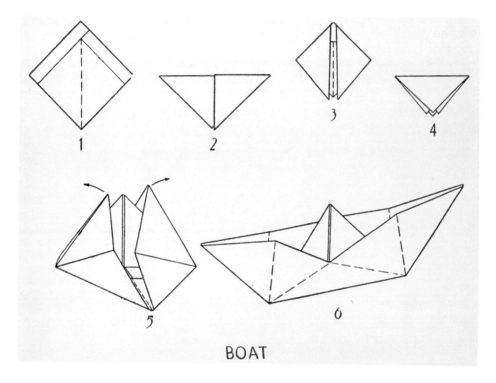

BOAT

or in a stream, and you can have great fun with it, as it will carry
small cargoes of earth or sticks. If you and your friends make
several of them, you can take them to a nearby brook and have
races. Do not try to make the boats of newspaper, or they will
break up in the water and disappoint you. And do not make the
boats too big, or they will be too "floppy" and become wrecks
almost directly after you put them in the water. If the brook goes

through a tunnel or pipe it is fun to put the boats in the water on one side and watch for them to come out at the other side. If you want to make sure that the boat will pass through without sticking somewhere on the way, try floating a few bits of stick through first. If you do not do this you may lose your boat.

3. CRAYON CASE

If you have odd pieces of chalk or crayons that you want to carry about without getting your fingers or your pocket handker-

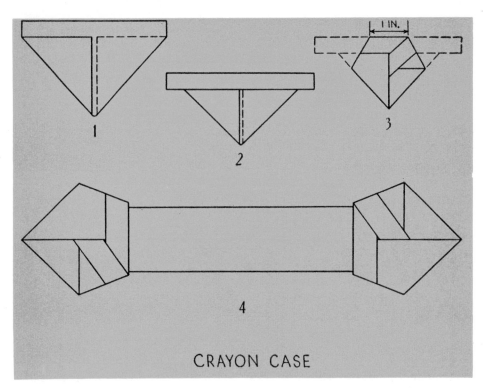

CRAYON CASE

chief coloured by them, you will find a crayon case useful. To make a crayon case you need three pieces of paper 4 inches wide and 5 inches long. There are two ends, which are made exactly alike, and these are joined by a roll or tube of paper between them.

To make an end you start as though you were going to make a

pointed hat, but when you have bent one corner up to the middle crease you turn your work over and bend the other corner to the crease on the back side. The bending is shown in (1), where the invisible flap at the back is indicated by a dotted line. Now you bend down the strips left at the top, one to the front and one to the back, just as though you were making a hat. Leaving an opening in the "hat" about 1 inch wide, you bend the corners as shown in (3), and tuck the ends into the pockets in the middle. One corner is bent towards you—you can easily see which one it must be— and the other corner is bent away from you. Do not flatten the creases at the bends finally until you have made sure that the ends tuck in nicely. Put your finger in the opening and work it into a nice round shape. On your finger the end of the crayon case looks like a hat called a mitre that is worn by bishops and arch-bishops.

You make two such ends and then you roll the third piece of paper to form a tube 5 inches long and about three-quarters of an inch in diameter. You put a "mitre" on each end of the tube and then your crayon case is complete, looking as shown at (4). To fill it with crayons, you remove one of the ends. If you want to make everything firm you can glue the seam of the tube when you have made its diameter just right, and you can glue the fixed end of the case on to the tube.

4. TRAY

Another toy can be made out of a single piece of paper longer than it is broad, and this is a shallow open box or tray. A sheet 8 inches wide and 10 inches long will make a tray 4 inches wide and 5 inches long. A sheet half this size will, of course, make a tray of half the above dimensions. The first thing to do with the paper is to fold it in half, making the two long edges come together. This gives a crease down the middle. Now the long edges are brought to the crease, as shown in (1), and two new creases made. The paper is then opened and folded in half the other way, making the two short edges come together. This gives a crease across the middle. Now the short edges are brought to the crease, as shown in (2), and two new creases made. The creases you made first of all are shown dotted in (2), and they are meant

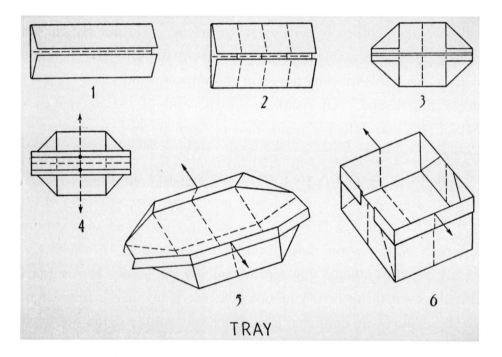

TRAY

to guide you in folding over the corners as shown in (3). The four corner flaps do not quite reach the edges of the paper running down the middle, but leave narrow strips which you must turn up and down over the flaps as shown in (4). After pressing down all the creases thoroughly, you put your two forefingers underneath the turned-over strips at their middle points and pull apart, as shown by the arrows in (4). The sides of the tray now begin to stand up, as shown in (5), and you can get your other fingers inside to help the corners to rise. After a little careful manipulation, you will find that you have a useful box or tray, like that shown in (6).

If you make a slightly bigger tray, using paper about a quarter of an inch wider and a quarter of an inch longer, you can use this as a lid, and then you have something like a chocolate box which will hold things without spilling. By using stiff paper, and gumming the strips shown in (3) before you turn them over into the position shown in (4), you can make a really strong job.

5. PICNIC CUP

You can make a paper cup that will really hold water or milk or tea if you have a sheet of good-quality notepaper or typing paper. From a piece 8 inches wide and 10 inches long you can make a cup which will be about 3 inches deep and 3 inches across the top when you have squeezed it into a round or circular shape.

First of all, you fold the paper as shown in (1), taking the bottom left-hand corner up to the top edge and creasing to keep it there. You will notice that, except for a strip on the right, the paper is double. You must tear off this strip to make the paper into a square with sides 8 inches long. Of course, if you have it, you can start with an 8-inch square of paper, and then you do not need to waste anything. All you have to do with your square at first is fold it along one of the diagonals; that is to say, you bring opposite corners together and squeeze flat to make a crease joining the other two corners together. You will need a square piece of paper for many other toys to be described presently, so look carefully at (1) and remember how to get a perfect square from an oblong piece of paper.

But we must not forget that we are making a cup. You take

the square piece of paper, folded in half to form a triangle, and you place it before you with the long creased edge at the bottom going from left to right, as in (2). You then pick up the left-hand corner and bend it over to touch the opposite edge. Before creasing the paper to hold it there, you must see that the line marked *A* runs parallel to the bottom crease. Parallel means like two railway lines

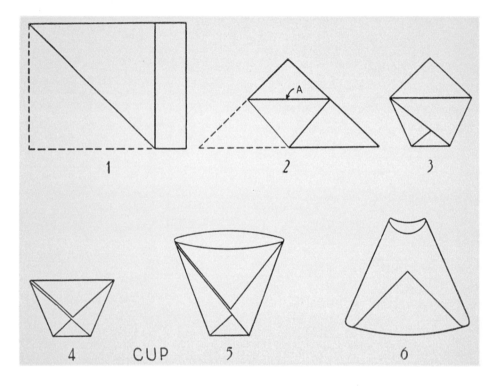

which go ever so far both ways without ever meeting. You next do the same thing with the right-hand corner, getting your paper to appear as in (3). Now you separate the overlapping points at the top and fold the front one over towards you and down, as in (4). The back one you fold away from you and down the back. You can now put your finger in at the top and open the paper out to form a cup, as shown in (5), which is drawn rather larger than (4). You can press the bottom in to form a dimple. This is shown in

(6), where the cup is drawn upside down. The dimple helps to keep the cup opened out. It is now ready for your drink.

You will notice that, when it is upside down, the cup looks like a smart hat. Well, if you use a larger piece of paper than one 8 inches square, a piece 20 inches square, shall we say, you will have your hat. As it comes undone rather easily, it is advisable to put a spot of gum or paste on the inside of the two triangular flaps turned over last of all. Better still, you can make two big stars or rosettes of coloured paper and gum them over the points of the flaps.

6. OPEN BOX

The open box you are going to make now is stronger than the tray, and if made of good-quality paper it will hold water without letting any escape. You need a square piece of paper, and if each side of the square is 8 inches long the box will have sides 3 inches long, and the depth will be a little more than $1\frac{1}{4}$ inches.

The first thing you do with your square piece of paper is crease it from corner to corner; that is to say, along the diagonals. You do this in order to find the middle of the square: it is where the creases cross one another. You now fold over each corner of the square to touch the middle as shown in (1). You then fold the paper along the dotted lines to bring the top and bottom edges to the middle, making it look like (2). The right- and left-hand edges are bent to look something like safety-pins. You now fold the bent edges over to meet in the middle, as shown in (3). While you are pinching the paper at each side to make the new creases, using both hands together, you can bend the whole thing into the shape of the letter W, by forming yet another crease in the middle, as shown in (3) by the dotted line. Looked at from the side, your letter W appears like the sketch (4). The corners marked with dots in (4) are now pulled out, one by one, in the direction shown by the arrows. While you are pulling out the right-hand corners you must pinch the sides of the W together firmly at the left, and, in the same way, you must pinch the W together at the right when you are pulling out the left-hand corners. After pulling out each corner, press the whole thing flat so as to make new creases where these are wanted.

If you do all this properly you will have the object shown in

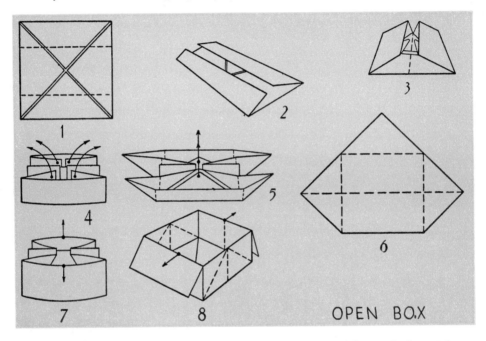

OPEN BOX

(5), which looks like two boats side by side. Inside each boat there is a little tongue of paper. These tongues are marked with dots in (5), and you must pull them out in the direction shown by the arrows. They may not come out easily, and you must be careful how you ease the paper, wherever it may stick, in order not to tear it. Pull out the nearest tongue first, to make your double boat disappear behind a single sheet of paper shaped like (6). Fold all three triangles towards the centre, on each side of the toy, using the creases already in the paper. These creases are shown in (6) by two upright dotted lines and another going across to join their tops. There is one more crease, shown in (6) by the long dotted line going across half-way up the upright creases. You must next fold the top part over the bottom part, using this crease. Having dealt with one of the pulled-out tongues in this way, you must turn the paper over to do the same thing on the other side. First you pull the tongue out and then you repeat the folding, as for the first tongue.

When you have finished all this you will have the object shown in (7). You put your two fore-fingers inside the two compartments and separate them as shown by the arrows. If you do this carefully, you will find that you have made the box shown in (8). You can actually boil water in this, using it like a saucepan over a candle, or a small spirit lamp. The paper cannot become hotter than the water in contact with it, and so it never burns, although it may get black with soot on the under side. If you make the box out of a sheet of stiff paper twice as large (16 inches square) it will be big enough to put on a small gas ring.

7. CHINESE JUNK

To make a small boat resembling a Chinese junk, you must first of all make an open box, as already described. You then press down the sides of the box, beginning in the way shown in (1). At (2) you can see how the pressing must be continued. Eventually you can flatten the whole thing down, as shown in (3). Now you put your fingers under the oblongs on top and turn them right over, following the indications of the arrows in (3). When you have done this, and flattened everything down again, you will have what you can see in (4). You now bend this up in the middle, as shown in (5), eventually pressing the sides together. Now you pinch the paper at the left-

hand dot and also, with the other hand, at the right-hand dot. You
pull your hands apart, and the toy stretches in a strange way, like

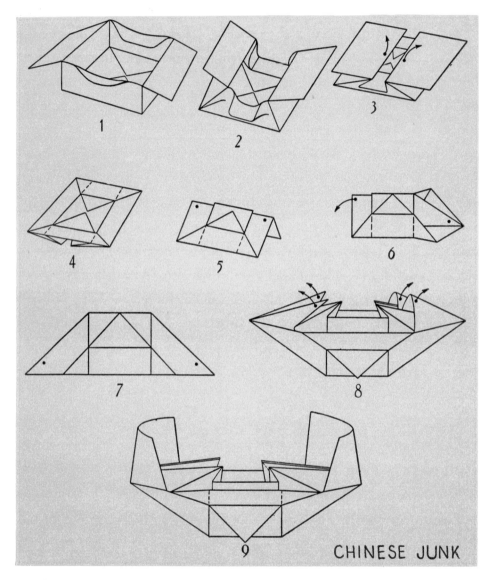

CHINESE JUNK

a telescope. If the right-hand end comes out first, you will have
the toy appearing as in (6).

You must pull again at the left-hand end in the direction of the
arrow in order to make the two ends alike. When you have suc-

ceeded in this your toy will appear as in (7) if viewed sideways. If you turn it over it will spring open to some extent and appear as in (8). You take hold of the points indicated by dots and pull upwards in the direction of the arrows. Your junk will now be finished and will appear as shown in (9).

In the water it is rather top-heavy, and you will have to put a weight of earth or some marbles in the bottom before it will float on an even keel. Altogether the junk is rather a complicated toy to make, because, starting with a flat sheet of paper, you must remember about fifteen different folds. One made from a piece of paper 8 inches square is about 5 inches long and 2 inches wide. It is rather easy to tear the paper, and make a leak in your junk, when you are pulling out the ends, as in (6), so be careful, and use good paper, not newspaper.

8. STEAMSHIP

You are now going to make a steamship, which is the most real-looking of all the paper models. You start with an 8-inch square of paper, crease it across the corners and fold the corners to the middle, just as though you were going to make an open box. This makes your paper look like sketch (1) on page 122. Now you turn the paper over, putting the four corner flaps towards the table, and you will see a plain square. You fold the corners of this to the centre, as in (1) on page 126, and then you turn the whole thing over and fold the four corners to the centre yet again, as in (2). Notice that you have done the same thing (i.e. folded all four corners to the middle) *three* times, turning the paper over between the first and second time, and again between the second and third time.

If, now, you turn over what you have at (2) you get the object looking as at (3), where you can see four little square flaps that can

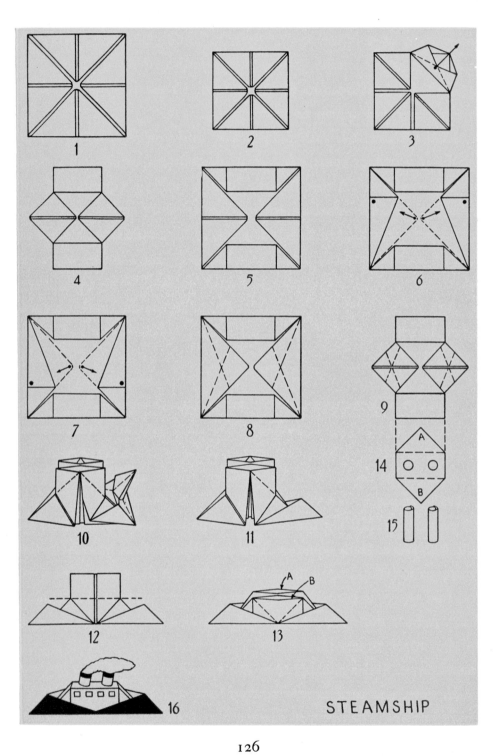

STEAMSHIP

be opened out. The top right-hand one is shown partly opened out already. You must open out the opposite one (bottom left-hand corner) as well. Flattening everything down, you now get (4), which looks more like a folded shirt than a steamer.

Well, you must partly undo this "shirt" by bringing up the four corner flaps at the back and flattening everything, as in (5). To your left and right you will see two triangular flaps which you must crease by lifting the points and moving them, as shown by the arrows and dots in (6), towards the upright edges of the square. Make the turned-up edges of the flaps lie neatly along the sides of the square, and then press down to make clear creases. Put the points of the flaps back in the middle again and repeat the performance, but taking the points of the flaps another way to the upright edges of the square, as shown in (7). Crease firmly as before, and return the points of the flaps to the middle. The creases you have made should be as shown by the dotted lines in (8).

You now put the corners of the square behind again, so that your toy looks as in (9). Now comes the more difficult part of your work. You fold the toy along the line running from left to right, and at the same time pick out the right-hand flap so that the whole thing looks like (10). Before you completely flatten the two sides of the toy together you must turn the flap "inside-out," as in (11), using the creases already made to help you. When you have done the same thing to the other end, your toy looks like (12). You now fold down the upstanding parts in the middle, along the line shown dotted in (12). The front one folds towards you, and has its corners tucked in at the front; the back one folds away from you and has its corners tucked in at the back.

The toy now appears as at (13), and all you have to do is make the decking (14) and the two funnels (15). The points (A) and (B) of the deck (14) are folded back along the dotted lines and tucked into the pockets (*A*) and (*B*) of the hull of the ship shown in (13). When you put in two little rolls of paper to form the funnels, your toy is complete. If you paint it and stick cotton-wool in the funnels, it will look very grand, as you can see by the sketch (16). It is a good idea to use a little gum or glue to hold things firm before you start painting. The parts you bend over to get (13) from (12) should be glued where you have to tuck them in. Points (*A*) and (*B*) of the decking (14) should be glued into the pockets of the hull. Lastly, the funnels should be glued at the bottom and where they go through the deck. You can glue the seams as well. The best colour to use for the outside of the hull is black. Inside the hull you can use brown. The upstanding parts inside can have windows drawn on them in ink and then they can be painted yellow. The funnels can be scarlet, with black bands round the top. A little glue inside the funnels will hold the "smoke" in position.

Do not try to float this toy in the bath, as it will only turn turtle and get spoilt. For imitation water use a piece of glass.

9. CRUET

The toy you are going to make now is sometimes called a cruet and sometimes a salt-cellar. It is rather a pretty flower-like object with four compartments in it to receive salt, pepper, mustard and anything else, such as sugar, that you fancy. You could, of course, fill them with different-coloured powder paints and use it as a paint box. It keeps its shape best if you make it of stiffish paper and not too big. A piece of paper 4 inches square makes one with compartments about 1 inch across.

You start in the same way as for Toy No. 8, the Steamship, by folding the corners of your paper to the centre, turning over and

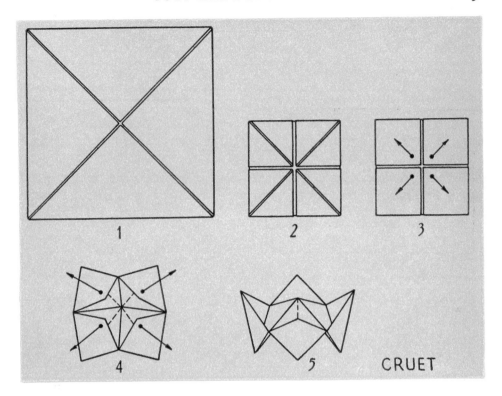

folding to the centre again. These two folds are shown at (1) and (2). After you have done both folds the toy looks like (3), at the back. You now try to pick up each of the little square flaps shown in (3) and pull them up and out as shown by the arrows. The paper is springy, and you may find that they do not want to come. But if you persevere, being careful not to crumple or dent the paper, you will succeed at last. Underneath the squares is a cross-like crease. The centre of this may at first go down when you pull the squares up. You must stop it from doing this and make it come up too, like you can see in (4). When you have succeeded in opening your cruet right out, it appears as you can see it in (5).

10. BASKET

To make a basket which will really hold light loads of sweets, berries, etc., you take a square piece of paper and crease it across the corners each way, as shown in (1) by continuous lines, and then down the centre each way, as shown in (1) by dotted lines. When

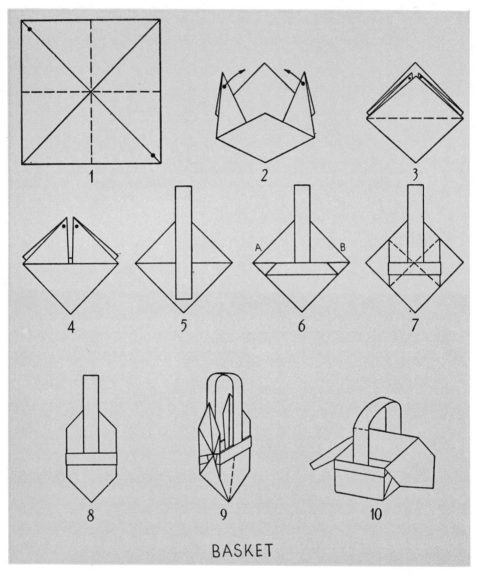

BASKET

you have made the corner-to-corner creases, you should turn the paper over before making the side-to-side creases, so that the paper will fold up easily in the manner shown in (2). You will see that the corners marked in (1) with black dots are being brought closer together in (2). Eventually, they must be made almost to touch, as shown in (3). At (3) you can see two upstanding triangular flaps, one in front and the other behind; you must fold these down. The front one is folded forwards and down, making a crease where you can see the dotted line in (3). The back one is treated in the same way, so that now your toy will appear as in (4). You now need a separate strip of paper, about twice as long as your folded paper is from corner to corner, and folded in half lengthwise to make it of double thickness, and therefore strong enough to serve as a handle. This long strip of double thickness must be bent in half, like a girl's hair-clip, and be passed over the folded paper with one leg in front and the other behind, as you can see in (5), which shows the front leg. You now pick up the triangular flap you have recently folded down, and you roll it up with the long strip inside. When you have done this, and flattened everything down, your toy appears as in (6). You must turn it over and roll up the other end of the long strip in the back flap, flattening this down too.

Now comes the part that is hard to do neatly. You must take the front two corners at (A) and (B) and turn them backwards and inwards towards the middle, so that they are in the position shown dotted in (7). They are drawn dotted because, really, you cannot see them. You now turn your toy over and fold the other two corners backwards and inwards in the same way. This gives you the shape shown at (8). If you hold your toy up by its handle, and look on one corner, it will appear as in (9). Already you can see that it is getting to look like a basket. You open it out wider, and at the same time you fold down the flaps at each end. Then, when you have poked the corners quite out, by putting your fingers inside, your basket is finished, and it appears as in (10).

If you want to make it strong you can gum the flaps before you roll them up with the ends of the handle inside. Also you can gum the end flaps to the ends and bottom of the basket. If now you gum a strip of card underneath the top loop of the handle it will not be so weak and easy to bend.

You can make a pretty little dolly's shopping basket from a piece of paper 4 inches square, and a useful one to hold your sweets from paper double the size. If you have a party you can make baskets to put beside the plates of your guests with jelly or something else nice inside. Your friends will be pleasantly surprised, and you can have some fun after tea showing them how the baskets were made. Children who know already can be invited to help you show the others.

11. BELLOWS

This is a working toy which can really be used to make a draught. You need good strong paper, not easily torn, and if you have an 8-inch square it will make a bellows 4 inches long. First of all you crease your square as though you were going to make a Basket (Toy No. 10). However, in folding the paper you do not pick up opposite corners, as for the basket, but opposite sides, at their middle points. You bring these together until your paper looks like (1). Now you flatten and fold down the corner marked X to the bottom point, as shown in (2). You do the same thing with the corner marked with a dot. You must now turn the paper over and fold down the two corners you can see on that side. When you have done this your toy will look as in (3). The next step, shown in (4), is to bend over the left- and right-hand front corners until they are in the middle, moving them in the directions shown by the arrows and making firm creases going from bottom point to points nearly midway along the top sides of the square. In the same way you must make creases running, as shown in (5), from the top point of the square to the points nearly midway along the bottom sides of the square. When everything is flattened again the creases will appear as shown in (6), which has been drawn large to make it clearer. You must turn your toy over and crease it similarly on the other side. Now pinch up the paper at the right- and left-hand corners, to make the short creases you can see as dotted lines

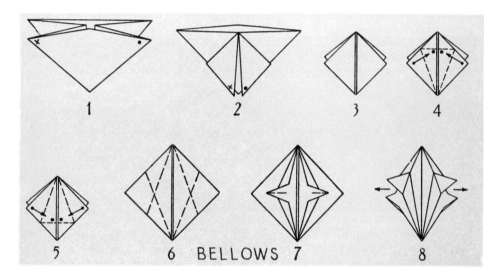

in (7). Go on pinching until you have made two little triangular ears sticking out at right angles to the main part of the toy. Turn over, and do the same thing on the other side. If you now look at your toy from one end, it will appear as shown in (8), quite finished.

All you have to do to work it is bring the little ears on the left together, so that they touch, and grip them between the thumb and forefinger of your left hand; grip the right-hand ears in the same way with your right hand; and then work your hands in and out as shown by the arrows in (8). A gust of air will come from the open end every time you bring your hands together. It may work better if you enlarge the hole at the end a little, snipping off a tiny bit of the point with scissors.

12. BOMB

On hot summer days, when you can get into bathing-suits and rush about the garden, it is fun to make paper bombs or hand grenades that you can fill with water and throw at each other. They can be put to mischievous uses too, but I will say nothing about that.

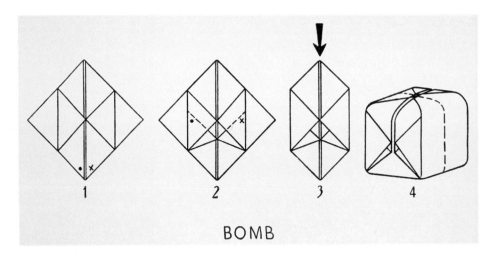

BOMB

A compact little bomb (about right for the ten-year-old hand) can be made out of a piece of paper (good quality) 5 inches square. You fold it as though you were going to make a bellows, getting as far as (3) for that toy. From here you do things differently. You first of all fold over the right- and left-hand corners in front until they are in the middle of the square, and then you flatten, so obtaining what you can see at (1). Now you pick up the points marked with a dot and a cross, and you tuck them into the folded-over corners, which you will find to be double at the bottom. When you have done this you will have (2), where I have indicated what has happened to the tucked-in points by dotted lines and the dot and cross as before. You now turn your toy over and repeat operations (1) and (2) on the back, obtaining the object shown at (3). All you have to do now is blow into your bomb from the top, as shown by the arrow, being careful to keep your hand closely round the outside in case you blow too hard and burst it open. The bomb will fill out nicely, like a toy balloon, until it looks like (4). You can now pour water in at the top.

If you want to make a store of bombs, it is best to leave them flat, as in (3), as you can pack many together into your pocket in this state. If you have already blown up your bomb, you can flatten it back into (3) again provided that you collapse the sides carefully.

13. KETTLE

This toy resembles the bomb in being blown out to form a receptacle for water, but it has handles at each side so that it makes a convenient kettle in which water can really be boiled. The handles enable it to be lifted away from the flame with boiling water inside, as they do not become too hot to hold.

A piece of paper 8 inches square will make a kettle having the water container in the form of a cube, each side of which is 2 inches long. To make it, you start as though you were going to make the bellows, folding your paper into the form shown in (3) for that toy. You then fold over the right- and left-hand front corners till they meet in the middle of the square, and press down to make firm creases. You then put the corners back again into their right- and left-hand positions, leaving the creases as shown by the dotted lines in (1). You now turn the paper over and make similar creases on the other side. Next, you pick up the point marked with a dot and lift it up and over until it occupies the position shown by a dot in (2). Now you swing it across from left to right, as shown in (3), using the crease already made when you do this. If, at this stage, you press on the corner indicated by the arrow, pushing it in the direction of the arrow, and at the same time pull down the top edge of the triangular flap, the crease shown in (4) by a dotted line running from left to right will begin to appear. Pull the top edge of the triangular

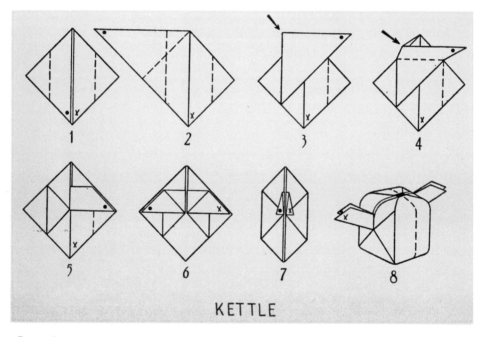

KETTLE

flap right down until it lies along the left to right diagonal of the square, as shown in (5), and then flatten to make all the new creases quite definite. The dot in (5) shows the same point as was marked by a dot in (2), (3) and (4). Next, you must pick up this point marked with a dot and bring it over from right to left, as shown in (6), creasing the paper to make it stay there.

You must now pick up the point marked with a cross and do the same things with this as you did with the one marked with a dot, so that it eventually finishes up in the position shown in (6).

You now turn the toy over and work on the back of it in exactly the same way as you have worked on the front. When you have done this, you should pick up the points marked by the dot and the cross and bring them together to form one of the handles of the kettle. You do the same thing with the corresponding points at the back. Holding the kettle by its two handles, you now blow into the opening at the top until it fills out into the form shown in (8). Your kettle is now finished and ready for use.

14. GLIDER

To make a glider that flies well, you should use a piece of thin writing or typing paper 6 inches wide and 8 inches long. This is the same as a 6-inch square with an extra strip 2 inches wide added to one edge. You crease the 6-inch square as in (1) for the basket. You then gather up the middle points of the right- and left-hand sides of the square and bring them together, making your paper look like (1) in the diagram below. Now you proceed, as when

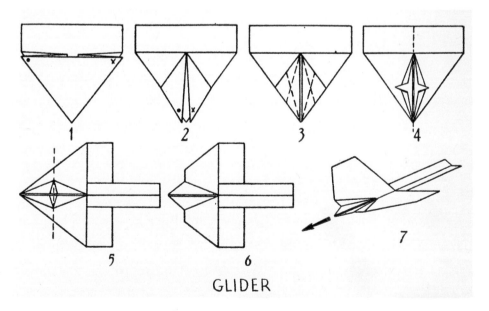

GLIDER

making the bellows, to fold down the points marked with dot and cross, as shown at (2), afterwards creasing them as shown at (3) and crumpling them as shown at (4). You must now fold along the dotted line in (4) to make a crease down the centre. The creasing should be done in such a way as to separate the little upstanding ears on the front.

After flattening the crease again, you slip into the point of the toy, as at (5), a strip of paper 9 inches long and 1 inch wide which has already been creased down the centre in the same way as the main plane of your toy. You now fold along the dotted line shown in (5). The triangular tip to the left of this line must go behind to make the toy appear as in (6). Your glider is now practically finished, only needing to be creased down the middle again to make it appear as shown pictorially in (7) which is a view of the glider in flight, as seen from the front and a little above.

To make it fly, you throw it gently point foremost, holding it level at the moment of release. If you throw too hard it will do silly things, but if you throw gently it should glide smoothly across the room, and still be some distance from the ground when it strikes the wall on the other side. If it flies to right or to left you need to correct some slight twist in the paper. If it dives, or keeps trying to climb and then stalling, it will be because the tail is bent up or down at the back end and needs straightening. You can learn a lot about the way a real aircraft works by altering the "trim" of your toy one.

In a large room or hall you can have a flying competition with your friends. Each of you makes the best glider he can. Then you mark off on the floor (with chalk, or by stretching two strings) a fairly narrow strip extending the length of the room. Each player stands at one end of this strip and throws his glider. The winner is the one whose glider goes farthest. Gliders which do not land between the white lines must be adjusted until they fly straight.

15. DART

Another flying toy is the dart. This is easier than the glider to make, and requires only one piece of paper about 12 inches long by 9 inches wide. The first thing you do is fold the corners at one end to the centre of your paper which, by the way, should be creased down the centre to start with. Your paper then appears as in (1). You now fold the newly formed corners, marked by a dot and a

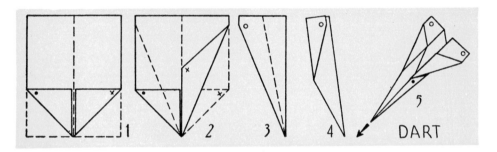

cross, to the centre. In (2) you can see how this is done, the one marked by a cross already being folded. When you have done the other corner also, you must double your toy up in the middle so that the corners marked with a dot and a cross are hidden inside, as at (3). You now fold over the blunt point marked O in (3), so that it lies to the right instead of to the left, as in (4). The crease made by this fold is shown in (3) by a dotted line. Behind the front point O in (3) there is a similar point at the back, and this must be folded behind before your toy can appear finally as in (4). Having flattened everything down firmly to make good creases, you must now let the two parts marked O spread out opposite to one another, as shown in the sketch (5). Your dart is now ready for flying. All you have to do to use it is hold it **between the thumb and forefinger** of one hand and throw it in the direction of the arrow, that is to say, point foremost.

16. PURSE

A piece of paper 9 inches square will make a purse 3 inches square. To begin with, you must crease your paper into three, first one way and then the other, thus dividing it up into nine 3-inch

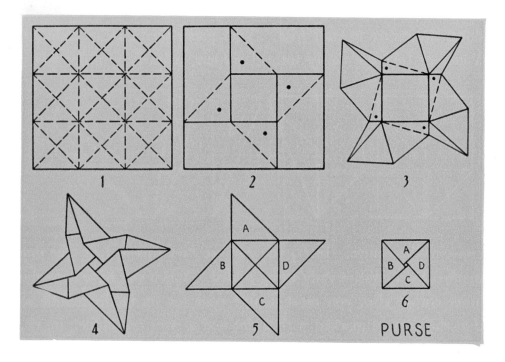

PURSE

squares. Now you must make all the diagonal creases, so that, finally, your paper looks as in (1). The next step is to make the creases of the central square very clear by pinching them between finger and thumb from *underneath* the paper. Now do the same to the diagonal creases running away from the four corners of the central square, as shown by dotted lines in (2), but pinching them from *above* the paper. You must now try to make the triangles marked by dots in (2) stand up so that, when viewed from above, they seem to shrink to a thin line. In (3) you can see the same triangles marked by dots when they are nearly upright. They look much narrower: when they are quite upright they will be visible from above only as lines because the paper forming them will then be viewed edgewise. The corners of the paper will make four things like a cat's ears, which you can help to form by pinching the creases in the way they want to go. When the triangles marked by dots are quite upright, you push them over towards the centre of the square, and if you make the various folds of paper overlap in the right order, your toy will appear as in (4), finally pressing down into the form shown in (5). To complete your purse, fold down the triangular flaps *A*, *B* and *C* in this order. Flap *D* is folded over *C* and tucked in under *A*, as shown in (6). To put a coin in your purse, you pull out flap *D* from under flap *A* and slip the coin under *A*. Then you put back flap *D*, at the same time shaking the coin down towards the bottom of the purse. If you study this purse carefully you will see that by putting a spot of paste or gum here and there you can make it into one which is fairly secure; but I should not advise you to keep your more precious silver money in it.

17. CLOSED BOX

The box you are now going to make is closed on all sides and makes a handy container for sweets. A piece of paper 8 inches square makes a box that is about $2\frac{3}{4}$ inches square on top and about $1\frac{1}{2}$ inches deep.

To start the box you fold your square of paper diagonally, both ways, in order to find the centre. You then fold all four corners to the centre, creasing well. When you have opened the paper again you will find that the creases make a small square inside a larger one. You now fold each corner of the paper to the mid-point of the opposite and more remote side of the small square. You can see this being done to one of the corners in (1). This makes four new creases. Now you fold each corner to the mid-point of the opposite and nearer side of the small square. You can see this being done to one of the corners in (2). Having made all the creases in your paper, you now use scissors to cut away eight small triangular pieces to give the outline shown in (3). You cut also along the thick lines

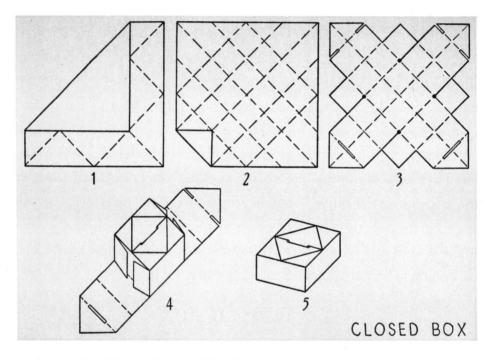

CLOSED BOX

as far as the black dots. Thirdly, you cut a narrow slit along the crease at the two bottom corners, as shown in (3), and you make nicks along the crease from each side at the other two corners. The width of paper left between these nicks should be equal to the width of the slit in the opposite corner.

If now you bend over the bottom right-hand corner to meet the top left-hand corner, fitting the nicked one inside the slotted one, you will have your toy looking like (4). At this stage it looks rather like a toy garage or aircraft hangar, and it can be filled with sweets or anything else you wish to put inside. The last step is to bend over the top right-hand corner to meet the bottom left-hand one, interlocking one with the other, as was done with the other two corners. Your box, which now appears as in (5), is finished. If you like, you can decorate it on the outside with paintings, but if you want to do this it is best to open it and flatten the paper while you are doing your painting. If you do open it, be sure you make some mark beforehand on the surfaces you intend to paint, as you may make a mistake otherwise and paint in the wrong places.

18. BIRD

The bird you are now about to make looks very real and, besides, if you waggle or pull its tail, it will flap its wings in a most life-like manner.

To make it, you need a square piece of paper, not too large. With thinnish paper the square should have sides not more than 4 inches long. If you have it larger than this the bird will not hold its shape very well and its wings will be too limp and "floppy."

You first crease your square along both diagonals and then down and across the middle. You now have a lot more creases to make, and you do this by folding the sides up to the diagonals, as shown in (1) and (2). The best way to make sure that you do all the creases shown in (3), without missing any, is to letter the four corners and then do the two folds shown in (1) and (2), keeping corner A at the bottom and on your left, afterwards repeating the process three times with corners B, C and D in the same position. You have eight new creases to make altogether, and then your paper appears as in (3).

It is now necessary to pinch all these creases firmly in the way you want the paper to bend. The creases I have shown by a continuous black line in (3) must be made clearer by pinching the paper from above; the rest of the creases must be made clearer by pinching the paper from underneath.

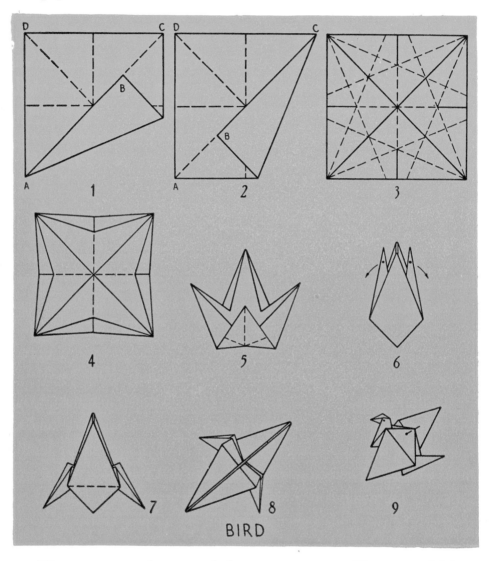

BIRD

The next part of your task is not very easy. You must fold up the middle points of the edges of your square so that they all move in towards the centre of the square. At the same time you must help the corners to rise up and approach the centre as well. If you watch all the creases to see that they fold in the way they were pinched to go, you should succeed in doing this, especially if you attend to only one side and two corners at a time. When everything has started going the right way, your paper should look like (4), when viewed from above. Later on, it makes the flower-like object you can see in (5).

When you have closed the petals of your flower closely together at the tips, you must flatten out two of them, choosing two that face one another; and the other two you must fold in two down their middles, making your paper appear as in (6). You must now pull down the folded petals, marked by dots in (6), following the arrows, so that they come into the positions shown in (7). As you pull them down they will try to turn inside out. You must help them to do this, and then make the creases needed to keep them in position.

You now fold towards you, along the dotted line shown in (7), the flattened petal that is nearest to you. The one farthest away must be folded away from you in the same way. Your toy should now look as in (8). It only remains for you to turn it up the other way and form the head of your bird at the end of one of the spikes. Your bird is then complete, as in (9). To make the head you bend over the end of the spike, helping it to turn inside out and creasing it firmly when you have made it as you want it. The bird looks more realistic if you put a black dot for an eye on each side of its head. If you hold it underneath at the front, you can make it flap its wings by pulling its tail in and out. You can make it stand on the table if you open out the creases underneath a little. To make it look as though it is flying you can hang it up by a piece of cotton. The hole for the cotton should be made with a pin, slightly in front of the point forming the bird's back, as shown in (9). A lot of gaily coloured birds hung up in a draughty place makes an attractive sight, just the sort of thing to please a baby lying in a cot or a pram.

19. TABLE MAT

What you are going to make now is a flat pattern or "cut-out," quite different from the folded objects so far described.

You start with a square piece of paper of any size but preferably

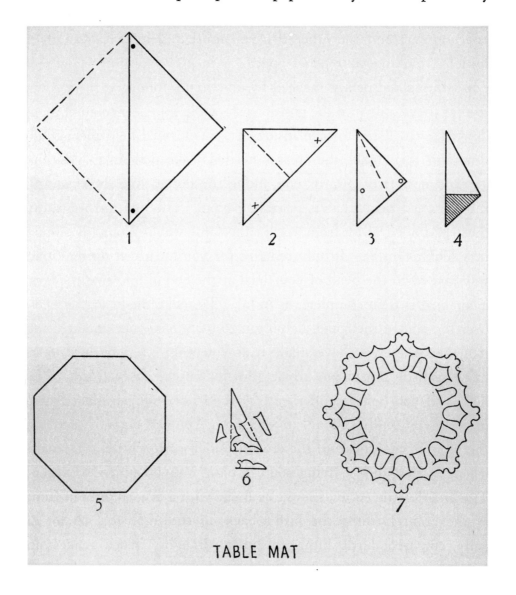

TABLE MAT

not too small and you fold it along a diagonal as shown in (1). Next, you bring the dotted corners together by folding the triangle in half. The paper (4 thicknesses) now appears as in (2). By folding along the dotted line and bringing the corners marked X together you get an object like (3), in which there are 8 thicknesses of paper. By making yet another fold, starting from the top point, as shown by the dots in (3), you bring the points marked O together and your 16 thicknesses of paper now appear as in (4). There is an 8-thickness triangular piece projecting, which I have shown shaded. You must cut this off. At this stage you might open out the paper again and then you would find you had an octagonal shape, as at (5). But to make a pretty mat you must leave the paper folded and then start cutting or tearing away pieces as shown at (6). You can cut or tear how you like, but the beauty of the final design will depend on the shapes you favour. Opening out the paper that is left, as at (7), you will see your finished Table Mat. There is no limit to the variety of patterns you can make in this way.

20. CHAIN

A strip of paper can be stretched to at least three times its original length by slitting it to make a " chain." In (1) you see a strip creased down its centre. This is folded as at (2) and then snipped from alternate sides. The cuts must not go right across the folded strip but leave an un-cut width of not less than an eighth of an inch.

When you open the paper out again, as at (3) you have a design that can be stretched lengthways to about three times the original length of the strip. You can make chains of 4 and more times the original length of the paper by making the scissor cuts closer together, but if you do this the chain may be rather frail and easy to break. Chains made in this way are useful for Christmas and party decorations.

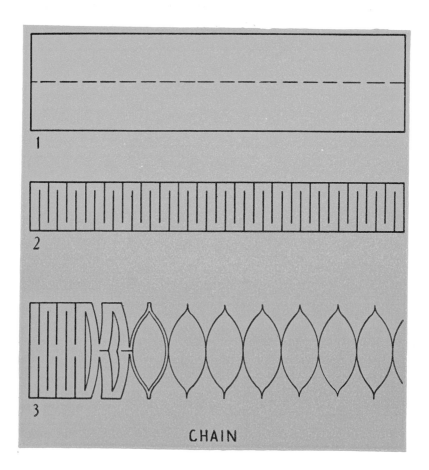

CHAIN

21. MAGIC POSTCARD

Tell your friend that you can make a hole in an ordinary-sized postcard big enough for him to go through, and he will not believe you. This is how you do it.

Fold the card down the centre, lengthwise, and snip it as though you intended to turn it into a chain. Then flatten the card again and slit it along the fold but not at the extreme ends. On either side of this central slit you now have a zigzag of card that you can stretch to a length of 18 inches, 24 inches or even more. Between these zigzags you can make an opening large enough for any person to pass through.

22. MAGIC RINGS

Here is a most mystifying conjuring trick. You

MAGIC POSTCARD

come upon the stage with three paper loops on your arm. They all look alike, but when you slit them down the centre with scissors you do not get the same result. The first ring divides into two narrow rings, which is what everyone expects to happen. The next one becomes a single ring of twice the original size and the third one makes a couple of narrow rings linked together.

Of course, the original rings are not quite alike, but if made large enough and "floppy" enough the differences will not be perceived by your audience. Ring No. 1 (see sketch) is made by gumming the strip ends together without any twist. This makes two narrow rings as shown at

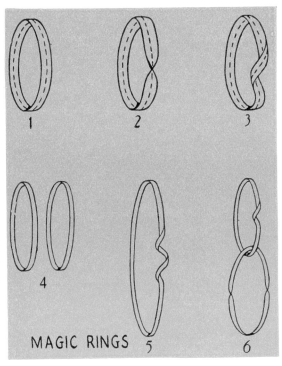

MAGIC RINGS

(4). Ring No. 2 is made with a half twist in the strip and ring No. 3 is made with a whole twist in the strip. The results of slitting rings 2 and 3 are indicated at (5) and (6).

23. HOW BIG IS A HOLE?

What a silly question! But now try this. On a piece of paper, not too thick, draw a circle the size of a sixpence. To make your circle you can draw round a sixpence with a sharply-pointed pencil. A halfpenny is a larger coin than a sixpence, but you can easily pass it through the sixpence-sized hole in your paper. How is this done? You fold the paper across the round hole and let the halfpenny hang as shown in the sketch. Grasping corners *A* and *B*, you bring them closer together as shown by the top pair of arrows. The paper will crumple up at the top and the hole at the bottom will become elongated, as shown by the lower pair of arrows. The halfpenny will fall through quite easily and without tearing or even stretching the paper.

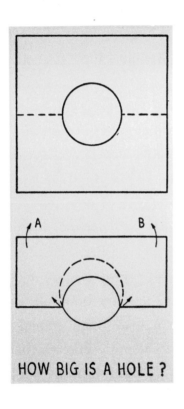

HOW BIG IS A HOLE ?

Section Seven: Home Entertainments

Chapter 2

A PAPER VILLAGE

IN the toyshops you can buy beautiful little models of every type of car. I am sure some of you who read this book will possess a number of "Dinky" toys. Made to the same scale are buses, bulldozers, cranes, tractors, ploughs and even farmyard buildings and animals. The smallest size of electric railway (gauge oo) is fairly closely in scale with all these things, so anybody who owns such a railway can add to its realism by surrounding it with the many things that can be seen near a real railway. If you do not have enough buildings to complete your layout you should try making some from good strong, white paper.

I know you can buy beautifully drawn and coloured cut-out sheets—even whole books of such sheets—but some of these cut-outs will be wrong in scale, or they may portray things you do not really want to make. The best way to obtain model buildings for your layout is to make them for yourself. In this chapter I will tell you how to do it.

Not all paper models are easy to make; in fact some are quite difficult to do. For this reason I am going to start with an easy design. When you have drawn your own plan, cut it from the sheet, and having folded the creases ready for sticking, you can decide how to colour it. Design No. 1, shown on the next page, will make a small

cottage, a garden shed or a garage for a "Dinky" toy car. Before
you make your flat pattern into a solid-looking "house," you should
draw in windows, doors and so on. You can mark out surfaces to
look as though they are tiled or made from bricks. Then you can
get out your paintbox and give everything a realistic colour. After

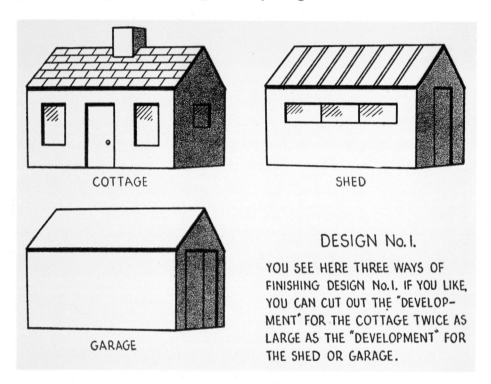

COTTAGE

SHED

GARAGE

DESIGN No. I.

YOU SEE HERE THREE WAYS OF
FINISHING DESIGN No. I. IF YOU LIKE,
YOU CAN CUT OUT THE "DEVELOP-
MENT" FOR THE COTTAGE TWICE AS
LARGE AS THE "DEVELOPMENT" FOR
THE SHED OR GARAGE.

colouring everything it will be a good idea to go over your lines with
pencil or pen again. Finally, you can re-make the folds, apply a
quick-drying adhesive to the tabs, and join everything together.

DESIGN No. 1

The cut-out pattern or "development" of a simple cottage, garage
or shed is shown on the next page. To make such a pattern you
need to use a ruler, a set square and a pair of compasses, because
everything must be drawn very accurately to the correct size. You

have to begin by drawing the FRONT VIEW and the END VIEW of your cottage at the top of the paper. For a large "Dinky" toy garage the proper size is 4 inches long and 2 inches wide. From ground to eaves the height should be 1½ inches, and the roof should add another 1 inch to the height. Notice how the two views are drawn standing on the same GROUND LINE.

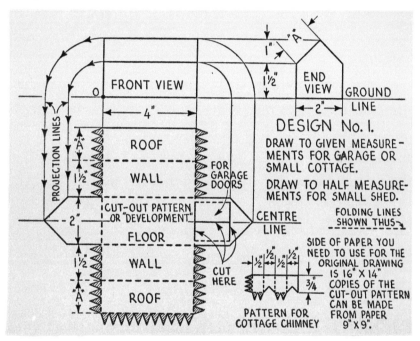

Parallel to the ground line on your paper, and fully 4 inches below it, you must draw a CENTRE LINE for your "development" or cut-out plan. The floor, 2 inches wide and 4 inches long, is divided down its middle by this centre line. Like wings, above and below the floor, you have flaps to form the side walls and the sloping sides of the roof. The wall portions are each 4 inches long and 1½ inches wide. The roof portions are of the same length, namely 4 inches, but the width must be taken from the END VIEW. It is the measurement shown as A. The end walls of the cottage go up to a point. When you draw them out each side from the floor you must copy the shape from the END VIEW or else use the compasses and set square to "project" the correct lengths down from the FRONT VIEW. I have drawn arrows all the way down the helpful projection lines in the diagram on page 153. Corner O of the FRONT VIEW is used as centre for your compasses when you draw the rounded portions of the projection lines.

You must leave a fringe of points along the edges of walls and roofs as shown. When gummed, these points serve to hold the model together.

The chimney is square in shape and $\frac{1}{2}$ inch each way. Its four sides are each rectangles measuring $\frac{1}{2}$ inch × $\frac{3}{4}$ inch, but out of two of them you must cut a " V " notch to allow for the angle of the roof. The angle of the " V " must be a copy of the roof angle in the END VIEW. You should bend the cut-out into a square tube and stick it up that way before you attempt to fasten it on to the roof with the remaining pointed tabs. These other tabs look neater if they are turned *inwards* so as to be hidden inside the chimney.

DESIGN No. 2

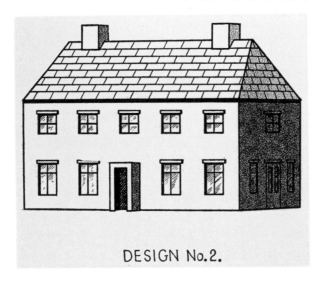

DESIGN No.2.

Shown on this page is a more elegant-looking house having two chimneys and a porch. You will not wish to vary this design to make of it a shed or a garage, but you may wish to add on dormer windows or extra wings so as to turn it into a really handsome mansion. I will tell you how to make the house you can see on the previous page, and afterwards I will tell you how to add to it.

At the top of your paper you draw, as before, full-sized views

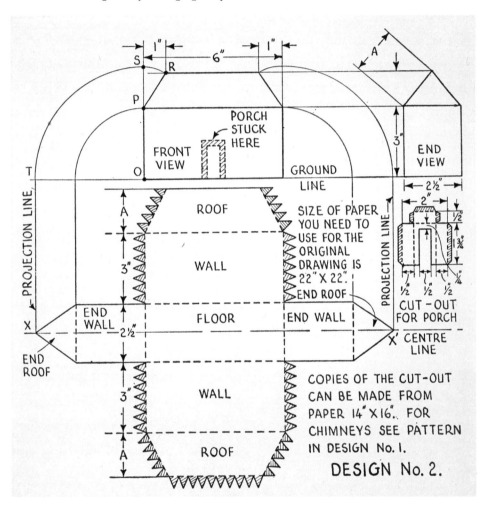

of the FRONT and the END of the house, standing on the same ground line. The centre line of your cut-out will have to be not less than $6\frac{1}{2}$ inches below the ground line on your paper. The floor, $2\frac{1}{2}$ inches wide, is divided in half by the centre line. Above and below the floor are rectangles 3 inches wide for the walls. The width A of the sloping side portions of roof is taken, as shown, from the end view. The height from eaves to roof ridge you can choose for yourself. In my drawing it is 1½ inches.

Extending 3 inches to left and right of the floor are the rectangles for the end walls. The triangular extensions for the end portions of the roof have their points located by projection lines as shown. To draw these projection lines you must use your compasses. Put the point at centre P and touch point R with the compass pencil to obtain the correct radius. Then draw the circular arc RS. Now move your compass point to centre O and stretch the legs apart so that the pencil reaches to S. Draw now the circular arc ST. Drawing the projection line down from T to the CENTRE LINE will give you the required position of point X. The same method will give you point X′ on the right-hand side.

Chimneys are made in the same way as before. A separate cut-out is shown for the porch.

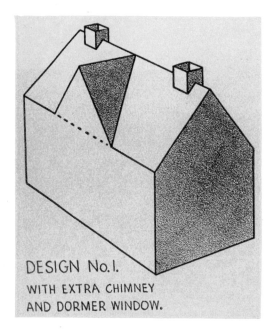

DESIGN No. 1.
WITH EXTRA CHIMNEY
AND DORMER WINDOW.

IMPROVEMENTS

Designs No. 1 and No. 2 can both be improved by small additions. On this page and the next you can see how the humble cottage in Design No. 1 can be turned into an attractive house by adding on a dormer window and another chimney.

The cut-out for the dormer window is drawn with the help of a new END VIEW showing the dormer, and a new FRONT VIEW. In the new FRONT VIEW the dormer is shown at B. You can choose for yourself the angle at the top of triangle B. When you have done so you must copy triangle B on the piece of paper that is to be your dormer window cut-out.

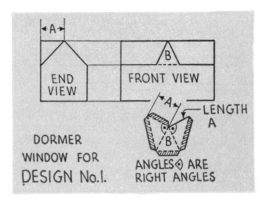

Going away from the top of the newly-drawn triangle you must draw two lines each of length A, as shown. You must take measurement A from the END VIEW. The direction in which you draw the two lines of length A is important. They must be drawn at right angles to the neighbouring sides of triangle B. I have clearly marked which angles must be right angles.

When you have drawn straight lines going from the bottom corners of triangle B to the outer ends of the lines of length A your cut-out is almost complete: it is something like a butterfly in shape. All you have to do is add narrow strips (or rows of

DESIGN No. 2.
WITH TWO WINGS ADDED.

pointed tabs) along the various edges, as shown. These will be needed for gumming.

Exactly the same method can be employed for adding a dormer window to Design No. 2.

If you wish, you can add a wing instead of a dormer. On the previous page you can see a house made to Design No. 2 with extra wings added on the front and the back.

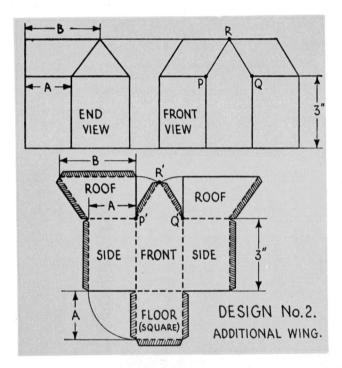

To make cut-outs for these extra wings you need to draw again the FRONT VIEW and the END VIEW of your house accurately to size. The appearance of the extra wing in these views is as shown on page 157. You may draw the triangle PQR to have any angle you like at the point R, but for the sake of a good appearance you would do well to make the slope of PR and QR the same as the slope of the roof at each end of the house. The amount the wing juts out is A and, here again, you can please yourself.

Having decided upon your design, you must make a faithful copy P'Q'R' of triangle PQR near the top of the piece of paper that is to be your cut-out. To complete the front face of the wing you must add on a rectangle below base P'Q' of the triangle; this will extend down a distance of 3 inches. On either side of this rectangle you must draw rectangles for the side walls of the wing. These rectangles will, of course, be 3 inches from top to bottom, and the width of each will be the distance A you have chosen to make the wing jut out in front of the house. The flap for the floor must also measure A in the up-and-down direction.

The roof flaps measure A at the eaves and B at the ridge of the roof, as you can see from the END VIEW drawing. The up-and-down measurement is obtained by compass, using P' for centre and P'R' for radius.

Narrow flaps or pointed tabs are added as shown along most of the edges of your cut-out, these being necessary for gumming.

CHURCH

No village or small town is complete without its church, so we will

CHURCH

make a really splendid one with a steeple. This diagram shows you how it will look.

The main cut-out, shown on this page, is cut-out No. 1; this is similar to the one for the humble cottage, shed or garage (see page 153, but it has a more steeply sloping roof, and its proportions are more dignified generally. The length of the sloping roof PQ=SQ is transferred by compass to positions PR and ST and then the whole length OR is swung round at right angles, as also is the whole length UT, to find the position of the roof ridge line.

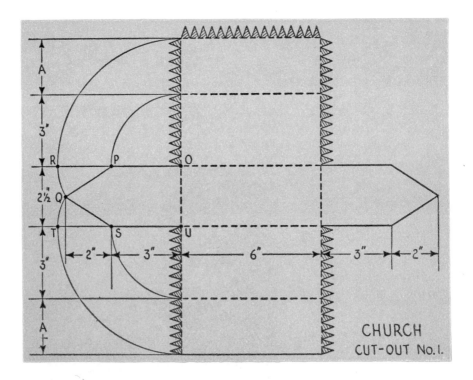

CHURCH
CUT-OUT No. I.

Cut-out No. 2, for the square tower, is shown on page 161. It is very easy to make but you must take care to see that the square flaps for the top and bottom are quite flat and truly at right angles to the sides after gumming in position. If the ends are crooked, then the tower will stand crookedly or, worse still, the steeple will lean over at an angle.

Cut-out No. 3, for the steeple, is an entirely new shape; it is made up of four triangles lying edge to edge. On the left of the actual cut-out is a side view of the steeple, which is 5 inches high. The triangular surfaces starting from the base and running up to a point, lean inwards slightly, so you do not see their true height in the side view. The true height of each triangle is OQ, which is a little more than 5 inches. With compass centre O, and radius OP, you must draw the arc PQ to cut the upright line going through O. The first

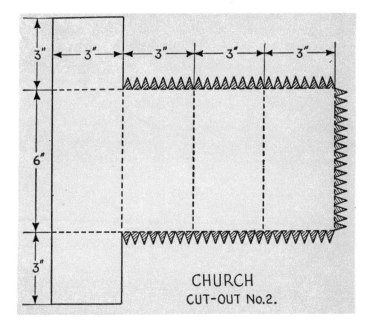

CHURCH
CUT-OUT No.2.

line drawn in your cut-out is line SA for the base of the first triangle; it is $2\frac{1}{2}$ inches long. Through the mid-point of SA you must draw the upright CENTRE LINE. The point of your first triangle is at R, found by projecting across from Q. Joining RS and RA completes the triangle. The other three triangles are copies of this first one, and you make them in this way. Taking R for centre and RS or RA for radius, you draw the circular arc SABCDT. To find points B, C and D, you must set your compasses to the length AS. With A as centre and radius AS, you cut the circular arc at B. Then you move the compass point to B, and, keeping the radius unaltered, you cut the circular arc at C.   Finally, you move the compass point to C and cut the circular arc at D.   Joining R to B, C and D completes the other three triangular sides of the steeple.   You then join A to B, B to C and C to D.   After adding gumming strips or tabs to the

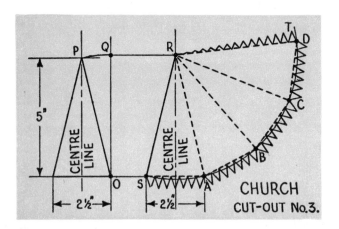

edges shown you can cut out the pattern for the steeple.   I have not shaded the gumming tabs in this diagram of the steeple cut-out because I wanted you to see very clearly the circular arc SABCDT.

SCHOOL, TOWN HALL, FACTORY

If you care to make three or more additional cut-outs, similar to the one for the church tower, they will provide you with blocks out of which you can construct a variety of buildings in the modern style.   Such buildings are usually made of concrete: when new, they may be dazzlingly white, so you do not need to paint your blocks. However, on two of the longer faces, opposite to one another, you may draw and colour a long line of windows.

On page 163 are suggestions for using your blocks.   Three of them will make a school or a factory.   Four will make a very splendid-looking Town Hall, which you can improve if you like by adding a steeple.

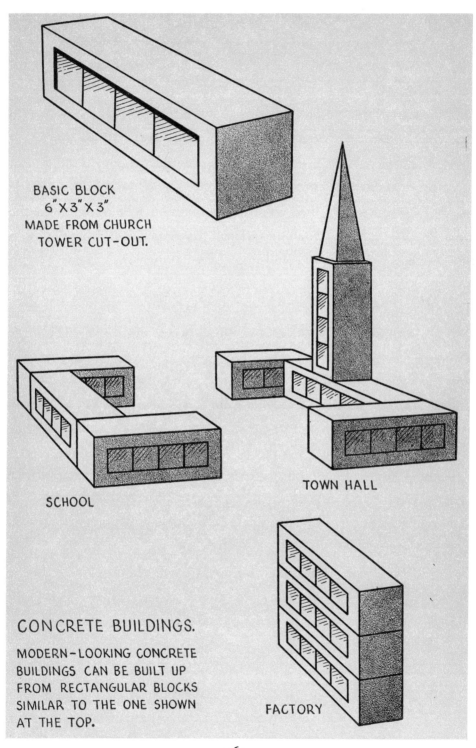

BASIC BLOCK
6" X 3" X 3"
MADE FROM CHURCH
TOWER CUT-OUT.

SCHOOL

TOWN HALL

CONCRETE BUILDINGS.

MODERN-LOOKING CONCRETE
BUILDINGS CAN BE BUILT UP
FROM RECTANGULAR BLOCKS
SIMILAR TO THE ONE SHOWN
AT THE TOP.

FACTORY

I do not have to tell you that the upright block forming the tower of the Town Hall could very well be decorated differently.　Instead of having two long lines of windows you could draw the four round faces of a clock.

We started this chapter with the intention of describing how to make the buildings for a paper village, but you will see now that enough cut-outs have been described to enable you to build a vast city—even a city of skyscrapers!　I hope that when you have made all the examples described in this chapter you will understand the rules for drawing cut-out shapes so well that you will be able to design and cut out quite original buildings of your own imagining.

HOW TO USE UP SMALL SCRAPS OF PAPER

When made in one piece a cut-out often requires a very large sheet of paper to begin with.　The church tower, for instance, if made in one piece, needs a sheet not smaller than 12 inches by 12 inches.　If you do not have such a large piece of paper to hand you need not be discouraged.　You can make the cut-out in two or more separate parts, so as to use any smaller pieces of paper you may have available.　Remember, however, that where the join comes you must put gumming tabs or strips on one of the two pieces.

If the building is at all complicated you may still feel the need for a large piece of paper on which to draw the original cut-out pattern by projection from the front and end views.　However, if you do not have such a large piece and cannot get one, then you can halve the scale of your drawing, making all the measurements in it one-half of the given measurements.　In an extreme case you might even reduce the scale to a quarter.　That way you could use a small piece of writing-paper to obtain the cut-out pattern for a very large model. Of course, the finished pattern would be only one-half or one-quarter

THE PAPER VILLAGE

(*Top*) Houses made to Design No. 1; and (*bottom*) houses made to Design No. 2.

THE PAPER VILLAGE

(*Top*) Church with house to Design No. 1 for comparison and (*bottom*) Town Hall
made from nine similar blocks with steeple added.

of the size you really wanted, but this need not worry you, because any pattern of a building is usually made up of rectangles and triangles and other simple shapes that are easy to copy two, three or four times the size of the pattern.

You will copy these shapes on separate scraps of paper, making them the required size; then you will add tabs where necessary and cut them out. The various pieces will be joined together with the aid of some gum, and in this way you will obtain a complete cut-out. It may consist of five or six pieces or even more, but the finished model will be the same as though it had been made from one large sheet.

The houses and other buildings shown in the photographs were all made piecemeal in this way from small scraps of paper to be found in any home.

Chapter 3

FUN WITH STRING

IF you have ever given a children's party, I expect you will remember how difficult it was to make a good beginning. The children did not come all together, but in ones and twos, and the first arrivals stood about shyly, waiting for the fun to begin. Perhaps you had planned to start with a game like Blind Man's Buff that would warm everybody up; you did not expect to have to wait so long before all your guests arrived. In preparing for a party it is always a good idea to have some amusing things to do with the first arrivals, and I have found that it is a great help to know a few easy tricks and puzzles that can be done with two or three lengths of string. The first child to arrive is asked if he can do the Ring Puzzle. While he is trying it, or being shown how to do it, more guests arrive, and they become interested in it too. Very often this one puzzle will keep the guests amused until everybody is present, but I will tell you some more puzzles to do with string, in case you need them.

RING PUZZLE

For this puzzle you need a piece of smooth string about three feet long, and also a finger ring. Any other sort of ring will do just as well. You must tie the two ends of the string together to make a loop. When you have made your preparations you pass the loop of string through the ring and then put your two thumbs through the ends of the loop. Holding your hands apart to keep the loop tight, you ask your friend if he can take the ring off the string without unhooking the string from either of your thumbs.

After your friend has made several vain attempts to take the

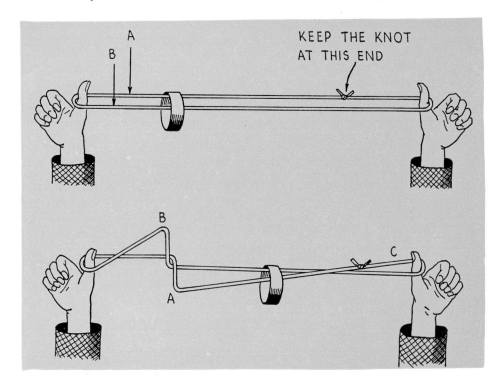

ring off the string you say, "Come, I'll put the string on your two thumbs, and then I'll do the puzzle myself." You then put the string on your friend's thumbs, taking care to have the knot in it near the thumb on your right. If the knot is to your left it may cause a hitch and spoil the trick. The string on your friend's thumbs appears as shown in the top sketch on this page. You must put both your hands above the left-hand end of the loop, keeping the ring on your right. You then take hold of the string at A between thumb and first finger of your right hand, at the same time taking the string at *B* between the thumb and first finger of your left hand. Now you pull your right hand towards you and push your left hand farther away. This crosses the string and gives it the appearance shown in the bottom sketch.

What you do next is quite easy to describe, but if I tried to draw it for you it would look difficult. You first of all put the loop *A*, which you hold in your right hand, over your friend's nearest thumb (the one on your left). All the time you must hold on to the loop *B* with your left hand. Your right hand is now free to do something else, so you put the first finger of that hand down through the loop at *C*, close up to your friend's other thumb. You must be careful to have the ring to the *left* of your finger when you do this. With this finger you now make a hook to hold the string which is nearest to you. You then run your hooked finger along to the left, pushing the ring over to the left and always holding on to the same string. You now put the loop of string on your hooked finger over your friend's thumb (again the one on your left). You are still holding on to the loop at *B*, and what you now have looks like a hopeless tangle. However, you tell your friend to pull the string as tight as he can and at the same time you let go of the loop *B*. To his great surprise (and to yours) the ring falls to the ground, leaving the loop of string on his two thumbs, exactly as it was in the beginning.

To vary this little trick, you can put the loop of string through a buttonhole in your friend's jacket instead of through a ring. The ends of the loop go over his thumbs, as before. You can go through the movements in the same way as for the ring, treating his jacket as the ring, and at the finish the string will still be on his thumbs but not through his jacket.

When you have let go of loop *B* it is quite a good idea to catch hold of your friend's two thumbs while he separates them, just to make sure that he does not let the string slip off them. If this happens the trick is spoilt and you will have to do it again.

ANOTHER RING TRICK

This is an easier puzzle than the last one. To prepare it, you pass the loop of string through the ring; then you put one end of the loop through the other end, as shown in the left-hand sketch, and pull tight, so that the ring is held by the string in the way shown by the right-hand sketch. Holding the doubled string fairly close to the ring, you give the ring to your friend and ask him to try to take it off the string. He may struggle with it for a long time, but the way to do it is

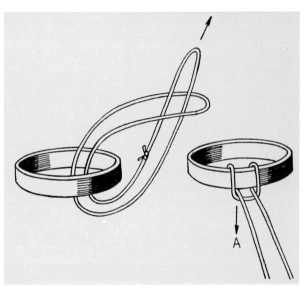

really very easy. All you have to do is pull the loop *A* down in the direction shown by the arrow, spread it out, and push the ring through it from back to front. The ring is then free from the string.

PRISONER

The last trick can be done in another way, using your friend as the ring; but if you want him to be puzzled by it you should not show him the ring trick first.

G. IV—6*

To make him your prisoner you will need a much bigger loop of string; one made from four yards of string will be big enough. You push one end of the loop through a buttonhole in his jacket, starting from the inside, and then you push the other end of the loop through the loop protruding through the buttonhole. You pull the string tight, as in the sketch, and, holding on to the free end, you tell your friend he is your prisoner, inviting him to escape. If he cannot do it, and says that he does not believe it is possible, you can offer to be his prisoner. When he is holding you a prisoner

you can tell him to shut his eyes, or you can blindfold him, and then you can make your escape. He may tell you that you have undone the knot or cheated him in some way, but you can assure him that you did nothing of the kind and repeat the performance, letting him hold the knot in his own hands.

After a while you can let him into the secret. All he has to do is pull down the loop *A* until it is big enough for him to step through. He passes it up behind his back and over his head, and then he is a free man.

HANDCUFFS

The puzzles described so far are useful for amusing one guest. When another arrives you can have great fun tying your two guests together and inviting them to escape from one another if they can. You need to have two pieces of string, each about three feet long. You tie the ends of one piece of string round the wrists of one of your guests, being careful not to tie too tightly, or too loosely. You then tie the other piece of string at one end round the wrist of your other guest. The free end you pass through the loop between the wrists of your first guest, afterwards tying it to the free wrist of your second guest. Your guests are now linked together, the two pieces of string being as shown in the top sketch. Near the parts encircling your friends' wrists I have written 1L and 1R for those going round

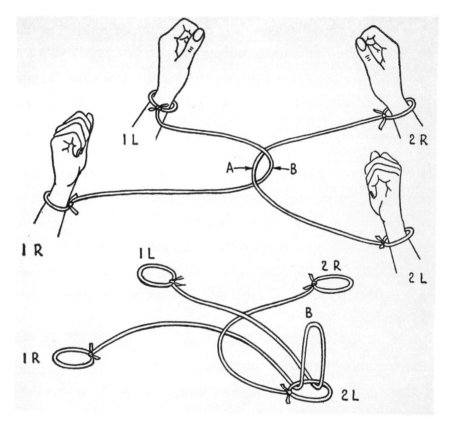

the left- and right-hand wrists of the first guest; and 2L and 2R for those going round the left- and right-hand wrists of your second guest.

In trying to escape, your friends will do all sorts of queer things, and they may make themselves into a fine tangle. If they stopped to think they would see that escape was really quite easy. Somehow or other loop B must be made to pass over 2R or 2L, or alternatively, loop *A* must be made to pass over IL or IR.   At first sight it would seem as though the string would have to pass through an arm in order to do this, but you can make it pass *over* and not *through* an arm.

Suppose you decide to make loop *B* pass over the left arm of your second guest.   You take the string forming loop *B* and bring it up against the left wrist of your guest, just below the encircling "handcuff."   He holds his hand up for you to do this.   You then pass loop *B* under his handcuff and pull it through until it appears as in the bottom sketch and is big enough to slip over his hand. When you have passed loop *B* over your friend's hand, it can be pulled away from him altogether, leaving your two friends separated.

If your friends have managed to get the loops twisted they can untwist them by raising their hands above their heads and then turning round.   If they have tried pulling loop *A* or loop *B* under a handcuff, but chosen the wrong handcuff, and so made matters worse than they were at the start, you can separate them by doing the correct thing, as already described, not once but twice.

If you have more pieces of string you can tie several couples together and keep the fun going with quite a large number of children for quite a long time.

You should practise all these string tricks with somebody you know very well before you try them out on guests.   If you are not sure of yourself, and make mistakes, your shyest guests will become more shy and awkward than ever.

Chapter 4

FUN WITH CARDS

A GREAT number of games and tricks can be played with a pack of ordinary playing cards. I shall not attempt to describe the games, because nearly everybody knows the best of them. Neither shall I describe any conjuring tricks of the kind that are intended to deceive anybody. The tricks I have chosen to tell you about are ones you can do anywhere, even with people pressing round you and watching you closely. You have nothing to hide from them except what is going on in your own mind.

SPELLING LESSON

For this trick, you must have a complete pack of 52 playing cards. You lay them out in four lines as shown in Sketch 1. Each line contains 13 cards, the first one having them in the order K (King), Q (Queen), J (Jack), 10, 9, 8, 7, 6, 5, 4, 3, 2, A (Ace). In the next line you miss out the King and start with the Queen. Then you miss out the Jack and put down 10, miss out 9 and put down 8, and so on, missing out every other card. In the third line you miss out two cards to start with, and put down Jack. You then miss out two more cards and put down 8. You go on like this, missing out two cards after each card you put down. In the fourth, and last, one you miss out three cards to start with and three after each card you put down. So far everything is quite easy, and you can allow your friends to help you. If each line finishes with an

K	Q	J	10
Q	10	8	6
J	8	5	2
10	6	2	J
9	4	Q	7
8	2	9	3
7	K	6	Q
6	J	3	8
5	9	K	4
4	7	10	K
3	5	7	9
2	3	4	5
A	A	A	A

SKETCH I

Ace, the cards are probably put down quite right, but check them over to make sure.

Now you must be careful and do everything yourself. You first of all pick up the right-hand line of cards after pushing the top ones down under the Ace at the bottom. Now you put this small pack, still facing Ace upwards, on the Ace of the next (or third) line of cards, and push the cards of this line down under their own Ace. You transfer all the cards to the Ace of the second line of cards and push these second-line cards underneath. Finally, you put the cards on the Ace of the first line, and push these down as well.

You now pick the whole pack up and turn it over, so that the top Ace becomes the bottom card and faces the palm of your hand.

The cards now have to be dealt out, face down, as shown in Sketch 2. The first 13 cards are laid out in three rows of 4, with the odd card making part of a fourth row. The order in which these 13 cards are laid down is shown by the top numbers in the oblongs of Sketch 2. The next 13 cards are laid on top of the first 13, but in the order shown by the second row of numbers in the oblongs. Thus, the first place is missed out, and the first card put in the second place. The third place is missed out and the second card is put in the fourth place. You go on like this, missing out a place each time, until at the finish you have put one card in every place and brought the number of cards in each pile up to 2. The second row of numbers in the oblongs will show you the order to follow. Now you put out 13 more cards, missing out the two first places, then two more places after the third, two more after the sixth, and so on. The order in which this 13 cards is put down is indicated by the third row of numbers in the oblongs. When you have finished, you will have 3 cards in every pile. The last 13 cards are put down in the same way, but missing out the first three places, then three places after the fourth, three places after the eighth, and so on. The fourth, or bottom, row of numbers in the oblongs shows you how to lay these cards out. In the end, you should have 4 cards to each pile and no cards left in your hand.

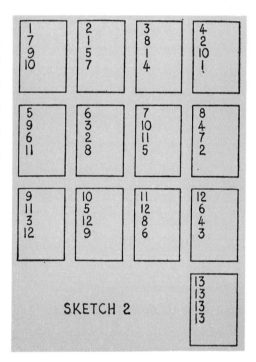

SKETCH 2

Now be careful how you pick up the 13 piles. Start with the one that has four 13's written in it in Sketch 2, and put this on top of the one above it. Pick the two up together and put them on the next to the left. Pick the three up and put them on the next to the left again. You go on like this until you have five piles together. These you put on the right-hand pile of the next row above, and you go on heaping by moves to the left as before. When you have "mopped up" the second row down as well, you proceed to "mop up" the top and last row in the same way.

Now you can give your spelling lesson. Holding the pack in your right hand, you count out the cards with your left. You say "O, N, E spells one," and while you say this you put down three cards on top of one another, the first two face down and the last one face up. The card you can see is a "one" (or Ace). Now you make another heap of cards, saying, "T, W, O spells two." As you say this you lay down a card for each letter, turning up the last one, which is indeed a "two." Now you make yet another heap, saying, "T, H, R, E, E spells three." If you put down a card for each letter and turn up the last one it will be a "three."

You can go on like this for all the numbers up to "ten." Then you must say, "J, A, C, K spells Jack"; "Q, U, E, E, N spells Queen," and, "K, I, N, G spells King."

Everyone is very surprised that it comes out so nicely, but really there is no mystery. If you will think of all you have done to make the pack you hold in your hand at the beginning of the "lesson," you will see that you have gone to a lot of trouble merely to arrange the cards in the order four aces, four twos, four threes, four fours, and so on. I will now write out the cards in their correct order, and put the letters underneath, so that you can see how the trick works.

1	1	1	1	2	2	2	2	3	3	3	3	4	4	4	4	5	5	5	5	6	6	6	6	7	7	7
O	N	E	T	W	O	T	H	R	E	E	F	O	U	R	F	I	V	E	S	I	X	S	E	V	E	N

7	8	8	8	8	9	9	9	9	10	10	10	10	J	J	J	J	Q	Q	Q	Q	K	K	K	K
E	I	G	H	T	N	I	N	E	T	E	N	J	A	C	K	Q	U	E	E	N	K	I	N	G

WHICH CARD WAS IT?

There are many ways of finding a card that somebody has hidden in the pack, but most of them depend on some special arrangement of the cards, and if you gave your pack to somebody else to shuffle or arrange, you could not afterwards find the hidden card. The way I am going to describe to you now does not have this disadvantage. You can give your cards to a friend; let him pick out his card, put it back in the pack and shuffle it to his heart's content.

You do not use a whole pack, but only twenty-one cards. If you are doing this trick for little children, it is best to have picture cards that are all different and more easily remembered than ordinary playing cards. When your friends have chosen a card, and hidden it among the other twenty, they give you back the pack. You then deal the cards out, face upwards, in three piles, putting them down on each pile in turn as shown by the numbers 1, 2, 3, etc., in Sketch 3. It is best to put the cards down so that they can all be partly seen when you have finished. Enough of the cards should show for your friends to be able to tell you in the end which of the piles has their chosen card in it. You ask them this question and they must tell you which heap it is in by pointing, or by letting you point and saying "Yes" when you have indicated the right pile. You now gather up the three piles, being careful to put them together *with the indicated pile in between the other two.*

Now you deal out the cards again, in exactly the same way, and ask once more, "Which pile contains the chosen card?" You gather up the cards, putting the indicated pile in the middle, as before.

You deal out the cards a third time, ask for an indication, and put the indicated pile in the middle once again. Now you are ready to find the hidden card.

You count the cards out silently to yourself, face down, on the table, but when you come to the eleventh, you do not put it down: instead you show it to your friends and say, "Here is your card."

1	2	3
4	5	6
7	8	9
10	11	12
13	14	15
16	17	18
19	20	21

SKETCH 3

You are bound to be right if you have done everything correctly, but if you have made a mistake somewhere, you can easily begin all over again.

How does it work? I will tell you, though the explanation may be a little difficult for you to follow.

When your friends tell you for the first time which pile of seven cards contains the chosen card, you put this pile between the other two, and you know then that the hidden card may be any one between the eighth and the fourteenth in your hand. Now you deal out again. You can make a sketch of what you have done, putting a number for each card as at *A* in Sketch 4. The hidden card is one of the ones with a ring round it. Now then, whichever pile your friends point out to you you are going to put between the other two. The hidden card is one of the ringed numbers in the *middle* seven. It is not one of the first seven cards, and it cannot be either of the next two cards because, whichever pile is put in the middle, it starts with two unringed numbers. But it might be the

1	2	3	•	•	•
4	5	6	•	•	•
7	⑧	⑨	•	•	•
⑩	⑪	⑫	x	x	x
⑬	⑭	15	•	•	•
16	17	18	•	•	•
19	20	21	•	•	•
	A			B	

SKETCH 4

tenth or the eleventh or the twelfth. It could not be the thirteenth or fourteenth because, whichever pile is in the middle, these will be unringed numbers. Very well, then, the hidden card may be any one from No. 10 to No. 12 in your hand.

Now you lay out the cards again. I have shown this at *B* in Sketch 4, making dots for all the cards except the tenth, eleventh and twelfth. For these I have put crosses. You will notice that each pile has a cross at the centre.

Now you ask which pile contains the hidden card; and you can see that whichever pile has to go in the middle the card marked as an X is going to be the eleventh from the top of the pack, eleven being the sum of seven and four.

HIDDEN PAIRS

You are now going to do a trick that will delight and surprise as many as ten people. You get a friend to put down twenty cards in pairs, face down, so that you cannot see them. If the guests are very young, you should use picture cards (all different), as little people find it hard to remember ordinary playing cards. You can easily make your own picture cards before the party begins.

Now you tell your ten friends that they are each to pick up one pair of cards, look at them and remember them so that they would know them if they saw them again. When they have looked at the cards and memorised them, they put them face down again.

In the meantime you can be out of the room, or looking out of the window, so that nobody can accuse you of watching.

Now you ask somebody to pick up the pairs and give the pack to you. The pairs can be picked up in any order, but paired cards *must* be kept together. The pack must not be shuffled.

You now lay out the cards face upwards in four rows in a rather mystifying way, and then you ask each friend in turn to point out in which row or rows his two cards appear. When he indicates the row or rows, you promptly tell him which are his two cards. You do this for all ten friends and, of course, they think you are a magician.

How is it done? I will tell you. While you are dealing out the cards you are thinking of the four words BIBLE, ATLAS, GOOSE and THIGH, and you imagine them to be written on the table as shown in Sketch 5. You will notice that ten letters are used to spell these four words, and each letter is used twice. You put the cards down smoothly and steadily, but dodging about in a mysterious way, and really arranging them in pairs. The first pair go down on the two B's, the next pair on the two I's, the next pair on the two L's, and so on. The order in which you put down the cards may be as

1	3	2	5	7	
B	I	B	L	E	ROW 1
9	11	6	10	13	
A	T	L	A	S	ROW 2
15	17	18	14	8	
G	O	O	S	E	ROW 3
12	19	4	16	20	
T	H	I	G	H	ROW 4

SKETCH 5

shown by the numbers over the letters, but you can vary it so long as you lay them down pair by pair. Do not hesitate between pairs, or you may give someone an idea of what you are doing. Whistle or hum a little tune while you are doing it so that nobody could guess you were spelling out any words.

When you ask your first friend to show which row or rows his two cards are in you have to think quickly which letter his two cards must cover and then put your two forefingers on his two cards.   Supposing he said "Top and bottom rows," you would know that the letter covered was I, and you would point out the second card in the top row and the third card in the bottom row. If he said "Both in the second row from the top," you would know that the letter covered was A, and you would put your fingers on the first and fourth cards in this row.

A good deal of practice is needed to do this trick well, but, in time, it becomes very easy.

Section Eight

THE FINE ARTS

Chapter 1

WHAT IS ART?

ALL children can enjoy a story or a picture, because stories and pictures make them think of real things that are exciting or pretty. If a story is well told, using the fewest and the best words, it is a work of art, but it is not a work of art if it is told clumsily. A picture is a work of art if it makes you think what the artist hoped you would think, and this means that the lines and patches of colour forming the picture must be of unmistakable meaning, giving you one idea only.

Most of us are quite good judges of a story, and can tell a bad one from a good one, but we are not so clever at deciding which pictures are worthy to be called works of art. The test is really quite easy, however. Look at an album full of ordinary snapshots, and compare them with photos made by someone who is really clever at photography. Imagine that you have found a snap of a little girl, net in hand, peering into a pool for tadpoles or tiddlers. If the picture is taken by just anybody, it is almost certain to be full of faults. Perhaps, when you first looked at it, you hardly noticed the little girl at all. It often happens that in a bad picture there are several things competing for your attention, all equally prominent. And matters may even be worse than that: there may actually be something to catch your notice first that is not anything to do with the subject at all. For instance, in the front of the picture, and larger than the little girl you are meant to look at, there may be a stray dog sitting down for a moment to scratch. Now that would be ridiculous, would it not? Yet many home-made pictures have silly things like that in them.

GOOD AND BAD PICTURES

A common fault in photographs is to have everything focused as sharply as the main subject, so that the picture might be taken as *either* one of a child fishing, *or* one of a particularly fine clump of bulrushes farther away.

It is rather difficult to make a perfect picture by photography, though it can be done by people with knowledge and patience. A man with pencil and paints has a task that, in some ways, is easier. When HE makes a picture of a little girl fishing, he can leave out the things that spoil the effect. If there is a fat man bathing nearby he need not take any notice, but, alas, the camera would put him in, bald head and all, making the picture stupid, with too much in it.

Every work of art, no matter whether it is a story, a picture or a statue, is intended to tell us something, and if it succeeds in telling us just that, and nothing else, it deserves to be called good. Of course, the something it is meant to tell us must be really *worth* telling. An artist may say to himself, "My goodness, what a divinely lovely face; I must make a picture of that." If people looking at his picture say at once, "My goodness, what a divinely lovely face," using the artist's very own words, then the picture is a success. But if people say, "Where, I wonder, did that girl buy that hat?" or, "If I had that brooch I'd put it in the fire," then the picture has missed its aim and is a failure.

Sometimes, of course, the fault is with the person looking at the picture, and not with the picture. Some ladies, for instance, cannot see faces at all, but look always at hats, hair styles, clothes, shoes, face paint and powder, and so on.

MUST A WORK OF ART BE BEAUTIFUL?

Does every work of art have to be beautiful? By no means. An artist may see the toil-worn face of a very old person, or the crafty face of a criminal, and say to himself, " There's an interesting character; I'd like to paint that." If his picture is well done, intelligent people will understand it. They will say at once of the old person, "Poor old body, I can see he's had a hard life," and of the criminal, " That's a nasty-looking fellow; I wonder what wickedness he's done? "

You see now that a work of art must have two qualities to be considered good. It must have a single and quite definite purpose to begin with, and it must, furthermore, be successful in fulfilling that purpose.

What shall I tell you about the weird pictures of the impressionists, the surrealists, the cubists and so on? What shall I say about Epstein's statues (two of which you can see facing page 206), or Picasso's paintings, many of which are of almost unrecognisable subjects? The artists in these cases have their ideas, but they may be ideas that you and I cannot receive from their work. There are people who say that they understand these oddities and, for them, the works are true and successful works of art, but for us they may be failures. We just have not got the same kind of minds as the sympathisers, but we need not worry about that. It is quite absurd to get angry or rude about the work of a man like Epstein. He has a perfect right to his ideas; and if we let ourselves be offended by his statues, I am afraid it only goes to show that we are silly, selfish people who want everyone to do only the things that please us, and who think they are wasting their time if they try to please themselves and their friends.

If you are a civilised person you will be tolerant of everybody's artistic attempts, provided they are not obviously stupid. After all, some pictures may be deliberately intended to convey the idea of confusion or chaos, or of horrible jangling discord. A Picasso may have been painted purposely to remind you of how you felt that morning you awoke with a headache and a fever and knew that you were going to have influenza. If it succeeds in doing this, it will have been a success, even from your point of view, though you may not have realised it, and though it may have been distinctly unpleasant.

MUSIC

Music is another form of art, and this too is intended to produce definite sensations in you. If it is modern music you may not like the sensations, but then, you know, you may not have been *meant* to like them. Some people enjoy a mild form of torture, and modern music gives them what they want. Do you not believe me when I say that people like torture? Well, please explain, if you can, why so many people enjoy playing with a machine for giving electric shocks, or riding on switchbacks that make them sick, or getting into difficulties on very high mountains.

The dreadfulness of some modern music is so truly and lastingly dreadful that it can be fascinating to listen to. You can get the excitement out of it that you may have got out of a terrific air-raid, or out of a ride in a runaway tram-car. You do not quite enjoy it at the time but when it is all over you say to yourself, "That was grand and exciting, and it will be something to tell my children

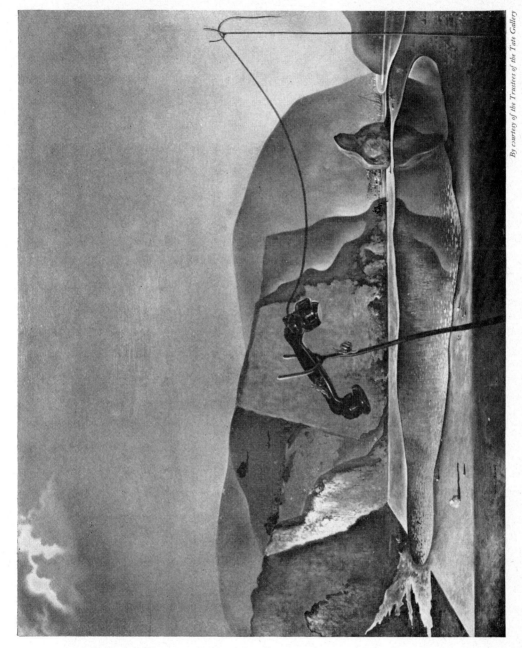

" Beach scene with telephone," by Salvadoor Dali.

"A Bronze," by Henry Moore.

about when I grow up, but I am not sure that I should want to experience it again."

There is one piece of music I know—the "Bridal Cortège" from the *Golden Cockerel*, by Rimsky-Korsakov—which reminds me of the start of a long journey in an express train. The noises one hears in a train are not tuneful or nice noises, but if they tell you that the train is getting up speed and making a splendid effort to take you home, or to someone you love best in all the world, why then, you like them and you think that they are lovely noises. The piece of music I am telling you about goes thundering along like a train that is travelling at a staggering speed yet can be depended upon to reach its journey's end dead on time. Of course there *are* pieces of music that suggest trains which break down or meet with constant signal checks. Such music seems good to those who get a miserable sort of satisfaction out of thinking themselves doomed to ill luck and disappointment. There really are people like this, though you might not believe it.

HOW TO ENJOY ART

In the pages that follow I shall tell you about great works of art and (in some instances) about the people who were their authors. Already, I think you will see that it is not difficult to understand or enjoy art. When people have difficulty it is because they go about with the fixed (and wrong) idea that every work of art has to be beautiful and has to appeal to them personally. "Well, I can't see it," they say, and look peevish.

There isn't any need to worry over art we cannot appreciate though it is a fact that if we really try to appreciate it, remembering at the same time that some art is meant to be tantalising, or even mildly painful, we shall often succeed. People do not like inhaling the fumes from a burning weed (smoking tobacco) or eating putrid flesh (high game) or drinking stale grape juice (wine) the first time they try, but after a while they find these things rather nice.   Much the same sort of thing applies to modern forms of art.   When you have become accustomed to them they do not seem so bad. Presently they begin to seem quite pleasant, and in the end they seem really and truly enjoyable.

ENJOYING MUSIC

Perhaps the best way to familiarise yourself with a queer piece of music is to buy a gramophone record of it and play it to yourself once a day for a week or a fortnight.   If you did this with a simple popular piece of music you would know the melody by heart after a day or two and, by the end of the fortnight, you would probably be unable to get it out of your head and be heartily sick of it.   This does not happen with the best music. You can listen again and again, and for a long time your enjoyment of it goes on growing and growing.   Some things may be so wonderfully done that you never become tired of them.   They are usually things that are quite impossible to hum or whistle, because they may consist of two or three tunes played at once, all cleverly harmonised together.   It is these pieces of music that you can continue to enjoy longest, because your memory does not become plagued with endless repetitions of them. You can hear them only when they are played for you properly by a big orchestra, or on a complex instrument such as an organ, a piano or a harpsichord.

ENJOYING BOOKS

A good book, like a good piece of music, is one that you can enjoy again and again.   A simple story book you may not want to read many times because you soon know by heart all that it is about. But when a story is told by a writer like Dickens or Mary Webb, it is not simple at all. You could probably tell it quite briefly in your own words, but it would not be the same. The great story-tellers have their own special and inimitable way of telling their stories, and really it is not the story we enjoy so much as the way in which it is told. Some of the stories told by Dickens are really rather poor, but they are told so magnificently, and the detail is so perfect, that one can always enjoy reading them again. People often pick up a book by Dickens just to read a well-loved page or two. In the chapter on "Great Books," I shall give you a short account of some famous books and tell you why I, and most other people, think them so fine.

ENJOYING PAINTINGS

In the chapter on "Beautiful Sculpture" I have said (page 194) you can look at a picture and see it all at a single glance. This is not quite true. Your eye takes it all in at once, I admit, but your mind may not. You may have to look at it many times before you feel that you know it properly. And then, if it is a good picture, you will probably find yourself still wanting to look at it again and again, just because it fills you with wonder every time you see it.

A fine picture is like a fine piece of writing: it speaks to us, and, though it may not have a lot to say, it says it so beautifully that we are never tired of taking it in. Besides, the thing it tells us may be something we find it hard to believe if we are far away and among ugly and dreary surroundings. You might, for instance, almost forget how lovely the country can be if it happens that you have to spend all your days in one of the uglier parts of a big town or city. One look at a really fine landscape painting will refresh your memory and fill your depressed heart with gladness.

Then again, you might, in a fit of gloom, grow to dislike the sight of hundreds and hundreds of people streaming along in drab clothes, all hurrying, all cross-looking. One look at some of the best paintings will remind you that people are not so bad after all. A painter paints what he loves and, if he is an artist, he will make you love it too. So when you feel depressed with everybody, go and stare at the pictures in an art gallery and they will probably put you in a kinder frame of mind.

ARTISTS ARE GREAT TEACHERS

Some children have to wrestle with ideas that should never have been put into their heads, ideas that, sooner or later, they will have to unlearn if they want to be happy. A misguided friend may teach them, for instance, that a wharf or a coal mine or a factory is always ugly and hateful, and that nobody should have to work in such surroundings. A visit to a gallery of fine pictures will show you that the artist can make these places appear romantic and even beautiful by portraying them in terms of light and shade and colour. No place is so ugly that sunlight or moonlight cannot sometimes give it a special glory or radiance of its own.

Disgruntled folk never see the beauty of what lies around them, but the artist goes about happily, seeing what others miss. As far as seeing goes we can be artists too—all of us. We may not be able to record what we see on paper or canvas, but we can remember, and be glad again and again.

Another wrong idea children may have impressed on them is that human dignity and grace are all a matter of fine clothes and careful grooming, but in a picture gallery you can see that many an artist has made a fine picture of ragged gipsies, toiling labourers, patient shepherds and other unfashionably attired folk. Such pictures may be expressive of sturdy independence, honest industry or merely the grace of the human figure. Most artists have been convinced that human subjects can sometimes be shown to good advantage in no clothes at all, and examples of their work occur in all picture galleries.

I should not expect you to care for everything you see in a picture gallery, but most of the paintings are worthy of more than a passing glance. The artists have done their work so well that they may succeed in making you like what they like, even though you did not like it before. So, in addition to cheering you up, the work of great artists may actually teach you something and make you wiser.

Paintings, statues, music and books that can fill cold hearts with kindness, angry hearts with forgiveness and despairing hearts with hope have a value too great to be measured in money, and we must be grateful not only to the gifted people who have produced these things but also to the foresight and generosity of those benefactors who have gathered them together and made them freely available for our enjoyment in galleries and museums everywhere.

Chapter 2

BEAUTIFUL SCULPTURE

WHEN you have had one look at a painting you have seen it all, but with a statue this is not so. You can walk round it and look at it from a hundred different viewpoints. Side by side on the plate opposite this page are two views of a charming statue called "Brother Kiss." If I had them, I could show you many more views of the same group.

Another thing you can do with a statue is move the lamps that shine upon it, so as to make the highlights and the shadows change places. If you walk round it now, under the altered lighting, you will see a hundred more new views of the statue to delight you.

When you have tried various kinds of lighting on a statue, and walked round it to look at it from all points of view under all conditions, you can still go on obtaining new views by putting it on a higher or lower pedestal or table, and seeing how it looks from below or from above.

The statue called "Music" that you can see opposite this page has been photographed from one side and low down, with a bright light shining on it from the front. I am sure that a hundred, or even a thousand, equally lovely pictures could be made from the same statue, photographing it from different angles and under different arrangements of lighting.

Brother Kiss, by Madrassi.

Brother Kiss, by Madrassi.

Music, by J. Börjeson.

The First Step, by Constance Roux.

"La Pietà," by Michelangelo.

"Moses," by Michelangelo.

Many statues, like the ones mentioned so far, are of homely subjects, not of anybody famous or anybody remarkable. Another of the same kind, called "The First Step," is shown in the next picture. It used to be in the Salon de Paris, a famous art gallery where there are other beautiful things. I expect you will like these homely statues best because there is nothing at all puzzling about them. The subjects all look like people you might meet anywhere, and they are all doing ordinary things.

STATUES OF HISTORIC AND HEROIC PERSONS

The statues shown in the next plate are much more famous because they are by one of the greatest and cleverest sculptors of all time, Michael Angelo Buonarroti, usually called Michelangelo, who lived from 1475 to 1564. He was an Italian, and besides being a brilliant sculptor he was a great painter and a great architect (see page 213).

While reading the Bible you may have pictured to yourself some of the people whose lives and actions are described in its many hundreds of pages. Already you will know that Moses, subject of one of Michelangelo's greatest and most famous pieces of sculpture, was the maker of our first laws and rules for good living. The other example of Michelangelo's work portrays the sadness of Mary as she grieves over the body of her crucified son, Jesus.

Michelangelo's best known work is probably the enormous statue of David, which he carved from a block of marble too huge to interest other sculptors. Instead of showing you this particular statue of David I want to show you two others, which were made earlier (see plate facing page 199). The statue by Donatello shows David with a large sword in his right hand and wearing a hat not unlike the " tin hats " used by British soldiers. Otherwise he seems rather unprotected. Notice the stone in the left hand.

Donatello, like Michelangelo, was an Italian; he lived from 1386 to 1466, and a young pupil of his named Verrocchio became equally skilled in the art of the sculptor. Verrocchio was 51 years younger than his master, and he died in 1488. You can see his statue of David in the picture to the right of Donatello's David. Already Goliath has been killed, and his head lies at David's feet. Verrocchio supposed that David wore some sort of battle dress, but he has no hat, and his sword is not much bigger than a knife or a dagger.

Facing page 198 you can see a statue of a man on horseback. This statue stands in Venice and it is thought to be the best equestrian statue ever made. It is quite old—in fact, it is another example of the work of Verrocchio. The rider is Bartolomeo Colleoni, an Italian soldier, who made fighting his profession in the days when all Italy was composed of little kingdoms under quarrelsome warlords. Colleoni fought for the master who offered him the biggest wage. He became a skilful commander and fought in the wars between Venice and Milan, sometimes helping one side and sometimes the other. Although his frequent changing of sides led to charges of treachery being made against him, he lived to the ripe old age of 75, unhurt by such enemies as he had made by his apparent want of loyalty. To him fighting was merely a profitable business and not a matter for sentiment.

Below the picture of Colleoni you can see statues of three more historical characters. The first is Diogenes, a Greek philosopher, who believed in living as simply as possible, more than 400 years before the Christian era. The second is Saint John as a child, and the third is of Saint Geneviève, the patron saint of Paris, who lived from 419 to 512.

Sculptors do not always choose to portray heroism or virtue or athletic vigour by modelling historic characters: sometimes they choose to represent people without any special claim to fame. There are two pictures of this more impersonal kind on the plate facing page 199. One of these, the very famous "Discobolo" or Disk Thrower, is of great antiquity. It came from Greece where, several hundred years before the Christian era, the sculptors were creating works of art that are still treasured to-day. They have often been copied but never bettered. Statues of this kind are not of anyone in particular, but they tell a dramatic or exciting story. There is good reason to believe that many of the old Greek statues portray legendary persons, like Hercules, Apollo, or Atlas, but their main intention is to show heroes in vigorous action, with all their muscles at work.

The sculptors of long ago were also fond of carving pictures in relief. By this I mean making pictures that "stand out" in the way that the Queen's head stands out on a penny. Sometimes the figures projected only very slightly from their background (bas-relief), but in other examples, the roundness of the figures was almost complete. In many museums of ancient art you can see plaster copies of battle and other scenes carved in relief by the Greeks or by the Romans.

You may have seen plaster copies of the Disk Thrower, but the original (with some parts missing and replaced by modern carving) can be seen in Rome at the Vatican Museum. It was the work of a famous Greek sculptor called Myron, who lived some hundreds of years before the Christian era. (Mirone in Italian spelling.)

Another very well-known Greek statue is the "Venus de Milo," whose picture I have omitted partly because pictures of her are seen everywhere, but chiefly because, like many other ancient statues, this one is broken, having no arms. Children do not like broken things and I do not blame them.

At the side of the Disk Thrower you can see a much more recent statue of the heroic or athletic kind; this was the work of the British painter and sculptor Sir Frederic Leighton, who lived from 1830 to 1896. It shows an athlete struggling with a python, and it is in the same style as the work of the Greeks. Most famous of all the statues portraying snakes is the group discovered at Rome in A.D. 1506 showing the legendary killing of Laocoon and his two sons by serpents. This is believed to have been carved by the Greeks, and Leighton may have taken it as his example.

WHY ARE SO MANY STATUES NAKED?

We have come now to an important question. Why are sculptors so fond of carving naked people? Some of my young readers may think naked statues dull or stupid, or even rude, but they ought to remember that there are no fashions in nakedness, whereas clothes, other than a simple piece of rag or cloth, belong to definite periods and look ridiculous only a few years after they were in fashion. Sculptors of thirty or forty years ago might have tried to make statues of the overdressed persons you can see in old family photographs, but they would have been sorry afterwards, because, although their work might have looked right at the time, it would be thought hideous to-day.

If a statue is to look pleasing now and for evermore it must be of a person quite naked, or with only some simple wrap to wear. The lovely statue of the "Ball Player," shown opposite page 202, will always look right and proper because her clothing is the sort of clothing that has always been worn at some time or another by everybody. You might take it for a nightdress. Perhaps the girl has jumped straight out of bed and is on the way to a bathing-pool in the bright morning sun. Evidently she meets a child or a pet dog

Statue of the 13th-century Italian warrior, Colleoni, by the Italian sculptor
Andrea del Verrocchio.

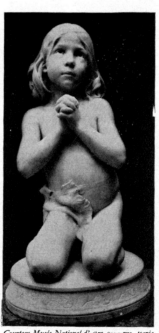

Diogenes, by E. Boisseau.   St. John, by J. Dampt.   Saint Geneviève, by
E. Benet.

Statue of David in bronze by Donatello.

Another bronze of David, this time by
Verrocchio.

" The Disc-Thrower," by Myron (or Mirone).

"Athlete Struggling with Python," by Leighton.

who wants a ball thrown. You can imagine all this about this statue, or you can believe that it is simply a modern example of Greek style sculpture showing a girl athlete playing some classic ball game of ancient times—a feminine equivalent of the Disk Thrower. It is not an old statue, nor a very famous one, but such was the intelligence of the sculptor in choosing the girl's dress that she does not look old-fashioned and comical, nor is she ever likely to do so. The same cannot be said of old statues made true to the fashion of their day.

The clothes worn by our great-great-grandparents were obviously intended to hide the human shape as much as possible. Ladies would rather let their skirts drag in the dirt than show the least little bit of leg. A statue of one of these people in full dress would be a sorry spectacle; it could only tell us how miserably shy they were of letting anything of themselves be seen except face and hands. Most portrait-sculpture of the last century has disappeared on account of its small value in an age when the fashions of dress are so different. Only the likenesses of such famous people as Queen Victoria, the Duke of Wellington or Abraham Lincoln have been preserved.

NATURAL BEAUTY

There is one other reason why the sculptor disapproves of clothing. The folds set an interesting exercise in carving, but there is a limit to what can be made to look real in stone. Hair is hard enough to make " alive," and the furry or frilly finishes used on some clothes are impossible to imitate. Finally, the main attraction of clothing may be its colour, and, of course, this will be entirely lacking in a statue. The ancients did sometimes paint their statues (even the Greeks did this), but it would be thought very crude to do so to-day. Consequently, except when clothing is needed to tell us who the person is, the sculptor prefers to leave it out. Statues of famous judges and statesmen are clothed because the clothes are an indication of their office. Michelangelo's great statue of Moses, the most famous of all law-makers, is clothed, and so are the more modern statues of people like Oliver Cromwell and Abraham Lincoln. But given free choice, most sculptors prefer to carve the natural shape of bare body and limb rather than the accidental and fortuitous lines of clothing.

The dance of the little girls in the group called "Danse Rhythmique" facing page 203 would usually be performed in some sort of ballet dress, but dress of any sort, especially a stone one, hides the secret of perfect balance by appearing to add weight where in fact there is none. There could be no excuse for loading the little figures of this group with huge marble frills and flounces.

The "Springtime of Life," by W. R. Colton, shows the adoration felt by a little girl of about eleven years old for her young brother. You can almost hear her say, "Please, Mr. Sculptor, make a nice one of our Jim." She obviously doesn't care a bit what she herself is going to look like, for you can be sure that, if she did, she would be sitting up straight, with her hands neatly folded in her lap. Between you and me, I think Jim was a bit of a wriggler, so that his patient sister had some difficulty in keeping him posed.

The next example, also of a brother and sister, is a foreign one. The children are more nearly the same age, and they are gazing at something on the ground in front of them, something very interesting. Like me, I expect you will be wondering what it is. It must be something amusing, because the children are smiling. Perhaps it is a kitten getting itself tangled up with the wools and cottons from Mummy's work-basket (plate facing page 203).

The three children sitting on a rock are another foreign example of sculpture. They have been having a lovely splash in a pool of water, and now they are gazing down into it to watch the little fishes swimming to and fro.

"The Kiss," shown opposite to page 202, is a relatively modern group in which you can see a lovely young mother being hugged by her baby daughter. It is the work of a British sculptor named Thornycroft, and is in the Tate Gallery, London. Like the other examples I have chosen to illustrate this article, it is wonderfully true to life, though I ought, perhaps, to add that truth alone does not make carved stone or moulded clay into a work of art. It is not enough to copy or imitate Nature, as machinery can be made which will do this to perfection. What the artist has to do is reveal to us the purposes in Nature, or his ideas about Nature. "The Kiss" is wonderful, not because it shows us accurate models of a woman and a child, but because it successfully portrays the feeling of child and mother for each other.

GOOD AND BAD STATUES

Sometimes you can see carefully and truthfully carved statues that do not please you, and that nobody regards as great works of art. They fail because they seem dead and expressionless, or because they show a rather trivial side of Nature as though it were something important. You could make a lifelike statue of somebody brushing her teeth, or giving the back of her neck a rub with a sponge, but unless you were a great genius your work would probably be ridiculous. The genius could choose a subject of this sort, no doubt, and succeed in creating a masterpiece. Shutting his eyes, he might visualise some earnest little girl trying to clean her teeth or bath herself for the first time. He might see how hard she was trying to be independent of help, he might see how proud she was feeling of her success, he might see that her movements were, as yet, a little strained and clumsy. If he put all this into his statue, it would be a great work of art, because it would succeed in lifting up the trivial act of toilet to the level where it would rank as high human achievement. It could very well be called by some such title as "Independence," and it would serve to commemorate one of the most important days in the life of every child—the day when she discovers that she can do difficult things for herself.

The real genius does not need to copy Nature faithfully. He can express his idea by hewing something quite simple and rough. Asked to make a statue of someone in the bath, the person of slight genius would very likely labour long and hard to create a lifelike copy of some beautiful young lady giving herself her daily sponge. The result would be pretty, no doubt, but trivial. The real genius would choose to do a statue something like the one I have imagined and called "Independence." It would be of great originality and a surprise to us. He might labour lovingly on the form of the child, making her true to life in every detail; but his work could succeed equally well if it took the form of caricature. In a caricature the work could be rough, and features could be exaggerated to make them plainer. The child could be made to look even more childish than the living model, and her attitudes could be made more expressive than in the original. The artist uses a live model to help him see his vision more clearly, but he does not always copy her. Much modern sculpture is very far from being true to nature, but it is very expressive all the same.

LIVING SCULPTURE

The sculptor is not always fortunate in the living model whose poses are his inspiration and pattern. Many human beings are sadly

" The Kiss," by Thornycroft.

" Ball Player," by Professor W. Schott.

"Figures on a Fountain," by Blondat.

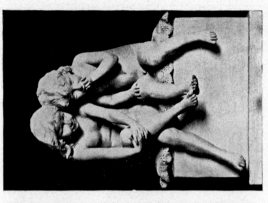

"Brother and Sister," by H. Goetschmann.

"Rhythmical Dance," by Madame Colinet.

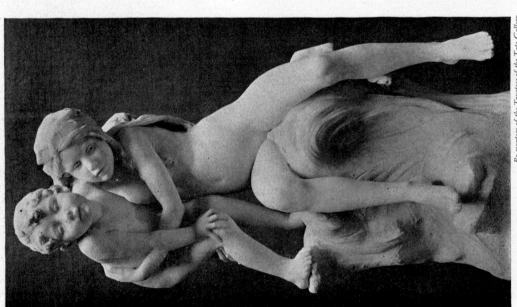

"The Springtime of Life," by W. R. Colton.

inelegant in their proportions from over-eating, lack of exercise and old age and so the majority of statues are portrayals of imaginary or ideal figures more beautiful than most of us ever were or hope to be.

When the sculptor portrays children, however, he may be able to take them as he finds them, for many are truly lovely. You would scarcely have been able to tell the difference between Nature and art if I had slipped in some pictures of live children among those of statues. Small children especially are so sure of loving glances and kindness that they are much less shy than grown-ups of being their natural selves. They have a grace and dignity that is all their own and they do not have to wear gaudy clothes and jewels in order to make a favourable impression. Older people are not so sure of the approval of their fellows and, consequently, they may hanker after purple robes and gold chains to give them a comfortable feeling of dignity.

Chapter 3

STRANGE SCULPTURE

MANY of the present-day sculptors have become tired of portraying natural-looking or idealised human figures, and they are doing work that you and I might feel inclined to call grotesque or ugly. In every age there have been works of art that might be called carica-tures—for instance the gargoyles carved as decorations on old churches—but in the nineteenth century there was definite rebellion on the part of clay modellers and stone carvers. While some of them endeavoured to produce work of perfect finish, the same as had been expected and required in every age hitherto, a small number began to offer rough and unfinished-looking figure studies as complete works of art.

In the works of Auguste Rodin, who lived from 1840 to 1917, this roughness was only superficial as the general lines of his subjects were preserved. You can see from his statue called "Despair" (opposite page 207) that the figure is recognisably human though there seems to have been a weathering of the stone and consequent blurring of all finer detail. It is the same in other examples of his work, and you may or may not like it.

The tendency to ignore reality and produce purely fanciful repre-sentations of people and things has continued, and an idea of how far it is leading sculptors from the literal truth can be gathered from looking at the works of Eric Gill or Jacob Epstein, which form the subject of the other illustrations to this chapter. These are as extreme as anything I wish to show you, because I do not believe you would want to see the latest examples in distortion and simplification that are accepted nowadays as sculptural masterpieces.

Epstein's work is sometimes reminiscent of the work of primitive African peoples and sometimes it may remind you of Egyptian art. The examples I have chosen to show you are easy to find if you happen to live in or near London. They are the allegorical figures of "Day" and "Night" on the great offices of the London Passenger Transport Board, immediately over St. James's Park Underground Station. When I tell you that silly people have gone to the trouble of throwing dirt at them, and abusing them, you may not be surprised. They are both art of a kind that is difficult to appreciate until you are accustomed to it. I am not sure that I can make you like them, but I will try (see plate facing page 206).

The statue called "Day" suggests wakefulness and youth. I think the funny-looking little boy must have tumbled straight out of bed at crack of dawn, eager to be tearing across a dewy lawn without waiting to put on any clothes. If it gives you any sort of idea like this, then it lives up to its name and to the intentions of the sculptor, and it is, to this extent, a success.

The statue called "Night" is of a sleeping child on the lap of a great strong-faced nurse or guardian angel. I think it is rather clever, because it works in the idea of sleep's mysteriousness, and especially of our own tendency to dream dreams of things like nothing on earth. I am sure that your dreams, like mine, are visions of mixed familiarity and strangeness. Considered as sleep's own nightmarish dream of a child on the lap of its nurse, I think "Night" is wonderfully effective.

There are other examples of strange sculpture on the great office building of the London Passenger Transport Board, and these, like "Day" and "Night," are clearly visible to passers-by, although they are rather high up. These high-flying figures are intended to represent the four winds, and they were carved by different sculptors. Two, namely, the East Wind and the North Wind, were carved by Eric Gill, and I have given you clear illustrations of these, on the plate facing page 207, because Eric Gill was a worker of great originality in several fields of art, and he has been acclaimed a great artist. He wrote several interesting and thoughtful books, one about the place of clothing in art.

HOW THERE CAME TO BE "UGLY" WORKS OF ART

People who really prefer the strange new sculpture to the old say that the old is too easy to appreciate, and that, like everything else easy, it gives little satisfaction. But, in its day, the beautiful sculpture I described in my last chapter was not at all easy to appreciate. In fact, it was not easily appreciated by you, because you were too young ever to have seen it before. You will remember, some of you, that its nakedness seemed silly and strange to you, just like the ugliness of Epstein's work is seeming strange to you now. Well, I explained why sculptors favoured nakedness, and you saw that they had quite complicated thoughts about the matter—thoughts that needed a lot of explaining.

Very many people know what the older sculpture stands for, and feel that there is enough of its kind to suffice humanity for the rest of time. It is these people who are doing, or paying for, the new and "ugly" kinds of sculpture. They want to be made to think new thoughts and, as the world is in many ways hideous and

"Day," by Jacob Epstein.

"Night," by Jacob Epstein.

"The East Wind," sculpture by Eric Gill.

"The North Wind," sculpture by Eric Gill.

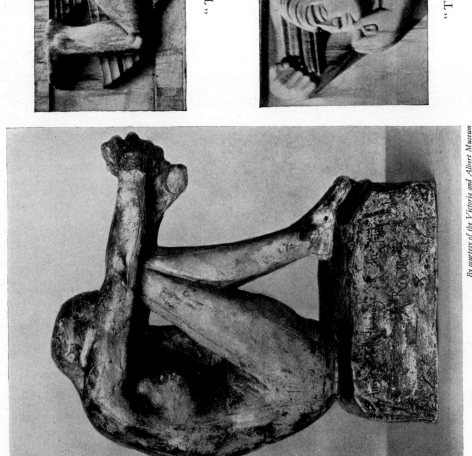

"Despair," by Rodin.

painful perhaps, they want to be helped to like hideous and painful things. By this I mean to say that they want to be able to make the best of what cannot be helped.

SOME GOOD NEEDS A HARD SEARCH TO FIND

Sculptors such as Dobson and Epstein and Gill have tried hard to make something attractive from commonplace models. Instead of carving lovely girlish figures, they have carved dumpy, fat, coarse-looking women, and all sorts of other subjects that are generally not thought worth looking at.

They seem to say by their statues, " Here is a creature you might condemn as gross and hideous, but behold, there is something rather massive and grand about it after all. See, this fat, enormous-limbed woman has the feelings of a good mother for her extraordinary-looking offspring. You cannot deny that God breathes the good life even into such monsters as this."

WHY WE MUST WISH SUCCESS TO STRANGE ART FORMS

I have never spoken to Epstein, or any of the other modern sculptors, but I think I can see what some of them may be trying to do. They may be trying to enlarge our capacity for loving so that it will take in everybody, including the ugliest and the unluckiest. If I am right, they are great and noble souls who deserve our highest praise and admiration.

There is some virtue in loving young and pretty creatures, but there is more virtue, far far more virtue, in striving to love where ugliness, imbecility and evil all stand in your way. The idea that we should try these difficult exercises in love is very old, but we have not hitherto had much practical help from our artists, most of whom have favoured the loveliest subjects they could find for their pictures and statues. That help seems to be coming now, however; through the work of the much-misunderstood and much-maligned artists of our own time.

As regards the very latest creations, by sculptors like Henry Moore, I do not think this explanation of mine applies. Fitting titles for works in this category would be "Shape with hole in it," "Rotten log in the form of a woman," "Pyramid stuffed into a cube," and so on.

To appreciate these things there must be contentment with mere shape and pattern, and possibly with surface texture and surface reflections of light. As babies lying in our cradles we learnt to like the look of things and the feel of them, with no idea of loving or hating. Perhaps we treasured an old bone because of its smoothness or the near-transparence of its thinner parts. The appeal of the most modern sculpture is the same as the appeal of the interesting-looking bone, but the grown-up idea of a beautiful bone differs from a child's idea. The bone needs to be much larger and it must look vaguely like a woman, or a horse, or a footballer in the act of scoring a goal. Instead of having the real thing put before them some people seem to prefer having the dim and suggestive shape or shadow offered to them.

Not being very warmly attracted to art of this indefinite kind, I cannot tell you any more about it. Neither can I tell you why other people prefer complicated contraptions made of wire to objects resembling old bones. This is a mystery you must investigate for yourself.

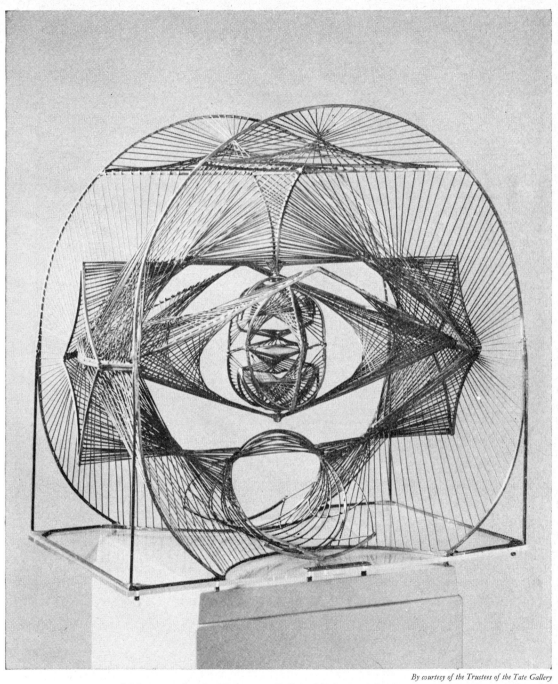

" Maquette for the Unknown Political Prisoner," by Peusner.

"Cock," by Picasso.

Chapter 4

BEAUTIFUL PICTURES

THE things it is possible to show in the form of sculpture are not many, and all of them must be beautiful by reason of their shape alone, because a statue is usually colourless. The painter has a far wider choice of subjects. Instead of restricting himself to representations of human beings, as most sculptors do, he can make pictures showing lovely stretches of country, or pretty cloud effects, or a storm at sea. You might be able to make a statue that would suggest a strong wind—a girl holding her hat on and her skirts flying out behind her, for example—but you could not depict rain or mist or lightning flashes by anything made of stone. The artist who makes pictures, whether they be drawings or photographs in black-and-white, or paintings in colour, can convey these ideas very well.

Before the days of photography it was natural that artists should wish their pictures to be true to life. Their wish was to record their impressions accurately. They worked hard to improve their skill at drawing or painting likenesses of people and things. Since photography was invented, artists have been rather vague as to their objectives. They no longer strive to make their pictures true to life in the photographic sense, because they realise that a man with a camera can imitate life to perfection. People to-day do not think so well of paintings and drawings that imitate Nature. To paint a picture that appeals to modern tastes the artist must make the most of any special advantages that the brush and pencil possess and that the camera does not.

A very great advantage in drawing and painting is that the artist can compose his picture so that, besides showing things in a realistic or characteristic way, it makes a pleasing design. The photographer must make pictures of things as they really are, but the artist can imagine the things to be moved about until they make the prettiest or neatest arrangement. In painting a country scene he can leave out trees that are awkwardly placed, or awkwardly shaped, and he can introduce new trees where these help to improve his design. The finished picture will, of course, have to have some such general title as "Landscape" or "Spring Morning." It could not be called by the name of any particular place. A picture called "Hampstead Heath," or "Brighton Beach," would have to be fairly accurate representations of particular places.

In writing of *English Painting from the Seventh Century to the Present Day*, Mr. Charles Johnson, M.A., Official Lecturer at the National Gallery, London, says that at the present time design and not subject-matter is regarded as the aim of good painting. He mentions a picture by the famous painter Whistler of Whistler's own mother which the artist called "An arrangement in black and grey." Evidently the artist was more concerned to portray the pretty pattern that his mother made than to create a faithful likeness.

This passion for design has proved so strong in some artists that they have been content to paint anything so long as it yields an attractive pattern. Herein lies the explanation why there are so many pictures of dull things, such as dustbins in back-yards, hats on chairs, cabbages in baskets and so on. The more enthusiastic a painter becomes about creating new designs the less does he care for painting real things. Many modern painters, such as the late Paul Nash, Picasso and Braque, alter the real shapes of things until they can hardly be recognised, and sometimes they create things that are merely intended to fill space and have no existence at all outside the artist's own mind.

If we agree that design is the main purpose of painting, we shall have to excuse and even like the weird works of these extremists, but most of us want pictures to be of interesting things, and most of us want them to be reasonably true to life. We do not want them to be less true than life; we want them to be more true than life. Of Mrs. Jarley's waxworks in Dickens's famous book, *The Old Curiosity Shop*, it was said that they were "as large as life, and twice as natural." Everybody laughs at the idea of a work of art being twice as natural as life itself; but the expression is not so silly as it sounds. Many things in real life are hidden from us, and this is especially true of a person's character. The ordinary person puts on a face suitable for every occasion in which he finds himself, and any artist who painted him wearing a particular expression would only paint what it was natural for him to see with his two eyes. A greater artist would overlook the pose and the falseness of the expression, and would paint the person in his true character. Of the painting of an artist like this it would be correct to say that it was more than natural, or more true than life itself.

My own opinion is that while every painting should be of good arrangement or design, its real aim should be to excel in truth the natural appearance of the things painted. If good design is taken to be the artist's main consideration, then many artists will go to absurd extremes and paint things that have no relation to truth at all. Others will keep close to truth, but will be content with what is less true than Nature. I think that the greatest artists, while careful to observe the rules of good composition or design, are mainly concerned to see "behind" Nature and paint what is not clearly visible to everybody.   They are not content to show people as the common man or woman sees them (and as the camera represents them); they want to show them with the light of their hopes and desires shining in their faces.

Portraits by such great masters as Hogarth, Reynolds and Gainsborough are true character studies of the sitters, not always flattering to them.   Asked to paint the portrait of a rich and conceited city merchant, all dressed up in his ceremonial robes and gold chains, the master artist would greatly outshine what a photographer could do with his subject.   His picture might be the embodiment of greed and cunning; yet, so clever would it be, that the sitter would be pleased with it.   Unconscious of the faults in himself that others could see quite clearly, he would pay the artist a hundred guineas or more for this dreadful advertisement of his inner ugliness.

Alas! the great portrait painters were obliged to paint more disagreeable people than pleasant people, because of the money they needed in order to live, but now and then they were set a subject worthy of their great talents.   Also, in their spare time they chose to paint their own children or religious subjects or interesting everyday characters such as beggars, fishermen, tailors and so on.   For portraits of well-known writers, some by great artists, the reader is referred to the chapter on Great Books.   Reference will now be made to the portraits accompanying this chapter.

PORTRAITS

In every age the artists have painted portraits of famous people in order to please them or to receive payment.   Also many portraits of ordinary or unknown people were painted; these people served as

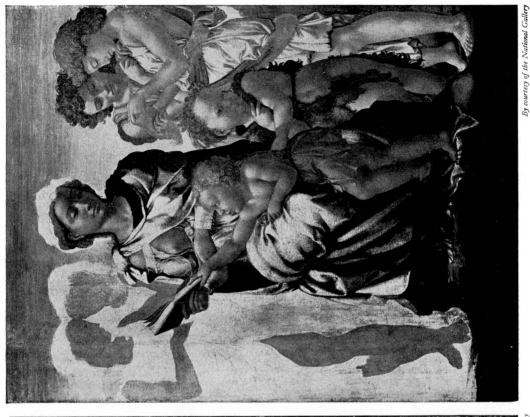

" Madonna and Child, St. John and Angels " (unfinished), by Michelangelo.

" The Virgin of the Rocks," by Leonardo da Vinci.

By courtesy of the Wallace Collection

"The Laughing Cavalier," by Frans Hals.

By courtesy of the National Gallery

"The Ambassadors," by Holbein.

models for the characters appearing in religious pictures, one providing the face of an angel, another the face of an apostle, and so on.

Most paintings 500 years old and more are not very pleasing to us to-day, because the faces are so smooth and round and wax-like that we feel they must have been untrue to life. However, it would be incorrect to say that all old paintings show this lifelessness. Among the greatest artists of all time were Leonardo da Vinci, who lived from 1452 to 1519, and Michael Angelo Buonarroti, who lived from 1475 to 1564. Also, though we may feel that no painter ever gave us a real portrait of the first Queen Elizabeth, we are satisfied to think that her father, Henry VIII, was competently portrayed by Hans Holbein, a German painter, who lived from 1498 until he died of the plague in London in 1543.

Leonardo da Vinci, like Michelangelo, was an Italian, and besides being a painter he was a sculptor, architect, engineer, mathematician and poet. Many of his great wall paintings failed to endure because they were done on a surface that flaked or crumbled, but some of his canvas paintings still exist, and one of these is shown facing page 212. There can be no question about the quality of Leonardo's work; it was superb by any standards. Leonardo filled many notebooks with sketches and drawings; some of these were subjects for paintings, some were of an architectural nature and some of mechanical inventions, including a flying machine. The excellence of his more finished work owed much to his skill and diligence as a draughtsman.

The example of Michelangelo's painting, portrayed opposite page 212, is unfinished; but here again you can see that in the excellence of the drawing there was the promise of a perfect painting. Michelangelo and Leonardo da Vinci were in some respects rivals, and Michelangelo is remembered chiefly for his wonderful sculpture (see page 195) and for his design of the dome of St. Peter's, the great church in Rome. This dome is still the largest in the world.

Holbein's work was as remarkable for accuracy of drawing and detail as Leonardo da Vinci's or Michelangelo's, and it is for this reason that we can believe in his portrait of Henry VIII. I shall not show you this well-known portrait but another painting called "The Ambassadors," in which you can see globes, sundials and other articles of scientific or artistic interest, all minutely drawn. The work in this painting is so exquisite, we can have no doubt that the faces are good likenesses also (opposite page 213).

Contrasted with the picture by Holbein is the famous portrait called "The Laughing Cavalier," by Frans Hals, a Dutch painter who lived from 1580 to 1666, the year of the Great Fire of London. This painting bears the date 1624 and it shows the same care for fine detail.

Living and working at about the same time as Hals was the Flemish portrait painter Van Dyck, who became the court painter for James I and Charles I of England. He lived from 1599 to 1641, and Charles I conferred a knighthood upon him, so that he became known as Sir Anthony Van Dyck. He was spared the unhappiness of seeing Charles I lose his throne and his head in 1649, because he himself died eight years before this tragic event. You can see Van Dyck's wonderful portrait of King Charles I on horseback in the picture facing this page.

Born in 1599, in the same year as Van Dyck, was one of Spain's greatest painters, Diego Rodriguez Velasquez. Many of his fellow painters were obliged by necessity (and by command) to confine their work to religious subjects, but Velasquez himself was favoured by King Philip IV of Spain and he became court painter, as Van Dyck had done in England at about the same time. You can see the

" Charles I on Horseback," by Anthony Van Dyck.

(*Top left*) "Don Baltasar Carlos in Infancy," by Velasquez. (*Bottom left*) "The Artist in a Cap," a self-portrait by Rembrandt. (*Bottom right*) "La Vieille au Chapelet," by Cézanne.

(*The Cézanne painting is reproduced by permission of the Nationa Gallery and those on the left of the page by permission of the Wallace Collection*)

charming portrait by Velasquez of Don Carlos Baltasar as an infant facing this page. I wonder how many little boys to-day would care to be dressed like this! Notice the sword on the right and the plumed hat on the left.

Only seven years younger than Van Dyck and Velasquez was another famous portrait painter, a Dutchman named Van Ryn Rembrandt, who lived from 1606 to 1669. Rembrandt became a rich man, and it is said that he had his pupils prepare copies of his paintings which he afterwards touched up and sold as his own work. Facing this page you can see a portrait he painted of himself.

For my next picture I have chosen one that was painted more than two centuries later by a French artist named Paul Cézanne (1839–1906). You will notice that in comparison with the work of Leonardo da Vinci, Hans Holbein and Van Dyck, the self portrait by Rembrandt is less meticulous in detail. Outlines are softer instead of being what the photographer would call " in sharp focus." The picture by Cézanne shows further progress in the softening of outline and cursory treatment of detail. Some of the artists of our own time have carried the simplification of portraits even farther, and it is doubtful whether their work will enjoy more than passing approval. That the art of detailed representation in portraiture has not been entirely lost is proved by the work of the modern painter Pietro Annigoni, whose beautiful portrait of Her Majesty the Queen is shown in colour opposite page 216.

For the sake of drawing an interesting comparison and showing the contrast between work of different periods I have made a jump from the time of Rembrandt (seventeenth century) to the twentieth century. Now I must go back to Thomas Gainsborough, who lived from 1727 to 1788.

Many of Gainsborough's most famous portraits are very large

and show very fine ladies. I have chosen to represent one of his
smaller works—an unfinished painting of his own little daughters
Mary (right) and Margaret (left). His earlier painting of the same
little girls, like older child studies generally, has an artificial character. The children are more like dolls. They are decorative but
hardly human, and even the interest of Margaret in a passing
butterfly does not prevent it from being rather stilted and conventional. The picture opposite page 218 is of children as we know
them, and as we know children always must have been, notwithstanding the puppet-like representations of children painted by some
of the Old Masters. I can imagine holding conversation with Mary
and Margaret; I can imagine romping with them or helping them
to make toys out of paste and paper. I have never felt the least
desire to make the acquaintance of the children portrayed by the
earlier artists, but these two little girls of Gainsborough belong to
the world of real and lovely things. I dare say you could see
children like them at your school—perhaps they bear some resemblance to favourite playmates.

Gainsborough never finished this charming picture, and if you
will look at it very closely, you will see that he intended to put a
cat on Margaret's lap. The faint outline of a rather wild-looking
cat has been sketched in.

Sir Joshua Reynolds, who lived from 1723 to 1793, is usually
regarded as the greatest of English portrait painters, and there are
many child portraits to his credit. The most famous of these is
called " The Age of Innocence." In a similar style were " Collina "
and " Viscount Althorp," and several more. My own view is that
Reynolds knew less about real children than Gainsborough. His
art was often a reversion to the classical cherubic but unreal infant.
One feels that the cherubs in the painting " Lady Cockburn and

A well-known portrait of the Queen, painted by Pietro Annigoni, commissioned by
The Fishmongers' Company.

"The Fighting Téméraire," by Turner.

her Children" (opposite page 219) are made to serve merely as decorations for their charming mother, whose face differs from theirs in being real portraiture. If you do not feel very interested in Reynolds' children, I shall understand why, because I am not very interested in them either. They are not profound character studies, and probably Reynolds was unaware that young children possess individual character. To many men all children look alike. In reality children differ more from one another than grown-up people do. People tend to become alike as they grow up because it is the purpose of education to make them think, do and wear the same things. Reynolds was at his best when painting portraits of men.

I will mention one more well-known painter of children. The picture entitled "Lady Georgiana Fane" was painted by Sir Thomas Lawrence, who lived from 1769 to 1830. His pictures of children are popular, and the one I have chosen is pleasing without, however, being memorable in the way Gainsborough's picture is memorable. The faces of Mary and Margaret live in one's mind like faces really seen. The little lady dressed in peasant costume is more like some-one seen on the stage in a play (opposite page 219). She is acting her part and showing us nothing of her true self.

The work of Lawrence is not much liked by those who are authorities on painting. They say that he was more concerned to please the sitter and make his portraits agreeable-looking than to reveal the truth. One of his most famous paintings, called "Master Lambton," shows a boy clad in a beautiful red velvet suit. The boy has a very girlish face, and nobody believes that he ever looked like his portrait. He may have been painted thus to please his mother.

My next portrait, that of "Doña Isabel Cobos de Porcel," opposite page 219, is by a Spanish painter, Francisco Goya, who lived from 1746 to 1829. Goya was a skilful painter who had lived an adventurous life, and he was no flatterer; consequently his picture may be considered a piece of honest work. The lady was clearly a beauty, but it is easy to imagine her sitting at a bull-fight in Madrid and watching this cruel scene with pleasure; her face is not a kindly one, despite her large liquid eyes.

Modern portraiture offers us a great variety of styles. There are artists who paint portraits like they paint country scenes and articles of domestic use with no intention of giving us a presentable likeness; the crudely drawn face is half a pattern and half a cartoon. At the other extreme there are artists who carry on the tradition of the great masters, making pictures that are at once likenesses and also magnificent designs. Augustus John has given us the portrait of "Madame Suggia playing her 'cello." This picture is dated 1921, and it reveals an absorption in music that is characteristic of the subject. It also makes a satisfying composition. I shall have a good deal to say about this picture later on.

PICTORIAL COMPOSITION

Artists were once in the habit of letting their pictures grow naturally, much in the way that children do. In course of time they noticed that the most pleasing pictures conformed to certain patterns or arrangements of the subject-matter. After making this discovery, they painted more self-consciously; that is to say, they chose one of the more agreeable patterns and arranged their subject-matter to give them this pattern. They called this "composition," and the painters of to-day all observe the rules of good composition. Some pictures have only their composition to recommend them, their drawing being bad and their subject-matter trivial. Other pictures combine the advantages of satisfactory composition with those of competent workmanship and significant subject-matter.

A portrait by Thomas Gainsborough of his daughters.

"Lady Cockburn and her Children," by Sir
Joshua Reynolds.

"Lady Georgiana Fane," by Sir Thomas
Lawrence.

"Dona Isabel Corbos de Porcel," by
Francisco Goya.

"Madame Suggia," by Augustus John.

Good composition requires the placing of all the parts of a picture on the canvas or paper in such a way as to give a real focus or centre of interest. Let us imagine that the centre of interest is to be a figure somewhere near the middle of the picture. It may be that a bright sky overhead tends to catch the eye and distract the attention of the onlooker. To balance this, the artist will paint something bright—a white hen or a little pool of water—near the bottom of the picture. A very small object may suffice. Then again, the lines in a picture—as for instance the two sides of a road, the folds of a dress, the sweep of a hill—can either help the composition or spoil it. The eye is led by lines, and whereas helpful lines may lead us to what the artist requires us to see, unhelpful lines may serve as a distraction.

"Madame Suggia" gives us a splendid object-lesson in skilful composition. The centre of interest is the 'cello, and the folds in the drapery all converge towards it, as also do the lines of the lady, who is so intent on her playing. A possible distraction to the beholder is the lady's brightly lit face. To offset this the artist has given us brilliant though small patches of reflected light from the lady's shoe and from the spike of the 'cello. If you will momentarily cover up these high-lights with your hand, you will see that your attention at once flies to the lady, and that the 'cello becomes an annoying distraction. The practice of covering up small parts of good pictures will soon teach you to appreciate their pictorial significance, and make you understand the importance of good composition.

A high-light that might easily have spoilt the general effect in "Madame Suggia" is the arm that wields the bow. Its attention-compelling power has been balanced, however, by the tremendous sweep of the lady's dress over the floor to the right of the picture. Only imagine for one moment that the dress was neatly gathered round the lady's feet, or tucked under her chair, and you will then see that the design would be ruined. You would have the feeling that the lady was falling over to the right and that she was throwing out her arm to balance herself.

LANDSCAPE PAINTING

The painting of landscapes and marine scenes underwent improvement in the same way that portraiture improved. I doubt if the work of the Old Masters would give you much satisfaction. The places they painted look dull and unreal and their masterpieces look very dark and dingy, mainly, no doubt, as a result of old age. The oldest scenic work possessing interest for our eyes is perhaps that of the Frenchman, Claude de Lorrain, who lived from 1600 to 1682. His work shows us real places with a vision akin to our own. The one example I am able to show you is a magnificent design in green and yellow showing a seaport at sunset. The picture shows us the way to the open sea lying between tall buildings and ships, which form a kind of avenue. This almost symmetrical design was made the basis of some of Claude's other pictures.

Bernardo Bellotto Canaletto, a Venetian artist, who lived from 1724 to 1780, chose somewhat similar subjects, and from his pictures we can form a very good idea of what Venice was like 200 years ago. Canaletto was an engraver as well as an original artist, so he knew the value of accurate line. From the example of his work facing this page you can see how excellent was his draughtsmanship.

The greatest of all English landscape painters, Joseph Mallord William Turner, who lived from 1775 to 1851, seems to have been greatly impressed by the work of Claude, and at one time in his life he made a conscious attempt to outshine Claude.

Turner is said to have drawn trees with a skill that has never

" The Canale di S. Marco from the Guidecca," by Antonio Canaletto.

" A Seaport at Sunset," by Claude.

Three scenes by John Constable, the famous English landscape painter. They are (*Top left*) "The Hay Wain." (*Bottom left*) "The Close, Salisbury." (*Bottom right*) "Flatford Mill." (*The painting at bottom left is reproduced by permission of Victoria and Albert Museum and the remaining two by permission of the National Gallery*)

been surpassed, but most children will prefer his paintings of nautical subjects. He had what might be called "the Old Master's eye" for the country, and he painted it in a style that hardly appeals to the youthful eye of to-day. In fact, most of Turner's paintings are rather too far from the literal truth to satisfy children. An exception is "The Fighting *Téméraire*," which shows an old wooden battleship being taken to harbour by a steam tug at the close of day. The sea is dead calm and there is a glorious sunset. Nobody but Turner would have dared to attempt such a difficult subject.

In this picture, shown in colour opposite page 217, one might expect the sunset and the battleship to compete for attention, but somehow or other Turner has managed to make the one picture do justice to both. Artists will ascribe his success to the use of a pattern in which the upright masts of the battleship and the side-to-side streaks of reddish cloud are both needed to fill the space effectively. Then again the light from the setting sun has been cleverly used to encircle the old battleship with an immense halo of glory. Part of this halo is in the sky, and the reflection in the calm sea continues it downwards. "The Fighting *Téméraire*" is said to have been Turner's favourite picture, and it was one that he refused to sell. Other pictures by Turner show stormy seas, the effects of which he used to study amidst great personal discomfort, memorising wave shapes to put down afterwards on his canvases.

A contemporary of Turner was John Constable, who lived from 1776 to 1837. Constable was also influenced by Claude, but he painted country scenes in a manner that is more easily appreciated than the style adopted by Turner. He was a painstaking draughts-man, not content with vague atmospheric effects such as Turner delighted to produce. All Constable's pictures are full of detail. They sparkle with the sunshine of a clear spring or autumn day, and his skies are invariably alive with moving cloud. Many of his pictures were painted in the neighbourhood of his father's mill at Flatford, in Suffolk, and the mill itself is shown in one of the pictures facing page 221. Constable did not achieve success or fame easily. His work differed from that of the Old Masters in being clean and fresh-looking, but it may have been this difference which made people slow to praise him.

More recent landscape painters have given us the impression of brilliant sunshine with considerable economy of effort. Thus the picture by Clausen entitled "A Road, Winter Morning," which was first exhibited in 1923, is as true to life as any one of Constable's great pictures, but there is far less detail. Admittedly the artist has chosen to view his scene with his face towards the sun, and has thus set himself an easier task than Constable generally did. Shadow hides nearly all detail when one gazes into the sunlight, whereas with one's back to the sun every detail is clearly seen. This avoidance of difficulty is practised a good deal by inferior artists, but Clausen is not one of these. His picture shows a master's eye for composition and a profound knowledge of drawing (opposite page 224).

PICTURES THAT TELL A STORY

From time to time artists have departed from their usual work of painting simple visions in order to tell a story. Hogarth went to the length of painting eight pictures to tell the tale of a foolish young man who wasted his time and his fortune on idle and wicked amusements. He also painted six pictures showing the progress of two young people at the time of their marriage. This, like the other, was a moral story with an unfortunate ending. Other artists besides Hogarth have painted story-telling pictures, but usually they have told their story in a single picture.

It was during the reign of Queen Victoria that the "story-picture" became really fashionable. Nearly all the well-known artists were painting them, though a few refused to do so, saying that it was not the purpose of painting merely to provide book illustrations and so take the place of the written word. Some of the story-pictures were very sentimental and silly, the subjects being unworthy of the skill and labour expended on portraying them; but others were of real interest, the artist having managed to say something more than any words could express.

Story-pictures are always interesting to children because they are easy to understand, and I have included three in this book. A possible fourth would be "The Fighting *Téméraire*," telling of the last hours of an old warship about to be broken up. I have already said a great deal about this famous work of Turner's, but now I will add that the subject, although a possible one for words, is a still more suitable one for painting. And this, I think, must be the test that distinguishes between good and bad story-pictures. If the subject is one that could easily be expressed in words, making a painting unnecessary, then the painting is bound to be trivial. If, on the other hand, the painter is able to show a momentary glimpse of fast-moving events that no writer, however skilful, could hope to describe, then I think the picture will justify itself in the sight of even the most critical. "The Fighting *Téméraire*" passes this test. The old ship goes to her doom with dignity, despite her subservience to a dirty little tug, and all creation appears to glow with radiance to do her honour in that sad hour. No words of mine would ever tell this story a tenth part so grandly as Turner's famous painting.

The story-picture opposite page 224 is of more doubtful value. Called "The Last In," and painted by William Mulready, it shows an incident in an old-fashioned village school. A little boy is late, and the master, who wears his hat when teaching, ironically raises it and, with mock politeness, says, "Good evening, young sir, we are indeed honoured by your visit." This is a well-arranged and well-painted picture, but the subject is too trivial to require painting. Charles Dickens, the novelist contemporary of Mulready, could easily have told this story to perfection, and his words would have done greater justice to the scene than any painting could possibly do.

Facing page 225, "All Hands to the Pumps," by H. S. Tuke, is more praiseworthy in its subject. It shows the efforts of some sailors to save their ship from sinking in a storm. The sails have been torn to ribbons by the gale, but someone is aloft trying to repair the damage. It would appear that his help is needed to make the pump work faster. Water has reached the inside of the ship and is being pumped up on deck, whence it can spill back into the sea. The picture poses some unanswerable questions, but, on the whole, it is a grand piece of work, and I do not think any words could have described this memorable scene so well.

The next picture, "Youth on the Prow and Pleasure at the Helm," by William Etty, is not a picture of any real happenings. It tells an impossible sort of story in order to point a moral. It is what you might call a "problem picture," and many of this kind (only more difficult to explain) are being painted to-day. The picture is intended to tell you that young people are not fit to be entrusted with great responsibilities. Perhaps the artist had been amused at hearing some young man say what he would do if he were made Prime Minister of England. The decorative ship may be intended for the Ship of State, and the original intention of the young people may have been to sail it safely and well through fair weather and foul. Plainly they have forgotten to take the ship seriously. It is burdened with too many pretty ladies, who obviously know nothing

"A Road, Winter Morning," by Clausen.

"The Last In," by William Mulready.

"Youth on the Prow and Pleasure at the Helm," by William Etty.

"All Hands to the Pumps," by H. S. Tuke.

about managing a ship and care less. Somebody has had the idea of bringing some nice flowering bushes from the greenhouse, and yet another individual has suggested bubble blowing as an amusing way of spending the time. And while all the young folk are disporting themselves in the ship, a fearful storm is brewing. You can see the imp of mischief at the top right-hand corner. In another moment he will blow so hard that the ship will be turned over and all the young people will be tipped into a raging sea.

This picture was painted about one hundred years ago, and we still prefer to choose relatively old men to be our Prime Ministers, fearing that in his "judgment on youth" Etty may have been right.

THE FUTURE OF PAINTING

In this chapter I have been able to tell you only a very little about the art of the painter. Most of the works I have described were painted in the pre-photography age, and therefore they were intended to represent Nature as faithfully as possible. When photography was invented, artists turned in disgust from painting Nature and concentrated on doing things the camera could not do. As I said in the beginning, they became very vague about their aims, different groups of artists having different ideas about what they ought to do; and some artists to-day are doing very queer work because they have queer ideas as to what is good art. Many strange pictures owe their existence to the idea that design is the important thing in a picture—design and not subject-matter. But many painters of queer pictures have been unkindly treated, and so you can now see queer pictures that, besides being designs, are expressions of dislike and contempt for ordinary people. Much of the work of Roualt is of this kind.

Nobody knows which kind of painting will find favour in years to come, so that my guess is as good as anybody's. I think it is probable that when artists have grown used to the camera, and have ceased to be so afraid of it, they will go back to their real work of painting pictures that are true to life, but more true than a camera can make them. A camera cannot lie, but it must copy lies; the artist can paint a false and lying subject with all masks and disguises torn away, and that is his proper mission.

The age of bizarre patterns masquerading as paintings will probably pass away and then artists will be found to have intentions again over and above those of mere designers.

WHAT CHILDREN CAN DO

An eye for good design and the happy use of colour may be possessed by anyone, and, consequently, if good design be the chief requirement in art, a child should be able to give us pictures of nearly as much value as the grown-ups. The children of to-day happen to be living at a time when great skill in drawing and the exercise of much thought in the choice of a subject do not seem to be required of artists. Almost anything appears to do as the subject of a picture, and it can be quite badly drawn so long as the final result is a pleasing design. I am not sure how long this state of things will go on, but many modern artists are delighted with the work of quite little children. In some instances they themselves seem never to have grown up properly.

The pictures following page 240 are by children. They reveal the courage and the instinct for good composition that every artist must have. They show also some skill in draughtsmanship, and they portray worth-while subjects. You may say of these pictures that they are full of faults and that you could do as well. I hope this is so, and I hope you will try.

You will notice that all the young artists have chosen quite difficult subjects and that their teachers have not compelled them to draw pencil-boxes or flower-vases or cigarette-cases. It is quite right that children should be encouraged to paint whatever is of interest to them. At the same time they should be given praise if they ask to be allowed to draw the small dull things. If they learn to draw well, their pictures will have the added advantages that good draughtsmanship brings in its train. The important thing is not to become so painstaking in drawing that you forget the whole picture in order to do a lot of perfect detail. Drawing should be the servant of the young artist, not the dominating passion. Boys often draw the parts of cars and other mechanical things very well, but this does not make them successful as picture makers. Quite little children who draw crudely may be able to beat them at making artistic pictures. If you once start making pictures you should go on doing so, but at the same time you should practise the drawing of things you know you do not draw very well—things like hands, feet, trees and so on. If you do not do this your pictures will never improve, and when you are twelve or thirteen you will become dissatisfied with your efforts and give up trying.

I do not think it will always be easy for artists to succeed with works of art like those being done at the present time by such artists as Braque and Picasso. Their art, like the art of children, is satisfying up to a point, but most people, even in these days, expect something more finished. They also expect worth-while subject-matter. I would not advise the young artist to continue painting like a child if he can possibly bring himself by constant practice to paint like a John Constable or a Thomas Gainsborough.

Chapter 5

BETTY'S PICTURE SHOW

OLD Miss Brown, the dressmaker, lived in a little cottage near the village school.   All the children who lived in the village had to pass her cottage four times a day, going to and from school.   On fine days Miss Brown used to stand at her gate to watch the children go by, for she loved them all, and she knew the names of every one.

Miss Brown had a lovely garden that was always gay with flowers.   She had a large apple tree as well, and in the autumn the branches of this tree were always weighed down by hundreds and hundreds of rosy apples.   In September Miss Brown filled a big washing basket with the best apples she could find, and she put it near her gate, so that the children going to school could help themselves to as many as they could carry.   She used to enjoy watching them, and sometimes she would say to a shy little girl or boy, "More —more—take more."   For some children helped themselves to only one apple, whereas others filled their pockets.

A friend said to Miss Brown one day, "I wonder at you letting the children help themselves in the way you do.   Are you not afraid that they will be greedy and start fighting one another?   Do not the bigger children get all your best apples?"

To this Miss Brown replied, "Oh no, indeed; they are always very good, and they never fight, for, you see, they know that there

228

will be plenty for everybody, and that I should never let even the littlest one go away crying and disappointed."

The friend shook her head doubtfully, and Miss Brown laughed. "Ah!" she said, "I can see that big crowds of children frighten you, because you are not used to them. A lot of people think that children are little savages and hard to manage, but if children know a person is fond of them, they behave beautifully, even to one an-other. There isn't a child in this village who would like to ap-pear rude and unkind in front of me—not even the terrible Teddy Bloggs."

Miss Brown had a tame parrot that used to talk a great deal, and sometimes she would invite children in to see it. "More, more!" it would say, directly it saw any little children; "take more, my little dears, take lots." For, you see, it had heard Miss Brown telling the children to help themselves to apples and it copied her. It always said the same thing, even in spring-time, when there were no apples but only blossom on the tree. Then the children used to look at one another and giggle. "No apples, Polly," they would say, "we cannot take apples." But the parrot would only shout the louder, "Go on, help yourselves, more, more, take more."

APPLES FOR ALL.

Suddenly Miss Brown fell ill. Day after day the children passed by her cottage without seeing her standing at her gate. They were sorry, but they did not worry themselves very much about it, because they felt sure that she would soon be seeing them again. But Miss Brown did not appear, and presently her garden began to look neglected. There were big weeds in her front path, and the lawn grew dreadfully long.

It was little Betty Perkins who first heard the sad story of Miss

MISS BROWN'S
PIANO IS TAKEN
AWAY IN A VAN.

Brown. At breakfast one day her Mummy said to her Daddy, "Oh dear, I'll never get my dress turned in time for the holiday. Miss Brown is still in bed, and she cannot do a thing. I hear that all her money is going too, poor thing. The furniture men were in last Wednesday to take away her piano. She had to sell it to get enough to pay her grocer and her milkman and her butcher."

"Oh, Mummy," interrupted Betty, almost crying, "hasn't Miss Brown got her piano now? We children did so enjoy it when she played to us and made us sing for her."

"Her piano's gone, dear," Mummy sighed, "gone for good, I fear."

Betty suddenly looked fierce. She swallowed down her breakfast quickly, and pulling her hat on to her head, she ran off down the road towards the school. It was really much too early, but a few children were loitering along, among them Teddy Bloggs.

"Teddy, Teddy!" Betty called out, "Miss Brown has had to sell her piano. She's ill and poor, not being able to work at her dressmaking, and the men are taking away all her things. What shall we do?"

Teddy was rather a dull boy, and he did not see that children could do anything. "We can't do anything," he said shortly.

"Oh yes, we can!" Betty retorted; "you can weed her garden for one thing, and you can cut her grass. I know where she keeps her mower, and I'll show you the place. If it's too hard for you to push by yourself, you can get that great lazy Billy Smith to give you a hand."

"That's an idea!" exclaimed Teddy; "I'll go and do a bit of weeding right now, and I'll do some more after school."

"I am going to give a picture show to get money for Miss Brown," Betty told her school friends, as they gathered in the playground before morning lessons. "I want every one of you to bring me the best drawings and the best paintings you have ever done. Daddy hasn't got a car now, so I am going to make him let me have the garage for my show. I shall tidy out all the things in there and clean it up, and then there will be room to hang lots and lots of pictures. I shall charge everybody threepence to come and see my show."

"Even the ones who've lent the pictures?" said Valerie doubtfully.

"Of course," answered Betty; "there will be everybody else's pictures to see, even though they've seen their own; and anyway, it's money for Miss Brown we want. Nobody will mind paying threepence, even if it doesn't seem very good money's worth."

When she got home after morning school, Betty bothered and worried her father so much that at last he said, "Very well, then, only I do not know where on earth we are to put all the garden tools and things."

"Just for that day I don't mind having them in the scullery," Mummy said; "and if it is fine, most of the things could be left out of doors."

That same afternoon all the children came to school with their best pictures. At play-time they brought them to Betty, who spread them out on the playground to have a look at them.

"Now then, children, start playing!" the teacher said, bustling up. But when she saw all the drawings, and Betty in the middle of them, she knew that something important was happening.

"Tell me about it," she said.

Betty explained her idea.

"That's splendid," said the teacher, "at this very moment there is a picture show in London. It is called the Summer Exhibition of the Royal Academy, and I went to see it last week. You must make yours as good. How are you going to choose the best pictures, Betty? There are too many to hang in your father's garage."

"I can easily pick out the best," Betty answered.

"Oh no," said the teacher, "you shouldn't do it yourself. If you do, some of the children whose pictures are left out might be offended. You ought to have a 'Hanging Committee.' What I mean is, that you ought to get three or four friends to help you sort the pictures into piles labelled 'Best,' 'Second Best,' 'Third Best' and so on. Then there will be nobody for the discontented ones to blame."

Betty followed out her teacher's plan. She let three of her friends help her divide the pictures into the several groups. There were many arguments as to whether certain pictures ought to be first or second, second or third; but in the end there were three neat piles

THE HANGING COMMITTEE

labelled first, second and third. Betty tied the piles carefully with string; and then the Hanging Committee marched off to Betty's house, carrying the piles with them.

First of all they prepared the " Exhibition Hall " by tidying out the garage. Then they started hanging the pictures. This they did with drawing-pins, of which Betty had bought a whole boxful on purpose. They found that there was room for all the pictures in the first pile, and all the pictures in the second pile, but only half the pictures in the third pile.

c. II —9*

"We shall need a notice to put up on the door," Betty said.

"I'll write one," said Molly, the youngest member of the Hanging Committee. So Molly turned over one of the pictures that had not been hung, and on the back, in large letters, she wrote:

XIBISHUN

2p.

"That won't do," Betty cried; "your spelling is all wrong; there ought to be an 'E' in front. So Molly added an 'E,' and Betty said, "That's better!"

The picture show was planned to open at nine o'clock on Saturday morning, and all the children were told about it at school on Friday.

"Bring your mothers and fathers and everybody," Betty said; "I shall be at the door to take your two penny pieces, and there will be a collecting-box with a big hungry mouth nearby, so that anybody who feels like giving more can do so."

Betty awoke at eight o'clock on Saturday to hear a great noise of chattering in the road outside. When she went to the window in her nightdress to look outside, she saw that a long queue of children had already gathered in the road opposite the garage. Teddy Bloggs was acting as policeman and making the children line up properly. Betty dressed quickly, and she found her mother downstairs with breakfast all ready for her. "Even though it is Saturday I thought you would want it early," she said.

"Oh yes, I do," Betty cried, and she started to eat. At half-past eight she took the garage key and went out to meet her friends.

"Well," she said, " as you are all so early, I'll open the exhibition now. I hope you have all brought your two penny pieces."

She unlocked the door, and the children started to file in one by one, giving Betty their money as they went past. Teddy Bloggs went inside to make the children walk round the garage one way only. When they had seen all the pictures they were made to go out or to sit on the long garden seat that Betty had put down the middle of the garage.

"If you sit on the seat for a few minutes, out of the way, you can go round again," Teddy explained. "We want you to enjoy yourselves."

By eleven o'clock some of the parents began to come. In the afternoon it was really crowded. Some of the children came two or three times, bringing aunts and uncles. "Look," they cried, "that's my picture over there."

Betty was busy taking money all day, and she noticed that a lot of people put something extra in the collecting-box. At meal-times Betty's Mummy brought her sandwiches and lemonade, so that she did not have to leave her post.

At six o'clock some of the very old people in the village came to see the pictures, and after that there was nobody, so Betty shut the garage door and hung a notice on the outside, saying:

EXIBISHUN

CLOSD

Then she went into her house with all the money. Daddy helped her to count it. In two penny pieces she had collected only £2.15p., but the collecting-box held quite a big treasure. Some grown-ups had put ten penny pieces and even fifty penny pieces inside. For everybody loved Miss Brown, and a great many people loved Betty too. Inside the box there was also a little letter which said:

"DEAR BETTY,—

"I will give you £1 for the notice on your door when the

EXIBISHUN is closed. I want it for a souvenir. I will call for it one evening next week.

"With much love from

"An Old Friend."

"Whoever can it be?" Betty wondered. She forgot to wonder when Daddy told her that the collecting-box contained £12.75p., but on Sunday she thought about the strange note again. She was still thinking about it on Monday morning at school, when her teacher, very stern, asked her to stand out in front of the class.

BETTY'S NOTICE

"Betty," said the teacher, "you have disgraced me and the whole school in the eyes of everybody."

Betty felt frightened, and then she saw a twinkle in the eyes of her teacher, and knew that she was not really angry.

"How do you spell 'Exhibition'?" the teacher asked her.

"With an 'E'," Betty answered.

"Like this?" the teacher asked, writing "EXIBISHUN" on the blackboard.

"N—no," stammered Betty, hanging her head.

"How do you write it, then?" the teacher persisted; "can anybody say?"

None of the children ventured to help, although the teacher held up her piece of chalk, offering it to anyone who cared to write the word on her blackboard.

"Very well," said the teacher at last, "you can all write the word

'exhibition' in your books twenty times. This is how you do it."
And she wrote:

EXHIBITION

very large on the blackboard.

"You can go to your place now, Betty," she added.

On Monday evening Betty and her Mummy and Daddy talked about giving all the money to Miss Brown, and they wondered how it would be best to do it. Mummy thought Betty ought to take it in an envelope, but Betty felt shy and said Mummy must go. While they were arguing, they saw someone open the garden gate and come up to the front door.

"Why, it's Mr. Pratt, the furniture man," exclaimed Mummy; "whatever does he want here? I don't know him at all, and I don't owe him anything."

Mummy went to the door, and Mr. Pratt took off his hat. "If you please," he said, "I've called for the notice." He was grinning all over his face. "Here's the pound I promised. And you can tell Miss Betty that I am sending back the piano to Miss Brown's cottage first thing in the morning."

"But I don't understand——" Mummy began.

"That's all right, Mrs. Perkins," Mr. Pratt hastened to explain. "No one need pay me anything to do it. I couldn't give her much for it, as it was an old-fashioned thing, and I reckon she's earned the price of it with all the fun and treats she's given our kiddies, my own among the rest."

"Mummy!" cried Betty suddenly, "couldn't we fix the envelope of money to the piano somehow, then nobody need go with it, and we needn't say it's from anyone special. We could just put on the envelope 'With love from all the village!'"

With luve from all the villiage to Miss Brown

AN ENVELOPE FULL OF MONEY.

"That's a grand idea," said Mummy. "Don't you think so, Mr. Pratt?"

"I'll fix it," said Mr. Pratt. "Just you write what you want on the envelope and give it to me. I'll have it tied on to one of the brass candlesticks."

Betty slipped Mr. Pratt's pound into the envelope, with all the other money, and then she wrote very large on the outside, "With luve from all the villiage to Miss Brown," and handed it to Mr. Pratt.

"Oughtn't it to be spelt properly?" Mummy said doubtfully.

"Oh no, indeed," Mr. Pratt cried, putting the envelope behind him hastily. "It'll do very well as it is. That way Miss Brown will know it's from a little child, and nothing could please her more. And she'll never know the piano came as a present from me. She'll think some of the money was taken out to pay for it. That's as it should be." Mr. Pratt's face beamed as he made this little speech. "And now," he concluded, "if you'll give me my notice, I'll be going. I want that notice specially, as I might be giving an EXIBISHUN myself one of these days—of old pianos maybe!"

He roared with laughter at his own joke and, notice in hand, went stamping off down the road, still going "HA! HA! HA!" as loud as anything.

Miss Brown very soon got well when she saw her piano come

back again and knew that, together with all the money, it was a present from the village.

"The dear children," she said, almost crying with joy, "to think that they should have repaid me so handsomely for all my apples. How true is the saying that kindness is never wasted, even when it is done without thought of any return."

The very next week Miss Brown got up and saw her nice tidy garden. She never found out who did all the work, and so she very wisely thanked all the children for everything by giving a huge garden-party. At that party she turned out cupboards and chests full of old dresses for the children to dress up in, and she banged out every dance tune she knew on the old piano, keeping the french window open so that the children could skip and dance to the music on the lawn. And all tea-time the old parrot kept screaming "More — more — take lots more—help yourselves, dears" in Miss Brown's own voice. Everyone said afterwards it was the best party ever given anywhere in the whole world—which may be true for all I know, though I've had some good ones myself.

"MORE!" SCREAMED THE PARROT "TAKE LOTS MORE"

Chapter 6

CHILD ART

FROM early infancy little children take great delight in wielding brush or pencil. Their earliest efforts might appear to be mere scribbling and daubing and of no special significance. The probability is, however, that they satisfy the little artist in much the same way as his seemingly inconsequential vocal utterances and constant movement satisfy him. They are modes of self-expression; products of the energy that is always animating him and forcing an outlet of some kind or another. To the student of child nature they have meaning, though to the average parent they just look a mess and a waste of good material.

In course of time, the child produces drawings or paintings, or modelled objects with clay, to which he gives a name, saying " man," " house," " tree," " lady " and so on. It would seem that he sees among his random scribblings some resemblance to the thing named, just as he sees animal or human shapes in shadows, in the configuration of trees and clouds, in elaborate old-fashioned wall-paper patterns, and in the embers of a fire.

Drawing, painting or modelling with the intent to represent definite things is the next phase, when the child becomes more purposeful in all he does. Speech becomes more definitely a communicating of meanings, and less an outpouring of sound for its own sake; movement becomes more definitely a going from one set place to another set place, and less a jig or dance enjoyable in itself. But the child's purposes are fleeting and of little real import to him, so that they do not entirely master him or canalise all his energy. There is an overplus of energy, and when interest in a particular project wanes, this energy is released in a riot of movement or sound. Thus, the drawing that was meant to be a man may

" Fairy and Witch Flying," by Merlith Morrison, aged 5.
(Ridings Park, Iver.)

(Prizewinner in The Caxton Publishing Company Ltd. Painting Competition.)

"Noah's Ark," by Bruce Stewart Kershaw, aged 7.

(Harlesden, London, N.W.10.)

"Fun in the Snow," by Diana Harris, aged 10.

(Gosport, Hants.)

"At the Circus," by Sarah Lewis, aged 12.
(St. Mary's School, St. Leonards-on-Sea.)

(*Prizewinner in The Caxton Publishing Company Ltd. Painting Competition.*)

"On the Pier," by Anthony Lucas, aged 12.

(Beckenham, Kent.)

"At the Seaside," by Sally Ansell, aged 13.

(Hackney Wick, London, E.9.)

" On the Station Platform," by James Millham, aged 13.
(Mid-Essex County Technical School.)

" A Roller-hockey Match," by Tessa Smith, aged 15.
(William Gibbs School, Faversham.)

at any stage revert to a scribble; the sedate walk on a pavement may become a zigzag hopping from side to side; the attempt to sustain intelligible conversation may be abandoned in favour of babbling or singing words and phrases that have no accepted meaning.

One of the time-honoured mistakes in child management—a mistake that is commonly perpetuated even to-day—is to try to hold the child to his purposes after they have lost their interest for him. "Don't scribble—finish your drawing properly." Do we not often hear people say this? In the street we hear people say, "Walk straight, for goodness' sake; you'll tire yourself out if you dodge about so." And, commonest of all, perhaps, is the injunction, "Stop that noise," or, "Don't talk nonsense."

Arising out of the mistaken view that a child should finish everything he starts, to the best of his ability, is the pernicious idea that he needs help and the force of example. "Not *that* way," says the too-conscientious parent, snatching away the pencil; "*this* way." Worse still, a parent may set some finished drawing, or some specific object, in front of the child and say, "You had better copy that."

By degrees the wrongly reared child acquires the idea that all his work has to give satisfaction to others, and then it loses its spontaneity, becoming self-conscious. Work that is done to curry favour, and that verges on plagiarism, is completely useless from the artistic standpoint; and the child who is being disciplined to do such work is merely being fitted to play some subordinate rôle in an office or factory.

True art springs from the urge to satisfy some inner need, and this is why all little children who are left to themselves can, and do, produce true works of art—works that give genuine satisfaction to those who are capable of understanding and interpreting them.

Judged by normal adult standards the artistic creations of small children are full of faults, but, then, so are adult works of art when judged from a small child's standpoint. The child tends to draw, not what he sees of a thing, but all he knows about it; consequently every human being has to have two eyes, two arms, and two legs, even if drawn in profile. Similarly, a four-legged animal must always be shown with four legs, an aircraft with all its wings, and so on. We must not make the remark to a child drawing a house that we cannot see the people and furniture in it from the outside—the child knows that they are there and so they must go into his picture.

Needless to say, true perspective, with the resulting foreshortening of lengths and the flattening of right angles into acute or obtuse ones, can play no part in art that has a different standard of veracity from our own. The grown-up is concerned to create the illusion of three-dimensional solidity on a two-dimensional surface, but it is a long time before the child becomes interested in trying to do the same, and he should not be forced prematurely to attempt what is, after all, only a mechanical trick. The wish to be able to do this may come in time, though to some artists, revelling in pure pattern and colour effects, this wish never matures. Herein lies the reason for much of the extraordinary work of modern artists—work that is incomprehensible to the average person, but full of meaning to kindred spirits.

The artistic productions of little children, despite their peculiarities, have found much favour among the accepted adult artists. It is said that child art displays tremendous strength of characterisation, and that the child's choice of colour is admirable. It is also said for the child that his work at the age of four or five years is likely to be far better than the drawings and pictures by others that are later set before him in picture books to influence his taste. The child of eight or nine may start drawing to some conventional professional pattern if he is persuaded to think it better than his own and he may choose to like what is in reality less good. Poor examples are plentiful enough. We have only to think of the worst kinds of comic paper and the poorest kind of Christmas card art.

The coloured illustrations accompanying this chapter show the work of children at its best. The eight pictures selected for reproduction are to be regarded as expressions of individuality. Their value lies both in their distinctiveness and their sameness. Children resemble one another markedly in some ways; in others they are more widely different than they will ever be again. The pressure that is normally brought to bear on them to make them into good conforming citizens seems to iron out much of this precious individual difference and, with it, the will to go their own unique way, doing and creating things that embody their own thought and feeling and nobody else's.

In the most advanced of modern schools the tendency is to allow children much more freedom than is customary elsewhere, the object being to avoid suppressing child enterprise and individuality. The excellence of the work done by youthful artists in such schools seems to provide clear justification for the policy of reducing to a minimum the use of force or compulsion in education.

The teaching of art in the school has been undergoing a great change in recent years. Children are no longer persuaded by the best art teachers to copy objects placed in front of them, and no longer constrained in the beginning to observe with punctilious accuracy the rules of proportion and perspective. It is, perhaps, true to say that in Europe the introduction of the more enlightened modern methods was due to Cizek, the famous Viennese protagonist of child art who conducted art classes for children some fifty or so years ago.

Cizek would not have any of his child pupils copy things from nature, and he was opposed to the policy of showing children too many ready-made picture-books and too many adult works of art. He believed in letting children make their own picture-books. His method of inspiring the child artist was to suggest a subject—gathering apples in an orchard, for instance, and then tell the children to shut their eyes and visualise it. Afterwards they were to draw what they had imagined. If their drawings were clear, they were allowed to paint them. Sometimes they were permitted to paint without drawing first. They were urged to work fairly fast, so that their work should be done before the mental image had faded, and so that their interest should last long enough to see the work completed. Nevertheless, a subject would often be made to occupy the children for two lessons. They would complete the drawing at one sitting and paint it at the next. The children frequently worked at benches or desks which were flat or only slightly inclined towards them; they did not always use easels.

Cizek insisted on the use of large pieces of paper, and he criticised children who were afraid to fill their paper completely. Figures in single-figure subjects had to touch the top edge and reach down to the bottom. Little figures he constantly ridiculed, saying, "We do not want to draw fleas here." Realistic drawings bearing the impress of the copyist of nature or of adult art made him impatient. "You may do work like that under instruction by other people," he said, "but we do not do work like that here." Nothing gratified him more than the dashing confidence of little children four or five years old, who would attempt anything and prefer their own achievements to anything anybody might show them.

Cizek was opposed to letting children try to complete images of things in one line. His pupils had to draw everything part by part. In drawing a human figure, body, head, arms and legs were drawn separately, the parts being added one to another. A tree had to have its trunk first, then its branches, then its twigs and finally its leaves or needles. The children were encouraged to believe that the childish way of doing things was preferable to the adult way. Cizek told them that the makers of children's picture-books knew nothing of children and nothing of making pictures.

When one of Cizek's pupils found the drawing of certain things easy, and tended to mannerisms or style, he was instantly given other things to do. It was Cizek's principle to keep the children contending continuously against fresh difficulties. In this he was conspicuously successful, while his pupils remained little. In their early teens, however, the children seemed less amenable to his lead. Notwithstanding what he told them, they seemed to lose their self-assurance, turning to the slavish copying of nature or of adult art. The great teacher had very little use for the artistic performances of children who had entered upon the phase of puberty. Something in the children seemed to him to die at the age of about fourteen or so, and he felt that he was unable to reach them any longer with his encouragement and advice.

In feeling a certain disappointment at the way children alter with the onset of puberty, Cizek can claim kinship with other great and generous hearts. Children tend to become worldly as a result of all the mundane influences that are brought to bear on them, and in the end they seem actually to despise the genius of persons who were their childhood's inspiration.

Chapter 7

GREAT BOOKS

Nearly all children learn to read for themselves before they are eight years old, and some are able to read quite well a year or two before this. At first all children read only for amusement, and

CURIOUS PEOPLE

they like their books to be full of bright pictures. In fact, their favourite books are of the kind in which pictures tell the story. Often they will spend their pocket-money on "comics," which are weekly or fortnightly papers, rather like the newspaper Daddy buys, but full of picture stories about the adventures and misadventures of curious people, or of still more curious animals. When children

245

become bigger, they can enjoy books with fewer pictures, perhaps no pictures at all.   But books with pictures are always preferred to those without, and even grown-ups like pictures in their books, although most of the books written for grown-ups do not have any.

When they were first written, many of the best and most famous books did not have any pictures.   They were printed again and again without any pictures, yet people went on buying them.   Then somebody had the idea of printing the old books once more, but with pictures put in to make them more popular still.   Some great books have been illustrated by very famous and very good artists, but it must never be forgotten that the pictures in these books are really a luxury and could be left out.

CURIOUS ANIMALS

Children who take down grown-up books from the bookcase often flick the pages over to see if there are any pictures, and then, not finding any, exclaim impatiently, "What a dull book!"   Sometimes they are quite right; it *is* a dull book.   But just as often they are wrong: the book, instead of being dull, is very interesting.

How can children tell which books are good to read and which are a waste of time?   At first they are quite unable to tell for themselves.   They have to be helped to choose their books by somebody grown up, who has already read most of the best books, and who knows the names of all the men and women who have written well.

People in charge of libraries can usually help children to choose good books that they will enjoy reading. Shall I pretend that I am in charge of a library and am taking you round to see all the books in it? I think that would be a very good idea.

CHILDREN'S BOOKS

The Juvenile Department of a big public library is a gay place, full of books for children of all ages. There must be hundreds and hundreds of picture books for quite little children, and besides these

CHILDREN'S LIBRARY.

there are travel books, adventure books, nature books and school-story books for older children. You are probably quite used to hunting among all these books for something interesting to take home, and so I should only be telling you what you knew already if I said that quite little children like the books about Ameliaranne and Milly-Molly-Mandy, or the great favourites with older children are the " William " books by Richmal Crompton and the " Dr. Dolittle " series. What you want to know about are the children's classics.

My dictionary says that a classic is a book of such excellence that, sooner or later, everybody wants to read it, so that it is never allowed to go out of print—not even when it is a great many years old. Some books that were written in Greek and Latin thousands of years ago are still being read by the scholars of to-day. Some books written for children fifty and more years ago are still great favourites with any young people who are fortunate enough to be lent or given copies. It is about these older books that I want to speak to you, because you ought to try to find them in your library and read them if you have not done so already.

It is no use going back a very long way in order to find nice old books for children, because few nice books were then written. A hundred years ago, and even less, the story books for children were mostly very dismal indeed. The title of one, written by James Janeway, who lived from 1636 to 1674, was *A Token for Children, Being an Exact Account of the Conversion, Holy and Exemplary Lives and Joyful Deaths of Several Young Children*. It contained thirteen life stories of thirteen good children, most of whom died between the ages of four and six years, and it was still being printed at the commencement of the nineteenth century. For entertaining stories the children were obliged to depend on the memory of their nurses or other kindly folk who had heard tell of amusing or exciting events in times past. The stories about Dick Whittington, Jack the Giant Killer, Tom Thumb and Robin Hood were originally handed on verbally from generation to generation in this way.

Most of the fairy stories that were to become such universal favourites were translations from French books. In 1698 there was published in Paris a book by Charles Perrault, containing the stories of Cinderella, Puss in Boots, Little Red Riding Hood and other well-known tales.

We owe *Goldilocks and the Three Bears* to the Countess D'Aulnoy, and *Beauty and the Beast* to Madame Jeanne de Beaumont.

The wonderful stories of the *Arabian Nights* appeared in French early in the eighteenth century and an English translation was soon made. In this way the more fortunate of children came to hear of the adventures of Sinbad, Ali Baba and Aladdin.

Meanwhile English rhymes, many of a rude or political kind, were turned into harmless nonsense for the amusement of children and eventually they were gathered together and put into the book of *Mother Goose*. At the end of the eighteenth century a moralising story about two boys and their tutor was to become famous. This was the tale of *Sandford and Merton*, by Thomas Day. Another very improving book, published in 1812, and again with additions in 1847, was the *Fairchild Family*. Nothing that happened to this family was missed by their Papa, who drew morals from every occasion.

Well, rather more than one hundred years ago, some grown-up people began to feel that the best way to make children good was not to lecture them and give them dismal stories about wicked children who came to bad ends, or about goody-goody children who went to heaven, but to treat them as they would treat their grown-up friends—that is, by doing something for them that they would like. And so they started writing more amusing tales and rhymes for children. In the beginning they were rather shy of writing anything quite without a moral, and so their first efforts were still rather improving in tone—like the old, old Fables of Æsop which, although quite good stories, were meant to teach people a lesson more than two thousand years ago. You should read *Æsop's Fables*, by the way, if you have not already done so.

Two sisters, Jane and Ann Taylor, were among the first to try
to please children as well as improve them.   Their book of *Original
Poems* was first published in 1804, and I do not think that nowadays
you would find it in any library, but it would be worth your while
to hunt for it in the second-hand bookshops. The copy I have, dated
1868, shows that these poems were printed again and again.   The
most famous poem in it, written by Ann, is called " My Mother."
It begins:

> " Who fed me from her gentle breast,
>   And hushed me on her arms to rest,
>   And on my cheek sweet kisses prest?
>   My Mother.

> " When sleep forsook my open eye,
>   Who was it sung sweet hushaby,
>   And rocked me that I should not cry?
>   My Mother."

I will miss out some verses here and quote you two later ones:

> " Who dressed my doll in clothes so gay?
>   And taught me pretty how to play,
>   And minded all I had to say?
>   My Mother.

> " Who ran to help me when I fell,
>   And would some pretty story tell
>   Or kiss the place to make it well?
>   My Mother."

The poem goes on like this for a long time, and then it says:

> "And can I ever cease to be
> Affectionate and kind to thee,
> Who was so very kind to me,
>   My Mother?

> "Ah no! the thought I cannot bear,
> And if God please my life to spare,
> I hope I shall reward thy care,
>   My Mother."

I paid only twopence for this little book, and I think that this one poem, by itself, was worth more than that, don't you?

There are dozens and dozens of others—some amusing, some sad and some very priggish, but all very moral. One amusing one is a libel on the duck, who, after all, is a pleasant and amusing bird though, I will admit, a noisy eater. It is called "The Notorious Glutton" and it begins:

> "A duck who had got such a habit of stuffing,
> That all the day long she was panting and puffing,
> And by every creature who did her great crop see,
> Was thought to be galloping fast for a dropsy;
> One day, after eating a plentiful dinner,
> With full twice as much as there should have been in her,
> While up to her forehead still greedily roking,
> Was greatly alarmed by the symptoms of choking."

I need not quote any more; the poor duck was punished for eating so fast.

Elsewhere in my twopenny bargain, under an attractive wood-
cut of a tortoiseshell butterfly, is the following short lesson:

> "The Butterfly, an idle thing,
>   Nor honey makes nor yet can sing,
>   As do the bee and bird;
>   Nor does it, like the prudent ant,
>   Lay up the grain for times of want,
>   A wise and cautious hoard.

> "My youth is but a summer's day;
>   Then, like the bee and ant, I'll lay
>   A store of learning by;
>   And though from flower to flower I rove,
>   My stock of wisdom I'll improve
>   Nor be a butterfly."

I do not need to tell you any more about this little book to
convince you that it was meant to do children good at the same
time that it amused them. There were many books of this kind,
but most of them were horrible books by people who tried to frighten
children into being good. One of the last of the moral rhyme books
is the famous *Struwwelpeter*, or "Straw-headed Peter." This is
still reprinted from time to time, and I am sure your librarian could
get it for you. You might think that the rhymes in this book were
of the kind intended to frighten children into being good, because
wrongdoers come to very bad ends; but their misfortunes are so
exaggerated that no child really believes in them. Instead of
trembling and looking frightened when they hear the end of each
fearful rhyme, little children roar with laughter. A boy who per-
sists in teasing animals is bitten by a dog; another boy who goes on

THE INKY BOYS

FLYING ROBERT

STRAW-HEADED PETER

CRUEL FRED

HARRIET

LITTLE SUCK-A-THUMB

THE LONG, RED-LEGGED SCISSOR MAN

LITTLE JOHNNY HEAD-IN-AIR

THE GREEN MAN

AUGUSTUS

FIDGETY PHIL

CHARACTERS FROM STRUWWELPETER.

sucking his thumbs like a great baby has them cut off by a " great, long, red-legged scissor man." Harriet, who plays with matches, is burnt to ashes; some boys who jeer at a black man are themselves made black by being dipped into ink; fidgety Philip, who cannot sit still at table, is buried at last under a heap of dinner things; Augustus, who will not eat his soup, fades away to a thread and dies. His thoughtful and persevering relations put the soup tureen on his grave! Little Johnny-head-in-air falls into a river; and silly Robert, who *would* take his umbrella out in a wind, is blown away and never seen again.

We come now to the mid-nineteenth century, which was an age of writers who wrote to please children—just to please them, nothing more. While some writers—Charles Kingsley, for instance—were still producing moral tales, new writers—for example, Robert Louis Stevenson and " Lewis Carroll "—were coming along with tales and verses of pure delight. *The Water Babies*, by Kingsley, is perhaps the last of the more enjoyable moral tales that were read by our grandparents and great-grandparents, and you will find much in it to enjoy reading to-day. I am sure you can get it in your library.

Robert Louis Stevenson, the son of a successful civil engineer, was always in poor health, and he could never live a very active life, so he started to write for his living. His stories *Treasure Island* and *Kidnapped* are among the most famous boys' stories ever written. They are stories about pirates and fighting, and even the girls like them. *Treasure Island* started a new fashion in books for children and thousands of similar stories have been written since, some very poor and others as good as *Treasure Island*.

Stevenson also wrote for quite small children. Thus, *A Children's Garden of Verses* is full of charming little odds and ends for the youngest of young people.

If Robert Louis Stevenson, with his love of fighting and adventure, was primarily a boys' author, Lewis Carroll (whose real name was Charles Lutwidge Dodgson) was his opposite number, because he definitely preferred girls, and made up all his stories for girl friends. His best-known and best-loved books are *Alice in Wonderland* and *Alice through the Looking Glass*. If you have not read these two books you should certainly do so, because you cannot be called an educated or well-read person without some knowledge of Alice. Even the grown-up books are constantly referring to something that happened in *Alice*. Adver-

— ALICE —

tisements and cartoons often show characters out of *Alice*—the Walrus and the Carpenter for instance, or Old Father William, or Tweedledum and Tweedledee.

If you enjoy *Alice* you will probably like Lewis Carroll's later tale, *Sylvie and Bruno*, though this is not so good. The portrait you can see of Lewis Carroll on this page was drawn by the man who made the pictures for *Sylvie and Bruno*.

Lewis Carroll wrote much that was just nonsense, but there was

"LEWIS CARROLL"
(By courtesy of the National Portrait Gallery)

another writer, called Edward Lear, who wrote *nothing but non-sense!* Fancy being famous for writing just *nonsense* and nothing else! His *Book of Nonsense* is a collection of absurd rhymes and pictures. Many of the rhymes are like the modern limerick, very

THE YOUNG LADY OF BUTE.
(EDWARD LEAR DREW HER
SOMETHING LIKE THIS)

short, and all beginning in the same sort of way. A specimen is given below:

> "There was a young lady of Bute,
>   Who played on a silver-gilt flute;
>   She played several jigs
>   To her uncle's white pigs,
>   That amusing young lady of Bute."

The best of Lear's poems are longer, and despite the absurdity of their subjects they are exceedingly good verse. Whatever your age may be, you will enjoy the poems about the Jumblies, the Dong with the Luminous Nose, the Duck and the Kangaroo, the Yongy Bongy Bo, and the Old Man in the Kingdom of Tess (who invented a purely original dress).

Edward Lear was really a serious artist, who made pictures of natural science subjects; he wrote his nonsense poems to amuse the children of his employer.

Still a tremendous favourite with all children who love animals is *Black Beauty*, by Anna Sewell. This appeared first in 1877.

If you are seeking for the favourites of great-grandparents and great-great-grandparents you must not forget the American writers. *Little Women*, first published in 1868, is still a favourite with girls: it was written in New England by Louisa May Alcott and the tale is continued in other books of hers.

In 1852 there appeared Nathaniel Hawthorne's *The Wonder Book* about old Greek legends. Shortly afterwards he wrote *Tanglewood Tales*. Younger children still read *Little Black Sambo*, by Helen Bannerman; this was published in 1899.

The wonderful fables about Brer Rabbit and Brer Fox and other creatures originated in a book called *Uncle Remus*, by Joel Chandler Harris, published in 1890.

Older children will be able to enjoy *Tom Sawyer*, a book for boys about boys, by the American writer known as Mark Twain.

In the library of my home town there are several books for children by an English writer much beloved by grown-ups—Rudyard Kipling. *Just So Stories for Little Children* is the name of one that will please very young people; two others are *The Jungle Book* and *The Second Jungle Book*. Some of the stories in these books are so nearly nonsense that I was reminded of them when writing about Edward Lear. Kipling wrote other books that were once very popular among rather older children—say ten years old and upwards.

They are in my local children's library too, and they are called *Puck of Pook's Hill, Captains Courageous, Stalky & Co.* and *Kim.* Kipling lived a great deal in India, and so most of his stories are of Indian people and Indian ways.

While you are hunting round for Kipling's name, which is on the "K" shelf, you are almost sure to run through the books whose authors begin with "G" and "H," and there you may see *Grimm's Fairy Tales* and also *Hans Andersen's Fairy Tales.* If you do not find Hans Andersen's books under "H," look under "A," because it may be listed as Andersen, Hans, the surname being Andersen and Hans only a christian name. Already you are sure to know some of the tales of these two great story-tellers—tales such as *The Tinder Box, The Little Mermaid, Hansel and Gretel, Snow White and the Seven Dwarfs.*

You will meet plenty of fairies, witches, goblins and giants in some of the older books for children, but not so many in the books written nowadays. However, there is one good story written in recent years that has a really nasty witch in it and also a giant. It is called *The Marvellous Land of Snergs.* It was written by E. A. Wyke-Smith, who was fortunate enough to have the *Punch* artist George Morrow make many splendid illustrations for his story. If this book had not been given such a queer beginning, I believe it would have become a classic, like *Alice in Wonderland,* as it is very amusingly written and the story is most exciting. My library has it, and I hope yours has.

A picture from *The Marvellous Land of Snergs*

(By courtesy of George Morrow, Ernest Benn Ltd., and Harper Bros.)

Many, many little books are being written for small children, telling of the adventures of rabbits and mice and squirrels and other small animals. They are illustrated by bright pictures of dressed-up animal characters, and all the animals talk like human beings. Some of these little books are very attractive, but

Mr. MacGregor chasing Peter Rabbit

From *The Tale of Peter Rabbit*, by Beatrix Potter (Frederick Warne & Co., Ltd.)

the best of their kind were those created upwards of sixty years ago by Beatrix Potter. These I am sure will always be popular and will bring pleasure to many homes. Your librarian will know them, and she will probably be able to find them for you on her bookshelves.

"Hush," said Christopher Robin to Pooh.
A picture from *Winnie-the-Pooh*
(*By courtesy of A. A. Milne, Ernest H. Shepard and Methuen & Co., Ltd.*)

The best ones are *Peter Rabbit* and *Benjamin Bunny*, which should be read in this order, as one tale is a continuation of the other. My second favourites are *Johnny Town Mouse* and *Squirrel Nutkin*.

Other books for little children that are sure to remain first favourites for many a long year are the Christopher Robin books by A. A. Milne. *When We Were Very Young* and *Now We Are Six* are books of verse; *Winnie-the-Pooh* and *The House at Pooh Corner* are stories about Christopher Robin and his teddy bear, who, though a very masculine creature, came in a strange way to have the strange name of Winnie-the-Pooh, which sounds girlish.

I had nearly forgotten to mention James Barrie and his old favourite *Peter Pan*. Peter has many adventures among pirates and fairies, and he shares most of them with a little girl called Wendy. Some of his adventures take place in Kensington Gardens, London, and so a statue of Peter Pan has been put up right in the middle of these gardens. Peter Pan is said never to have grown up, but to have stayed a little boy for ever and ever. Most grown-up people know the story of Peter Pan as well as they know the story of Alice, and when they call anybody a Peter Pan, they mean that, although he has grown up, he still goes on behaving like a small boy, expecting to be liked in spite of his childishness. They are usually thinking of the bad kind of childishness, such as temper tantrums, expecting to be given treats and never to do anything in return, expecting to be excused even for quite serious crimes, expecting to be able to romp about and play silly jokes. They do not mean that Peter Pan was bad, because everyone knows that Peter Pan was just an ordinary little boy; but they think it a mistake for people to stay like little boys for always, and so it is when that means showing all the weaknesses of a child and not having any of the child's good points. Very good and very clever people are like children in some ways, but only in the good ways. And being like children themselves (though not naughty), they are always very fond of children and very patient with them.

In some libraries you can find the books of Mrs. Molesworth. They are rather old-fashioned, with stories that go rather slowly, but they are worth reading. *The Cuckoo Clock* is about a little girl called Griselda who goes to live with two old aunts who have a cuckoo clock. The cuckoo comes to life and gives Griselda some interesting adventures. Without the cuckoo her life with the aunts would have been rather dull. Mrs. Molesworth's other best-known story, called *Us*, is about two little children who are kidnapped by gipsies.

Frances Hodgson Burnett wrote a book about a sadly overdressed little boy called Lord Fauntleroy, and also a rather exciting one called *The Secret Garden*.

Last of the famous books for children I shall mention is *The Wind in the Willows*, by Kenneth Grahame. This is another book about animal characters that talk like human beings, and it first appeared in 1908.

GROWN-UP BOOKS THAT ARE CHILDREN'S FAVOURITES

Among the countless books that have been written for the delight or instruction of grown-up people, there are several that have given great pleasure to children. The first real English novel ever to be written is one of these; its name is *Robinson Crusoe*, and it made its first appearance in 1719. It is about a sailor who lived alone for many years on a small island, and the story was so well told by its author, Daniel Defoe, that many people believed it to be the true account of a real adventure. There was, in fact, a sailor called Alexander Selkirk who suffered experiences similar to those described in *Robinson Crusoe*. If ever you visit Largo, on the Fife coast of Scotland, you may be shown the cottage where Selkirk lived.

ROBINSON CRUSOE,
FOR 28 YEARS PRISONER OF THE
SEA ON A DESERT ISLAND.

Dr. Johnson, a great man of letters, and the compiler of a famous dictionary, greatly enjoyed *Robinson Crusoe*, and also two other books which have since delighted children. "Was there ever anything written by a mere man," he asked, "that the reader wished longer except *Robinson Crusoe, Don Quixote* and the *Pilgrim's Progress?*"

When you are much older you may care to read Boswell's *Life of Johnson.* It is the true account of a man whose learning and wit were very great, so that he was much liked by other learned people, although much feared by those who pretended to be clever and who were in the habit of giving themselves airs. Dr. Johnson was not at all a handsome man; in fact, he was very ugly in appearance, as you can see by his portrait, which was painted by that great master, Sir Joshua Reynolds. He had a voice of thunder, and could be terribly snubbing, but at heart he was good and kind, and there was nothing in him of which a child need have been afraid. In fact, like all great men, he was very much a child himself, and this is perhaps why he picked out for his favourite books three which have proved pleasing to children.

Don Quixote was written more than one hundred years before *Robinson Crusoe* by a Spaniard, Miguel de Cervántes Saavedra, who led an adventurous life but made little money out of either adventuring or writing. He lost the use of an arm in a sea battle in 1571, the Battle of Lepanto; later he was captured by pirates, who took him to Algiers and kept him a slave for five years. *Don Quixote* has been translated into English, and various abridged editions have been published for children. It is the tale of a quaint old Spanish gentleman who, having confused his mind with reading too many old tales of knighthood and chivalry, starts off on adventures of his own. He rides a scraggy old horse called Rosinante, and is accompanied by a squire called Sancho Panza. Sancho is a country bumpkin and he rides a donkey. The two make a queer sight roaming over the land of Spain, more especially as Don Quixote imagines windmills to be giants, flocks of

DON QUIXOTE AND SANCHO PANZA.

sheep to be invading armies, inns to be enchanted castles, and so on and so forth. He is full of learning, but of all the wrong kind of learning. He makes beautiful, and sometimes quite sensible, speeches to shepherds, innkeepers, strolling beggars and other people, who cannot understand a word of them, and who usually end by jeering at him or pelting him with stones. It is a story that is funny and sad at the same time, but more funny than sad. To enjoy it to the full you need to be able to read old Spanish, but the English translations by Jervis and Smollett are quite good, and some parts you would like to have read to you just as they are, without anyone trying to make it easy for you by shortening them and putting easy words in place of hard ones. Gustave Doré has made hundreds and hundreds of wonderful illustrations for *Don Quixote*, and one day you may be fortunate enough to see a copy of the book containing these pictures.

Pilgrim's Progress was written in prison by John Bunyan, an English preacher, nearly fifty years before the publication of *Robinson Crusoe*. Bunyan was put in prison for teaching religion differently from the churches of his day, and *Pilgrim's Progress* is a story with a religious purpose. It was read by children a great deal at one time, when all children's books were of a moral or improving kind; it was a favourite of theirs because it was not so dull as their other books. Nowadays it is not read by so many children.

There is one more old book of the grown-ups that is a favourite of the children, and that is *Gulliver's Travels*. This was written at about the same time as *Robinson Crusoe* by Jonathan Swift, Dean of St. Patrick's, Dublin. Gulliver's adventures are described in the same plausible way as Robinson Crusoe's, but nobody could ever have supposed them to be true. At first Gulliver is shipwrecked among the Lilliputians, who are people as tiny as rats and mice;

then he finds himself in a place called Brobdingnag among huge giants. For a while he is on an island called Laputa that floats in the air and that can be moved by its inhabitants over other people they regard as their enemies to cut off the sunlight and provide an opportunity for dropping "bombs" on them. Gulliver meets the Struldbrugs—people who cannot die but grow older and ever older until they are utterly tired of being alive. At the finish he finds himself in a land where horses are the masters and men are the slaves. Some of the horses treat him very well, but the others think him a disgusting little creature and so he has to leave the country.

Swift did not write *Gulliver's Travels* to please children. It was really a political tract full of sly digs at people he did not like. All the same, it is a grand story, and it owes its lasting fame to the fact that it is not merely an attack on the few particular enemies of the author, but also one on the whole of mankind. It pokes fun at man's love of fighting, at his selfishness, at his vanity and his meanness of heart. It is, in its queer way, a moral book, and it preaches a lesson that is still needed as much as it was in Swift's time, there still being much of pugnacity, greed, bumptiousness and spite in human nature.

You must not think from what I have said here that *Gulliver* is a dull or priggish book; on the contrary it is an amusing and exciting book. One of the nicest parts is where Gulliver is given by the giants as a plaything to a "little" giant girl called Glumdalclitch. This great strong man becomes dependent upon the kindness of an infant; he has to rely on her to save him from the mischievousness of her other pets and her playmates. There is a frolicsome puppy, the size of an elephant, and a horrible baby brother who nearly swallows Gulliver whole. Gulliver is a vain creature when he first falls among the giants, but his pride suffers many an indignity as

C. IV—10*

the days pass. He is kept rather like a caterpillar in a matchbox, only his "little" mistress, out of kindness, has an extra-strong and well-furnished box made for him eventually. Luckily for poor Gulliver, a big bird takes a fancy to his box and he is carried away from Glumdalclitch for ever. He is borne through the air a tremendous distance, and is then accidentally dropped by the bird into the sea, whence he is rescued by a passing ship belonging to ordinary humans. In describing the rescue, Swift delights to magnify the difficulty the sailors would have had in getting Gulliver's box on board the ship. Although the "little" giant girl carried it about as a toy, the strong swaggering sailors had to abandon it to the waves, after removing what was of value from its interior.

Swift wrote many more books and papers to express his disapproval of things and people, but some of his writing is very savage and rude, and only *Gulliver* is now read to any great extent. There have been some beautiful modern editions of *Gulliver's Travels* with numerous illustrations. The film cartoon that was made of *Gulliver* was nothing at all like the original story, and I should be sorry if you supposed Swift to be in any way responsible for it.

An old novel sometimes given to children to read is Oliver Goldsmith's *The Vicar of Wakefield*. The author was born ten years after *Robinson Crusoe* was published, and *The Vicar of Wakefield* appeared in 1766. The story tells of a good clergyman and his family. All are virtuous to the point of being a little simple, and so they are sadly cheated and ill-used by more wicked people. In the end, however, virtue is triumphant, for, thanks to their patience with one another, they find happiness.

Goldsmith himself seems to have been a very likeable man, though not at all a thrifty one. He adventured on the Continent with only his wit and a flute to help him on his way. In fact, his early manhood seems to have been spent like that of the hero in a famous French story book called *Gil Blas*. If you will read about the lives of the great writers you will find that most of them did very queer things before they settled down to writing. In this way they gained a wide knowledge of life, and discovered interesting things about people and places. They would never have given us such wonderful books if they had been content to work in dull offices. The portrait of Oliver Goldsmith you can see opposite page 268 is a copy of one by Sir Joshua Reynolds.

I shall mention only one more writer for grown-ups whose books have found favour among children, and that is Charles Dickens, who lived from 1812 to 1870. The work of Dickens best known to children is his story *A Christmas Carol*, which tells of the astonishing things that happened to Ebenezer Scrooge, a very mean old man who refused to wish anybody "A Merry Christmas." At this point I will stop talking about children's favourites and say a few words about books for grown-ups.

GROWN-UP BOOKS

When you are passing from childhood to the adult state—say at thirteen to sixteen years old—you will suddenly begin to find some of your parents' books interesting. You may at first prefer the exciting tales of the French novelist Alexandre Dumas, who wrote *The Three Musketeers*, *The Count of Monte Cristo*, *The Man in the Iron Mask*, and lots of other books. Eventually, however, you are likely to come back to Dickens and enjoy such stories as *David Copperfield*, *Oliver Twist* and *The Old Curiosity Shop*. Other books by Dickens that you will like are *Great Expectations*, *Barnaby Rudge*, *Nicholas Nickleby*, *The Tale of Two Cities*, *Martin Chuzzlewit* and *Dombey and Son*. When you are grown up you will probably want to read *Pickwick Papers*, *Little Dorrit*, *Bleak House*, *Hard Times* and *Our Mutual Friend*.   I had read all these with pleasure before I was seventeen years old.

Dickens wrote mainly about the people of his own time and of his own country.   The people he described were, moreover, of the kind that had to work for a living—workmen, fishermen, tradesmen, lawyers, servants, bank clerks and so on.   He rarely describes people of great wealth and leisure, and when he tries to depict the aristocracy, he is usually rather unsuccessful.

Dickens himself started from humble beginnings and had to work very hard to achieve success.   At one time he was a newspaper reporter.   The portrait shows him as a young man.

For tales about more distinguished people it is necessary to read the novels of Thackeray; of these, *Vanity Fair* is probably the favourite.   It is doubtful whether you will care for any of Thackeray's books until you are grown up, and if you then become an ardent reader of Dickens, who wrote with a generous liking for humanity, you may never care for Thackeray at all, as his pen seems often to have been moved by a feeling of superiority.

Sir Walter Scott, the famous Scottish novelist, died in 1832, when Dickens was only twenty years old.   He wrote a great number of very fine historical novels, and many children have enjoyed reading *Ivanhoe*.   For me the most interesting story of Sir Walter Scott is a short episode in the writer's own life.   He was greatly attached to a little girl called Marjorie, who was a constant companion of his until she died at the early age of nine.   He had a greatcoat, such as huntsmen wear, with a pocket or pouch for holding trophies of the hunt, and in this pocket he would carry " Pet Marjorie."   Sir Walter Scott was the author of many enjoyable poems as well as a great novelist.

Dr. Samuel Johnson, 1709–1784.

Sir Walter Scott, 1771–1832.

Jonathan Swift, 1667–1745.

Robert Louis Stevenson, 1850–1894.

Charles Dickens, 1812–1870.

Oliver Goldsmith, 1730–1774.

All reproductions on this page are by courtesy of the National Portrait Gallery

The proper way to read a large book.

Treated with care, books will last for many years; those shown here are very old.

Famous women writers were Jane Austen, George Eliot and the Brontë sisters, Charlotte and Emily. You may meet the work of these ladies when you start studying English literature for examination purposes; in the meantime you might care for Charlotte Brontë's *Jane Eyre*; this is quite an exciting story, in which a horrible mad woman appears at dead of night to terrify the heroine. *The Mill on the Floss*, by George Eliot, is sometimes given to children to read, and so is *John Halifax, Gentleman*, by Miss Mulock.

The works of a lady figure among the best books that have been written in the past forty or so years, but you will need to be much older before you can expect to enjoy them. I am thinking of the books of Mary Webb, more especially of *Precious Bane, Gone to Earth* and *The Golden Arrow*. To read these books is to hear again the sounds of the countryside and be filled with the scented country air. The people described by Mary Webb are of the earth, earthy; and mingled with the scents of rose and honeysuckle you get the rank odours of cow parsley, elder and ground ivy. It is the real country that Mary Webb describes, the country that includes great sprawling weeds, stinging nettles and fungi, as well as buttercups and daisies. I cannot think of anybody else who has written so truthfully of what it feels like to be part and parcel of rural surroundings. People bred in towns do not care for the works of Mary Webb, probably because they cannot understand them if they have only known the country as holiday picnickers.

HOW TO TREAT BOOKS

Books are our best friends, and if we treat them well they will give us pleasure all our lives, and then give pleasure to others who come after us. Little children are very rough with books because they do not know any better, but sometimes an older child is not so

TOO LAZY TO FETCH
AN OLD CHAIR!

careful as he might be. At school he may use many books he dislikes — his Latin Grammar, for instance—and besides writing in this and turning down the pages to save remembering the number of his homework exercise, he often throws it about the room or uses it to stand on when he wants to reach something on a high shelf. The habit of ill-treating books, once fostered at school, may last throughout life. You can see from the state of the books in any public library that many people are not at all particular how they treat the volumes they read. Sometimes the cover is marked with an ugly ring where it has been made to serve as a stand for a wet beer glass or a cup of hot tea. Sometimes the pages are stuck together with jam by a person whose habit it is to read at mealtimes. Torn and crumpled pages are very frequently seen.

A BOOK IS NOT MEANT
FOR THIS

Holes are often burnt in books by people who are careless with their cigarettes.

A real lover of books hates to see a book ill-treated, and he rejoices in a really old book that still looks as good as new. I have a beautiful old Spanish edition of a story I have already mentioned —*Gil Blas*; it is in six volumes, bound in leather and dated 1797. Just

DO NOT LEND YOUR
BEST BOOKS TO THIS GIRL

A NASTY WAY OF TURNING
THE PAGES OF A BOOK

think of the wonders that have come to pass since this book was printed! Queen Victoria was not yet born in 1797; another eight years had to pass before Nelson won his famous victory at Trafalgar. The book was already eighteen years old when the Duke of Wellington defeated Napoleon at Waterloo; and it was

RIGHT   WRONG

KEEP YOUR PLACE BY USING A SPILL
OF PAPER OR A CARD; DO NOT TURN
DOWN THE PAGE AT ONE CORNER.

thirty-two years old before George Stephenson taught the world at Rainhill what his famous locomotive engine, the "Rocket," could do. No steamship had yet been seen on the seas in 1797 and, of course, my books are over one hundred years older than any but the earliest and most primitive motor-car or aeroplane. I cannot tell you what adventures and escapes the six slim little volumes have had in the century and a half of their life.

These grand old books are beautifully printed on a parchment-like paper that has hardly changed colour at all except at the very edges. Inscriptions inside them show that they were originally bought in Cadiz, near the seaport from which Christopher Columbus set sail on his famous voyages of discovery to the New World. Would it not be a sad and dreadful thing if, after all these years, my precious old

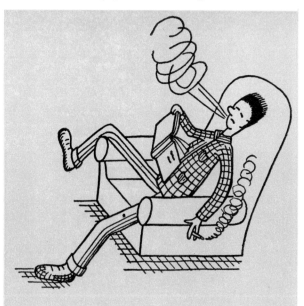

HIDE YOUR BEST BOOKS FROM
THIS YOUNG MAN.

books fell into the hands of some destructive boy to have their pages torn or disfigured by crayons? Many and many are the beautiful books that have met their end after long years of existence by being entrusted to children. Mothers who are at their wits' end to gain a moment's peace from the whining of an infant will sometimes give their babies the first thing that comes to hand, and often it is an old book that they believe to be of no more value to anybody. I am not

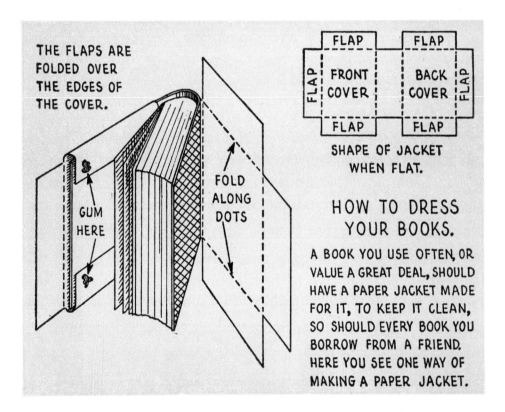

THE FLAPS ARE FOLDED OVER THE EDGES OF THE COVER.

GUM HERE

FOLD ALONG DOTS

FLAP · FLAP

FLAP · FRONT COVER · BACK COVER · FLAP

FLAP · FLAP

SHAPE OF JACKET WHEN FLAT.

HOW TO DRESS YOUR BOOKS.

A BOOK YOU USE OFTEN, OR VALUE A GREAT DEAL, SHOULD HAVE A PAPER JACKET MADE FOR IT, TO KEEP IT CLEAN, SO SHOULD EVERY BOOK YOU BORROW FROM A FRIEND. HERE YOU SEE ONE WAY OF MAKING A PAPER JACKET.

easily annoyed by children, but there are two things that excite my anger: seeing children being cruel to younger children or animals, and seeing them being wantonly destructive or careless with good toys and books.

All books should have paper dust covers made for them if they are to be handled often; and if they are big fat books, they should be

laid on a table when they are being read.   Children frequently break
the backs of heavy books by attempting to read them while lounging
in an armchair or on a sofa.   If you want people to think of you as a
cultured person, I advise you to start treating books carefully right
from to-day.   Get out of that slovenly habit of lounging and sprawling around with a book in one hand and a stick of toffee or a piece of
cake in the other.   Give yourself to your reading as you give yourself to your music or your play—wholeheartedly, and not trying to
do several things at once.   *And do not lick your thumb to make it
turn the pages more readily.*

THE BIBLE

There is one great book I have not yet mentioned, although it is
still sold in greater numbers than any other book.   I refer to the
Bible.   It was once the custom to give every child a Bible when he
was quite small, and, to this day, most children sooner or later have
Bibles given to them. The Bible is great literature, being beautifully
written in a pure clear style of English.   The language seems old-
fashioned now because our present Bible dates from the days of King
James I, more than three hundred years ago; but there are very few
places where it is difficult to understand.   Shakespeare's writings are
not much older, but they are not nearly so easy to follow.

Chapter 8

BOOK LAND

"THERE," said old Mr. Potter, "I've worked my last working day, and now I am a retired man. I've made quite a heap of money, and we can live in comfort for the rest of our days somewhere down in the country."

"Oh dear," sighed Mrs. Potter, "sixty-five you are already. Your life's nearly over. How you'll hate the quiet of the country! I always do. You'll feel buried. In a month or two you will wish you were back at work again."

"Fiddlesticks!" cried Mr. Potter; "I am going to have the time of my life. You see! This is what I have been waiting for this twenty years past."

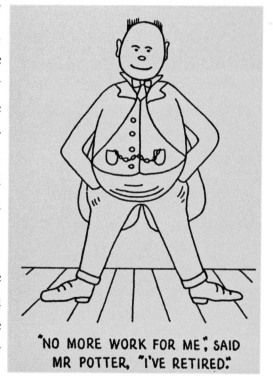

"NO MORE WORK FOR ME," SAID MR POTTER, "I'VE RETIRED."

Every day during the next month Mr. Potter set out after breakfast from his flat to go to the railway station—the same station to which he had gone day after day for twenty years to catch his train to the office.

"Poor dear," said Mrs. Potter to herself, "he can't break himself of the old habit. He's pining for the office again already, I do believe. Lots of men are the same when they retire."

Every evening Mr. Potter came home at six, just as in the old days, but he never said anything to Mrs. Potter. He just looked very happy, that's all.

"When are we going to the country?" Mrs. Potter asked him one evening as he sat gazing thoughtfully at the ceiling.

"Soon, soon, very soon," Mr. Potter said, twiddling his thumbs round one another cheerfully.

"I don't believe you want to go," Mrs. Potter said suspiciously; "You're deceiving me. You've found another job for yourself now, haven't you?"

"No indeed," exclaimed Mr. Potter. "Every day this past month I've been taking the train into the country. For the first fortnight I went to a different place each day. I've been seeing the world, I have."

He stopped speaking and smiled to himself.

"Well?" said Mrs. Potter, "and what have you been doing in the last fortnight?"

"Oh," went on Mr. Potter, "about two weeks ago I found the very place I wanted. It's

EVERY DAY MR POTTER TOOK THE TRAIN TO A DIFFERENT PLACE.

By courtesy of Polytechnic Touring Association Ltd

The Castle of Chillon, Lake Geneva, was the scene of events described in a poem by Lord Byron.

By courtesy of Polytechnic Touring Association Ltd.

Robert Browning yearned for the English spring, but spring abroad can be beautiful too, as this picture of Lake Lugano in Switzerland clearly shows.

ENGLAND'S GREATEST POETS

William Shakespeare, famous chiefly for his thirty-seven plays written in blank verse.

John Milton, author of poetical and prose works, of which the chief are *Paradise Lost* and *Paradise Regained*.

By courtesy of the British Museum

in a big village about forty miles from here. Quite a tiny cottage really, only there's a large summer-house made of two old railway carriages knocked into one."

"Gracious me!" cried Mrs. Potter. "Whatever do you want a couple of old railway carriages for? You're surely not going to play at trains at your age?"

"Oh no," answered Mr. Potter, "I've had them lined with shelf upon shelf—lots of shelves. And I'm having another couple of carriages added on with tables in them. I got two with corridor connections all complete. You'll be able to walk from end to end. And I've had a snack bar fixed up at the far end of the last carriage. You'll be able to have light refreshments."

"Indeed!" said Mrs. Potter. "But suppose I prefer to take my refreshments in my own dining-room?"

Mr. Potter chuckled and rubbed his hands. "There are a hundred and fifty children in the village," he said; "I've had them

150 CHILDREN.

counted, all but three, who were in bed with the measles, and one cripple, who has to lie on her back and can never get up at all."

"Oh!" said Mrs. Potter; "and how many dogs and cats may there be in your village? You didn't have them counted too, I suppose?"

"No," said Mr. Potter, "I didn't. But I had an inventory

taken of all the books. You wouldn't believe it, but there wasn't an *Alice in Wonderland* or a *Robinson Crusoe* between the lot!"

"How many brooms and buckets have they got?" Mrs. Potter asked, waxing more sarcastic than ever.

"Couldn't say," answered Mr. Potter; "but I've had to buy the tables and chairs here and get them sent down by rail. I couldn't buy a single one locally."

"Haven't we got enough already?" Mrs. Potter asked.

"We?" queried Mr. Potter; "oh yes, but I'm not thinking of us. It's *them* I'm thinking about—the children, I mean."

Mrs. Potter put her hands on her hips and poked her face very close up to Mr. Potter's. "Now what is all this going on?" she demanded rather crossly; "have you adopted a colony of orphans or something? You wouldn't be so mad as that, I hope?"

"I'll explain," answered Mr. Potter. "In these little old villages the children never have any books to speak of, so I thought I'd open a reading-room for them and stock it with books. That's what I've got the railway carriages for—see. There's a thousand of the best books going in before the end of next week—new and second-hand. The reading-room's going to be open every evening, Monday to Friday, from five o'clock to seven o'clock, and on Saturdays from two o'clock in the afternoon. I'm going to mind it to begin with, but later on I might get some of the bigger children to help take turns."

Mrs. Potter sat down on the sofa with a flop. "What a man you are for doing mad things," she said. "Whatever have the village children done for you that you should go and spend hundreds of pounds on them? It isn't as if you even know any?"

"It's not what they *have* done for me," said Mr. Potter, "it's what they're *going* to do for me. They're going to keep an old man from getting idle and bored. They are going to help him grow young again. Oh yes, indeed, it's a good time I'm going to have now I'm retired."

A month later everything was arranged to suit Mr. Potter's plans. Mrs. Potter was delighted with her lovely little cottage. It

MR POTTER'S NEW COUNTRY HOUSE.

had a long garden in the front, and just near the path was the train of carriages that were to belong to the village children. The school-teacher knew what was happening, and she was very pleased indeed. The Vicar rubbed his hands together gleefully and said, "Splendid notion, splendid notion!" The children guessed something was being done for them, and they were always hanging about in the road near the end of Mr. Potter's garden. Every time Mr. Potter saw two or three standing and gaping in the road he called over the gate to them, "You *would* like to know what's going on, wouldn't you, HA, HA?" Then he gave them a tremendous wink and disappeared behind the hedge. A moment later he peeped out again. "If you want to find out," he said, "call here next Wednesday at five o'clock. W's for Wednesday and also for Wonders—don't forget that! And it's five fingers you've got on each hand—one to suck, one to poke in your eye, one you're not to point with, one to stir your tea with, and a thumb for putting in the Christmas pie and pulling out the plum."

The children looked at each other and giggled. Then they ran off. But one and all remembered the time—five o'clock on Wednesday, and at the right moment they came trooping into Mr. Potter's garden. The Vicar and the teacher stayed away, however. "Better not let the children see us," the Vicar had said; "they know we want to improve their minds, and they might think there was a catch in your library idea if we were there. You're to be the Fun King here, so go ahead with it in your own way. We'll come and read your books too some day, if the children will let us!"

So at five o'clock on Wednesday, Mr. Potter received all the children by himself. Mrs. Potter was in the last carriage, behind the refreshment bar. She was pumping up the machine that was to make the ginger beer.

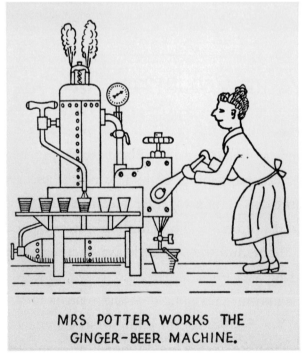

MRS POTTER WORKS THE GINGER-BEER MACHINE.

"Come along, all you young people," Mr. Potter called out, "it's all yours. Go in and have a look at it."

The children trooped into the first carriage. When they saw the little tables and chairs—just like in a glorious big doll's house —they shouted with joy. And at the sight of all the hundreds of gaily-coloured books on the shelves in the next carriage their rapture just left them gasping.

"Coo!" said one, "and I've only had one book in all my life?"

Mr. Potter stood behind the children and beamed all over his face. "There's pirates in those books," he said, "and engines, and aeroplanes, and fairies, and giants. You can go to the North Pole in those books, or to Africa, or anywhere you like. And it's all free for you, so long as you don't spoil anything. Just here beside me there's some little wash-basins where you'll wash your hands when you first come in. And over there you can get a bun and a drink for a penny. Only, if you have anything sticky, you'll have to wash again before touching the books. And no eating while you read. You sit to read, and you stand to eat. You stand over there at the snack bar. This evening you are all going to have a bun and a drink free. Then you can go past the wash-basins and afterwards you can start reading right away—or looking at pictures if you can't read. You go to get your book in the end carriage and then you come back into these others to sit down at a table and read it. When you have done with it you put it back where you found it. If you forget where it was, you go by the colour of the round spot I've had painted on each one. All the greens go on one shelf, all the reds on another and so on. Now for the snack bar!"

The children crowded round, and Mr. Potter helped Mrs. Potter to serve the drinks and the buns. Afterwards he superintended

"THERE'S PIRATES IN THESE BOOKS", MR POTTER SAID, "AND ENGINES AND AEROPLANES AND FAIRIES AND GIANTS!"

the washing. Before long, most of the children were either choosing books or reading them. "What about Margaret?" one of the children said suddenly, "she couldn't get here."

"That's the one who's always on her back, isn't it?" Mr. Potter said. "Did she want to come?"

"Oo, yes!" chorused several of the children; "she cried ever so when she heard we were to have a surprise. And the funny thing was she said, 'I hope it's books—I do so love books.'"

"When you go you can take a parcel of books for her," Mr. Potter said; "I will tie up some nice ones. Tell her she can keep them for two weeks and then she can have another lot."

At seven o'clock Mr. Potter gave a parcel of books to the girl who had remembered Margaret, and then he said, "Now, children, it's time you went home. Put your books back. If any of you want to mark your places I have some paper strips here. Just slip one in between the leaves. Your books will be here waiting for you after school to-morrow, and if it isn't a very nice evening for playing out of doors I shall expect to see you here. Come when you like—stay away when you like. It's all yours."

The children got up to go, and most of them remembered to say "thank you" to Mr. Potter as they went out. Mr. Potter went to the gate with the last of them. He waved "Good-bye," and then he turned back into his garden, where he met Mrs. Potter. She had started cutting some flowers for the cottage. "Well, you silly old man," Mrs. Potter said, lovingly putting an arm through her husband's; "are you satisfied?"

"Oh yes," answered Mr. Potter. "But there's just one thing I don't like. On really lovely evenings the children oughtn't to go stewing over books, and I shan't encourage them. But that means we shan't have any children here on the best evenings. Couldn't we make a bit of the lawn into a playground, and get a few swings and slides and things to attract them?"

"You are going to be a very busy man if you go on like this," Mrs. Potter replied.

"Busier and busier," agreed Mr. Potter. "I'm going to be busier than I've ever been in all my life. It's lovely to see so many children. All that colour, all that cheerfulness. Fine, fine!"

So Mr. Potter's place became the play centre for all the village children, and Mr. Potter became the happiest man in the world.

Every now and then, in the evenings, when all the children had gone home and couldn't see him, the Vicar came to have a turn on the swings, and the school-teacher as well. And both of them borrowed Mr. Potter's books to read. The Vicar's favourite was *The Naughtiest Boy in the School*, and the school-teacher's favourite was *On a Camel through Darkest Africa*.

WHILE CHILDREN SLEEP.

One half of Mrs. Potter liked having all the children very much, but the other half said that it gave her a headache. She didn't mind pumping up the ginger beer machine, but she refused to help in any other way. "It's your idea of fun," she said to Mr. Potter, "not mine. Give me flowers, and you can keep your children."

Chapter 9

POETRY

THE RIGHT USE OF WORDS

EVER since men started speaking to one another they have been improving their language and learning to use it more skilfully. The language of everyday use needs to be clear, and this means that the speaker must choose the right words to say what he has in mind, not words that could be taken for something else; also he must arrange them in sentences that are easy to follow and pleasant to hear. The difference between bad English and good English is that bad English is hard and tiring to follow, whereas good English is easy to understand and pleasant to hear.

THE MUSIC OF WORDS

When a writer or speaker starts using words for the pleasure that their sound gives him, he may make up poetry. Babies enjoy words for their sound long before they understand the meanings, and very small children often babble meaningless nonsense just for the pleasure of hearing themselves speak. There is real music to be made with words, and people have been making this word music for thousands of years. Some word music is just sound without sense, like Lewis Carroll's *Jabberwocky*:

" 'Twas brillig and the slithy toves
    Did gyre and gimble in the wabe:
    All mimsy were the borogoves,
    And the mome raths outgrabe."

Another example of sound without (or nearly without) sense is the old nursery rhyme:

"Hey diddle diddle, the cat and the fiddle,
    The cow jumped over the moon,
    The little dog laughed to see such sport,
    And the dish ran away with the spoon."

A person who wrote nonsense really beautifully was Edward Lear. *The Dong with the Luminous Nose* and some other compositions of his are poetry that might have ranked with anything Tennyson ever wrote had the subject-matter been less absurd.

Lear knew that he was writing nonsense, and intended it to be funny, which it certainly is. Many modern poets are writing nonsense, but they take themselves very seriously, and the result is not funny at all. These poets put sound before sense, just as some modern artists put design before subject-matter when painting their pictures. Unfortunately for poetry, modern ideas are not clear about which sounds are pleasant or unpleasant. The most amazing orchestral clattering and hooting passes for music. Melody seems to be thought old-fashioned and in bad taste. So much the worse for both music and poetry! You will find verses in the magazines of to-day that are neither metrical, meaningful, nor melodious. The poets themselves confess sometimes that their work has no meaning, but is the result of sudden impulse or feeling—what more old-fashioned people would call inspiration. Grown-up people enjoy puzzling over these riddle-like poems, but children prefer clear-cut thoughts plainly yet musically expressed.

POEMS THAT TELL A STORY

In all poetry books printed for children—even the most up-to-date ones—the editor has avoided new poetry, and served up, once again, the old favourites that delighted him in his own childhood. Among these are sure to be the poems that tell a story. A good example of this kind of poem is *The Diverting History of John Gilpin*, written in 1782 by William Cowper (pronounced " Cooper ").

Gilpin was a very respectable and dignified person who met with an unexpected adventure on the twentieth anniversary of his wedding-day. The day before, Mrs. Gilpin said to him:

> " To-morrow is our wedding-day,
>   And we will then repair
>   Unto the Bell at Edmonton
>   All in a chaise and pair."

She plans to have a feast at this old inn. However, she remembers that the family will be too many for the chaise to hold, so she adds, not very grammatically:

> " My sister, and my sister's child,
>   Myself, and children three,
>   Will fill the chaise; so you must ride
>   On horseback after we."

Gilpin borrows a friend's horse, and after seeing his family set out for Edmonton in their chaise, he prepares to make the journey himself. He is delayed, however, by seeing customers enter his shop, and then by his maidservant Betty, who calls after him that Mrs. Gilpin has gone without taking the wine with her.   Gilpin has to take the wine with him on horseback in two stone bottles, which he fastens on to his belt:

> "Each bottle had a curling ear,
>   Through which the belt he drew,
>   And hung a bottle on each side,
>   To make his balance true."

At last he was off.   The horse was impatient of the delay and would not go slowly.   The poet says:

> "But finding soon a smoother road
>   Beneath his well-shod feet,
>   The snorting beast began to trot,
>   Which galled him* in his seat."

The trot then turned into a gallop, and although Gilpin was feeling so uncomfortable, he could not check the horse:

> "So stooping down, as needs he must
>   Who cannot sit upright,
>   He grasped the mane with both his hands,
>   And eke with all his might.

> "His horse, who never in that sort
>   Had handled been before,
>   What thing upon his back had got
>   Did wonder more and more.
>   * Gilpin.

" Away went Gilpin, neck or naught;
    Away went hat and wig;
    He little dreamt, when he set out,
    Of running such a rig."

His cloak comes unbuttoned and flies away, so that everyone can see the two wine bottles, but still the horse rushes on:

"The dogs did bark, the children screamed,
    Up flew the windows all;
    And every soul cried out: ' Well done!'
    As loud as he could bawl."

Gilpin charges a toll gate across the road, where he should have stopped to pay a penny. The man opens the gate to prevent an accident, and on flies the unhappy man. Then, alas, the wine bottles work round his belt and come together:

JOHN GILPIN.

"And now, as he went bowing down
    His reeking head full low,
    The bottles twain behind his back
    Were shattered at a blow.

> " Down ran the wine into the road,
>   Most piteous to be seen,
>   Which made his horse's flanks to smoke
>   As they had basted been."

Gilpin rides at full tilt into Edmonton, where the family party is waiting for him:

> " At Edmonton, his loving wife
>   From the balcony spied
>   Her tender husband, wondering much
>   To see how he did ride.
>
> " 'Stop, stop, John Gilpin!—Here's the house!'
>   They all at once did cry;
>   'The dinner waits and we are tired: '—
>   Said Gilpin—' So am I! '
>
> " But yet his horse had not a whit
>   Inclined to tarry there;
>   For why?—his owner had a house
>   Full ten miles off, at Ware."

Poor Gilpin was carried on to Ware, and the owner of the horse, very surprised to see him arrive, asks why he has come:

> " I came because your horse would come;
>   And, if I well forbode,
>   My hat and wig will soon be here,—
>   They are upon the road."

The friend, amused by Gilpin's joke, lent him another hat and wig. He also invited him to stay and eat, but Gilpin would not stay:

> " Said John,—' It is my wedding-day,
> And all the world would stare,
> If wife should dine at Edmonton,
> And I should dine at Ware.' "

He turned his horse round and galloped back towards Edmonton. Once again the horse refused to stop, but raced on past Edmonton until it was back at the starting-place in London. Poor Gilpin lost his hat and wig on the way, and at the finish of his ride he was no nearer to being with his wife at Edmonton than he was at the beginning. It was all very funny to the bystanders, but Gilpin was not likely to see the joke until many months later.

A more difficult " story " or " narrative " poem is *The Rime of the Ancient Mariner*, by Samuel Taylor Coleridge, who lived from 1772 to 1834. The story of this is not funny, but rather gruesome.

A very old sailor man, like a beggar, stops a young and elegantly dressed youth who is going to a wedding feast and begins to tell him a long story:

> " He holds him with his skinny hand,
> ' There was a ship,' quoth he.
> ' Hold off! unhand me, grey-beard loon!'
> Eftsoons his hand dropt he."

But if the old man does not hold the younger with his hand, he holds him with his eye, which has hypnotic power. The wedding guest is forced to hear how the old sailor, many years before, had set sail one fine day upon a voyage that had had a tragic ending. The ship was a sailing ship, and for a while it ran uneventfully over sunlit seas. Then it runs before a storm into the cold waters of the south:

"The ice was here, the ice was there,
   The ice was all around:
   It cracked and growled and roar'd and howl'd,
   Like noises in a swound!"

Suddenly an Albatross appears.   An Albatross is a huge bird, and
sailors believed that it was very unlucky to hurt one:

"And a good south wind sprung up behind;
   The Albatross did follow,
   And every day for food or play,
   Came to the mariners' hollo!"

The Ancient Mariner confesses that he mischievously shot the
Albatross with his crossbow. This was the beginning of his own
misfortunes and the ship's. At first no harm seemed to befall. The
ship is driven by a good wind into the Pacific Ocean:

> " The fair breeze blew, the white foam flew,
>   The furrow follow'd free;
>   We were the first that ever burst
>   Into that silent sea."

Now, however, the ship's troubles begin, for the wind slackens and fails:

> " Down dropt the breeze, the sails dropt down,
>   'Twas sad as sad could be;
>   And we did speak only to break
>   The silence of the sea!

> " All in a hot and copper sky,
>   The bloody Sun, at noon,
>   Right up above the mast did stand,
>   No bigger than the Moon.

> " Day after day, day after day,
>   We stuck, nor breath nor motion;
>   As idle as a painted ship
>   Upon a painted ocean."

Eventually the drinking water in the ship is all used up, and the sailors become thirsty. Also the ship's boards, for want of sea spray or rain, begin to get dry and crack. There is plenty of water all around, but it is of the wrong kind, salty and useless:

> " Water water everywhere,
>   And all the boards did shrink;
>   Water water everywhere,
>   Nor any drop to drink.

> "And every tongue, through utter drought,
>   Was wither'd at the root;
>   We could not speak no more than if
>   We had been choked with soot."

After a long and terrible time the sailors see another ship. At first it appears very small, but it moves towards them. They wonder at its movement, because there is no wind to move it; nevertheless, they are very excited and pleased, for they think they will be saved from dying of thirst. Then they all receive a horrible surprise. The sun is setting and the strange ship draws quite near:

> "The western wave was all aflame,
>   The day was well-nigh done!
>   Almost upon the western wave
>   Rested the broad, bright Sun;
>   When that strange ship drove suddenly
>   Betwixt us and the Sun.
>   And straight the Sun was fleck'd with bars
>   (Heaven's Mother send us grace!),
>   As if through a dungeon-grate he peer'd
>   With broad and burning face."

Like their own ship, this one had drifted into seas where no wind ever blew. All on board her had died long ago, and the ship herself had become a hulk with the top planks scorched off by the hot sun to leave only the ribs showing underneath. To the sailors it seemed to be a ghost ship, and they saw, or fancied they saw, all sorts of horrible things. One and all turned to curse the man who had shot the Albatross; for they knew now that they too were about to die. Continuing his story, the Ancient Mariner tells how his two hundred companions perished. Eventually he was the only man to be left alive on the ship, and he lasts just long enough to be saved. The experience makes him look grey and old, and it leaves him a little funny in the head. He feels compelled to tell everyone he meets about his dreadful last voyage and that was why he stopped the wedding guest.

I will describe to you a third story poem you may like to read. It is called *The Pied Piper of Hamelin* and it is by Robert Browning, a poet who lived from 1812 to 1889. According to legend, the town of Hamelin in Germany was overwhelmed in the year 1284 by a plague of rats. Here is Browning's description of the plague:

> "Rats!
> They fought the dogs and killed the cats,
> And bit the babies in the cradles,
> And ate the cheese out of the vats,
> And licked the soup from the cooks' own ladles,
> Split open the kegs of salted sprats,
> Made nests inside men's Sunday hats,
> And even spoiled the women's chats,
> By drowning their speaking
> With shrieking and squeaking
> In fifty different sharps and flats."

The people of Hamelin asked the Mayor to rid the town of its plague, but this was easier said than done. The Mayor could not think of a plan. Then a strange piper appeared in the town, and he offered to charm away the rats by his playing. "If I do this for you, will you give me a thousand guilders?" he asked. "Not one thousand guilders but fifty thousand," came the reply. So the Pied Piper went into the street and he started to play on his pipe.

" And ere three shrill notes the pipe uttered,
    You heard as if an army muttered;
    And the muttering grew to a grumbling;
    And the grumbling grew to a mighty rumbling,
    As out of the houses the rats came tumbling.
    Great rats, small rats, lean rats, brawny rats,
    Brown rats, black rats, grey rats, tawny rats,
    Grave old plodders, gay young friskers,
    Fathers, mothers, uncles, cousins,
    Cocking tails and pricking whiskers,
    Families by tens and dozens,
    Brothers, sisters, husbands, wives—
    Followed the piper for their lives."

The cunning piper led all these rats to the River Weser where, in their excitement, they all fell in and were drowned. The people of Hamelin were delighted to be so quickly rid of the plague of rats, but when the Pied Piper went to the Mayor to claim his reward of one thousand guilders he was met with a rebuff. " Our promise was only a joke," the Mayor said; " we will give you fifty guilders."

At this the Pied Piper became very angry, but he saw that it was useless to argue, so he stepped out into the street once more and began to play a different tune. Then—

" There was a rustling that seemed like a bustling
    Of merry crowds justling at pitching and hustling,
    Small feet were pattering, wooden shoes clattering,
    Little hands clapping and little tongues chattering;
    And, like fowls in a farmyard when barley is scattering,
    Out came the children running."

All the children in Hamelin town ran after the Pied Piper, who led them into the mountains, and there a cave mysteriously appeared. Into the cave went the Pied Piper and after him went all the children except for a lame one, who was left behind. The cave closed as mysteriously as it had opened and the children of Hamelin were never seen again. The Mayor sent out messengers to look for the Pied Piper, and no doubt he put advertisements in the paper too, but all to no purpose. The piper intended that the people of Hamelin should learn a lesson they would never forget.

DESCRIPTIVE POETRY

Poetry is often written to describe things that thrill us with their loveliness. If the words of a description make music, we shall like them all the more. Here is a little piece Robert Browning wrote to say how grand it feels to be young and to wake up on a fine spring morning:

> " The year's at the spring,
>   And day's at the morn;
>   Morning's at seven;
>   The hill-side's dew pearled;
>   The lark's on the wing;
>   The snail's on the thorn;
>   God's in His heaven—
>   All's right with the world."

Once, when he was living abroad, Browning was very home-sick and, thinking of springtime in England, he wrote the following lines:

> " Oh, to be in England
>   Now that April's there,

And whoever wakes in England
Sees, some morning, unaware,
That the lowest boughs and the brushwood sheaf
Round the elm-tree bole are in tiny leaf,
While the chaffinch sings in the orchard bough
In England—now!

"And after April, when May follows,
And the whitethroat builds, and all the swallows!
Hark, where my blossomed pear-tree in the hedge
Leans to the field and scatters on the clover
Blossoms and dewdrops—at the bent spray's edge—
That's the wise thrush; he sings each song twice over,
Lest you should think he never could recapture
The first fine careless rapture!
And though the fields look rough with hoary dew,
All will be gay when noontide wakes anew
The buttercups, the little children's dower
—Far brighter than this gaudy melon flower."

One of the greatest makers of word music was Alfred, Lord Tennyson, who lived from 1809 to 1892. If you have failed to hear the music in the poems already quoted of Cowper, Coleridge and Browning, you will surely hear it in this description of a summer scene at the beginning of *The Lady of Shalott*:

"On either side the river lie
Long fields of barley and of rye,
That clothe the wold and meet the sky;
And thro' the field the road runs by
To many-tower'd Camelot.

And up and down the people go,
Gazing where the lilies blow
Round an island there below,
    The island of Shalott.

" Willows whiten, aspens quiver,
Little breezes dusk and shiver
Thro' the wave that runs for ever,
By the island on the river
    Flowing down to Camelot.
Four grey walls, and four grey towers,
Overlook a space of flowers,
And the silent isle embowers
    The Lady of Shalott.

" By the margin, willow-veil'd,
Slide the heavy barges trail'd
By slow horses; and unhail'd
The shallop flitteth silken sail'd
    Skimming down to Camelot."

There you have a marvellous word picture of an animated country scene in which there are waving fields of barley and rye, quivering trees with silver-backed leaves, and a swiftly running river over which little ripples are sent scudding by a fitful breeze. Besides all this, there is human interest; people on a road, barges pulled by horses, sailing-ships and, finally, a lady shut up in a castle on an island surrounded by water-lilies. No prose description of mine or anyone else's could paint the scene in our imagination one-tenth part so well as the verse of Tennyson, and why not? The reason is quite simple. A scene such as Tennyson describes fills us with gladness—with the desire to sing and dance.   The words of a poem sing and dance, but the words of ordinary prose just crawl along and are not worthy of so happy a subject.

I will quote another wonderful fragment of word music taken from Tennyson's works.   In reading this you must imagine that you are standing at sunset by a great lake surrounded by mountains which, together with the castles and other buildings thereon, are tinged with the glory of the last red rays of the sun.   Actually Tennyson was thinking of the Lakes of Killarney, in Ireland, when he wrote this poem. (See plate on reverse of plate facing page 265, Volume II.)   You can hear the thunder of distant waterfalls, and somewhere in the mountains a shepherd or a huntsman blows a horn.   The sound is thrown from crag to crag, and it is as though the whole vast scene becomes full of men calling to one another with horns.   Then the echoes die away.   This is how Tennyson felt about it all:

> "The splendour falls on castle walls
>   And snowy summits old in story:
> The long light shakes across the lakes,
>   And the wild cataract leaps in glory.
> Blow, bugle, blow, set the wild echoes flying,
> Blow, bugle; answer, echoes, dying, dying, dying.
>
> "O hark, O hear! how thin and clear,
>   And thinner, clearer, farther going!
> O sweet and far from cliff and scar
>   The horns of Elfland faintly blowing!
> Blow, let us hear the purple glens replying;
> Blow, bugle; answer, echoes, dying, dying, dying.

> "O love, they die in yon rich sky,
> They faint on hill or field or river:
> Our echoes roll from soul to soul,
> And grow for ever and for ever.
> Blow, bugle, blow, set the wild echoes flying,
> And answer, echoes, answer, dying, dying, dying."

Sometimes you will be made to read long poems or even learn them by heart, but all the time you know in your own mind that it is only bits you understand and like. When I was quite tiny I was given *Hohenlinden*, by Thomas Campbell (1777–1844), to read. It described a horrid battle, but I loved the opening verse, which tells how the place looked before the shooting began:

> "On Linden, when the sun was low,
> All bloodless lay the untrodden snow,
> And dark as winter was the flow
> Of Iser rolling rapidly."

The words go to almost the same tune as *The Lady of Shalott*, and perhaps this is why I liked them. The poem tells how the white snow, glowing with the red light of sunset, soon was made to glow with the red of men's blood, while the waters of the Iser were stained in the same horrible manner. The poet uses more solemn-sounding words than Tennyson, turning a gay rhythm into a sad one.

Another fragment that pleased me was the opening part of the long moral poem known to all school children as Gray's *Elegy*. The poet (he lived from 1716 to 1771) is sitting on the wall of an old churchyard at eventide, thinking about all the dead men who lie close at hand in their graves. He describes the time and place very well in the first three verses:

" The curfew tolls the knell of parting day,
 The lowing herd winds slowly o'er the lea,
 The plowman homeward plods his weary way,
 And leaves the world to darkness and to me.

" Now fades the glimmering landscape on the sight,
 And all the air a solemn stillness holds.
 Save where the beetle wheels his droning flight,
 And drowsy tinklings lull the distant folds:

" Save that from yonder ivy-mantled tow'r
 The moping owl does to the moon complain
 Of such as wand'ring near her secret bow'r
 Molest her ancient solitary reign."

Poets are fond of describing beautiful ladies as well as beautiful scenes; also they describe their feelings in verse, especially when those feelings are sad ones. You would not be greatly interested in any of this poetry, and so I shall not quote you any. Later on, however, your teachers may try to make you read poetry of feeling. Then you will be told about the poets Shelley, Byron, Keats and Wordsworth, all of whom wrote poetry of this kind. You will probably be given the much older poetry of William Shakespeare as well.

Shakespeare wrote several long poems and over 150 sonnets (a sonnet is a short poem of only fourteen lines). He is, however, principally famous for his plays, of which he wrote thirty-seven. These may be described as poetry because they are written in verse. As Shakespeare lived from 1564 to 1616, the language of his plays is a little old-fashioned to our ears. Moreover, the use of verse and of many elaborate figures of speech makes everything seem rather unreal to young people. Shakespeare's plays are often given to older school children to read, but the best introduction to them for younger children is the story book generally known as *Lamb's Tales from Shakespeare*. Here the events of the plays are simply told in everyday language. In some of the plays as originally written there are little rhyming songs sung by sprites or fairies, and even quite little children can understand how happy is Ariel (in the play called *The Tempest*) when he sings:

> " Where the bee sucks, there suck I:
> In a cowslip's bell I lie;
> There I couch when owls do cry.
> On the bat's wing I do fly
> After summer merrily:
> Merrily, merrily, shall I live now
> Under the blossom that hangs on the bough."

It must be fun to be small enough to hide in the bell of a cowslip or ride on the back of a bat!

Also from *The Tempest* comes the sad report about a drowned man:

> " Full fathom five thy father lies;
> Of his bones are coral made;
> Those are pearls that were his eyes:
> Nothing of him that doth fade,
> But doth suffer a sea change
> Into something rich and strange:
> Sea-nymphs hourly ring his knell;
>   Ding-dong.
> Hark! Now I hear them——
>   Ding-dong bell! "

How deep was the water? A fathom is six feet; consequently the water was thirty feet deep.

John Bunyan, who lived from 1628 to 1688, is chiefly remembered for his great book of adventure, *Pilgrim's Progress*, but he was something of a poet as well. In your hymn book, bearing the number 676, is a hymn about the courage needed to make a good steadfast pilgrim. What is a pilgrim? The dictionary says that a pilgrim is a traveller going to a sacred place to worship or do homage. Hymn 676 assures us that nothing will deter the good pilgrim from making his journey. He will brave bad weather, lions or other wild beasts, and even goblins and fiends in order to reach his destination.

The language of some poetry is difficult to understand because it belongs to a bygone age. Already I have said that Shakespeare's verse is sometimes hard to read, but much more difficult still is the poetry of the great English poet Geoffrey Chaucer, who lived in the fourteenth century. Even in those far-off days Canterbury was the meeting-place of pilgrims from many parts. Some of them could tell of exciting travels and strange adventures. In his work, *Canterbury Tales*, Chaucer relates the stories of many lively characters, but I am afraid you would learn nothing from his verses unless they were translated for you into modern English.

The poems of the national poet of Scotland, Robert Burns, make difficult reading to many for another reason. Burns did not live so very long ago—it was in the last half of the eighteenth century—but he grew to be a man in the company of people who spoke with a regional dialect, using words that are quite unknown to people in the greater part of Britain. Known throughout the world, however, and sung at every New Year's party to mark the end of the old year and the start of a new one, is *Auld Lang Syne*. Another small piece by Burns that everybody knows is the song that opens with the words: " O, my Luve's like a red red rose."

Much more to a child's liking is the poem by Burns, *To a Field Mouse*, which begins:

> " Wee, sleekit, cow'rin', tim'rous beastie,
>   O what a panic's in thy breastie!
>   Thou need na start awa sae hasty,
>   Wi' bickering brattle!
>   I wad be laith to rin an' chase thee
>   Wi' murd'ring pattle! "

Burns goes on to tell the mouse he is sorry that men have given it cause to hold such a poor opinion of him as he means it no harm. At the harvest the poor mouse's house was broken and scattered and nothing was left with which to build a new one. With winter on the way and all the fields laid bare what can a mouse do? The poet goes on to say that the mouse was not the only one to go to much trouble for nothing:

> " But Mousie, thou art no thy lane
>   In proving foresight may be vain:
>   The best laid schemes o' mice an' men
>   Gang aft a-gley,
>   An' lea'e us nought but grief an' pain
>   For promised joy."

" The best laid schemes of mice and men——" these words have come to be quoted so often now as to be thought of as a proverb. I wonder how many of my readers knew that they came from a poem by Robert Burns?

DIFFERENT KINDS OF VERSE

From the pieces of poetry I have quoted you will see that all poetry is not the same. The words dance to different measures, and although the last words in the different lines rhyme with one another, the rhyming lines are not always arranged in the same way. In Gray's *Elegy* the rhyming is between the last words of alternate lines; thus, in the first verse we have "day," "lea," "way" and "me" for the four words giving us the rhymes.

In *The Lady of Shalott* the rhyming is between the last words of the first four lines, between the last words of lines 5 and 9, and between the last words of lines 6, 7 and 8. For the first verse the rhyming words are "lie," "rye," "sky," "by," "Camelot," "go," "blow," 'below,' "Shalott." In the verses beginning "The splendour falls on castle walls" Tennyson employs yet another arrangement of rhyming words.

You cannot fail to hear the rhyming of Tennyson, as it is insistent, but other poets have given us verse that may have to be read aloud two or three times before the rhyme strikes us. In his little piece "The year's at the spring," Browning may have failed to please you immediately. You may have thought, "But this does not rhyme at all!" Well, look at it again, or better still, read it out loud once again. If you still miss the rhyme, try writing down the last words of the eight lines, putting the last four under the first four, thus:

> Spring, morn, seven, pearled,
> Wing, thorn, heaven, world.

You can *see* it now, can you not? If you read the poem through once or twice more you will surely *hear* it as well.

In the longer poems of *John Gilpin* and *The Ancient Mariner*, the poet has been more economical of rhyme; usually there are only two rhyming words for every verse of four lines.

Some of our greatest poets have dispensed with rhyme altogether and given us what is called "blank verse." The verse of Shakespeare's plays is blank verse; and so is the verse written by John Milton, greatest of English poets, in his famous *Paradise Lost*, a very long poem which was finished in 1665. Telling, in great detail, the old story of Adam and Eve in the Garden of Eden, it begins:

> "Of Man's first disobedience and the fruit
> Of that forbidden tree, whose mortal taste
> Brought death into the world and all our woe,
> With loss of Eden, till one greater Man
> Restore us and regain the blissful seat,
> Sing heav'nly Muse . . ."

You probably will not care for this at all, but will wonder how it can be called poetry when there is no rhyme. Well, the other ingredient of poetry is *rhythm*, and Milton's lines are rhythmical. I said that the words of a poem danced along in slow measure or in fast, and you will see that the syllables of the words in Milton's poem fall naturally into pairs. In each pair the first is lightly spoken and the second more heavily spoken, so that the words have a kind of te-tum, te-tum, te-tum te-tum rhythm. I will write the syllables in their pairs and underline the "tum" ones.

> (Of <u>Man's</u>) (first <u>dis</u>-) (o-<u>bed</u>-) (ience <u>and</u>) (the <u>fruit</u>)
> (Of <u>that</u>) (for-<u>bid</u>-) (den <u>tree</u>), (whose <u>mort</u>-) (al <u>taste</u>). . . .

Each pair of syllables is called a foot, and each line consists of five feet. Feet of the "te-tum" kind with two syllables, of which the last is accented, are called "iambics." There are other kinds of feet; for instance "trochees," which are also of two syllables, but with the accent on the first instead of the second, as in the word "penny." A well-known line consisting of three trochees is:

(Sing a) (song of) (six-pence).

I will now quote you some lines of Thomas Hood in which the feet are of three syllables, with the accent on the first:

(One more un-) (for-tu-nate) (wear-y of) (breath)
(Rash-ly im-) (por-tu-nate) (gone to her) (death).

You can see now what I mean when I say that the words of a poem trip or dance along. You can get this dancing without rhyming, and Milton definitely preferred to do without rhyme. In fact, he was quite rude about rhyme, and excused himself from it in *Paradise Lost* with the following little introduction. Notice the queer old-fashioned spelling and the frequent use of capitals:

The measure (of *Paradise Lost*) is "English Heroic Verse without Rime, as that of Homer in Greek, and of Virgil in Latin; Rime being no necessary Adjunct or true Ornament of Poem or good Verse, in longer Works especially, but the Invention of a barbarous Age, to set off wretched matter and lame Meeter; grac't indeed since by the use of some famous modern Poets, carried away by Custom, but much to thir own vexation, hindrance, and constraint to express many things otherwise, and for the most part worse, than else they would have exprest them. Not without cause, therefore, some both Italian and Spanish Poets of prime note, have rejected Rime both in longer and shorter Works, as have also, long since, our best English Tragedies (Shakespeare's?), as a thing of itself, to all judicious eares, triveal and of no true musical delight; which consists only in apt Numbers, fit quantity of syllables, and the sense variously drawn out from one verse into another, not in the jingling sound of like endings, a fault avoyded by the learned Ancients both in Poetry and in all good Oratory. This neglect then of Rime, so little is to be taken for a defect, though it may seem so perhaps to vulgar readers, that it rather is to be esteem'd an example set, the first in English, of ancient liberty recover'd to Heroic Poem from the troublesom and modern bondage of Rimeing."

People may agree with Milton in their minds, but few do so in their hearts, for nearly everyone prefers " riming " verse to blank verse, and good poets persist in writing it. At the risk of being classed by Milton as " a vulgar reader," I will express my own preference for rhyme. Tennyson wrote both rhyming verse and blank verse; I like the rhyming verse best. One of the last of England's great traditional poets, Rudyard Kipling, wrote splendid rhyming verse nearly three hundred years after Milton tried to restore the ancient preference for blank verse with his *Paradise Lost*.

Now you know enough about poetry to have some fun reading it and deciding which kind of poetry it is.

Children should read poetry out loud to one another, paying more attention to the meaning and the punctuation (commas, full stops and so on) than to the rhythm, and if they will keep on reading a poem until the meaning is clear to them, they will then read it correctly and the rhythm will come by itself. Nothing sounds more dreadful than the sing-song way of reading poetry, with a stop at the end of every line, whether there is really a punctuation mark there or not. Perhaps it would be best to keep reading a poem silently to begin with, and only try reading aloud after the meaning has been fully understood.

Chapter 10

PROVERBS

MIGUEL CERVANTES, the celebrated Spanish author of *Don Quixote*, defined proverbs as "short sentences based on long experience," and it can be said without doubt that an understanding of many of the better-known proverbs will bring benefit to us all. Boys and girls of all ages learn to take their place in the world from their parents, their teachers, and from books, and these proverbs form part of the guidance that is given.

There are so many proverbs that it would be quite impossible for you to memorise them all. In this chapter, however, you will find quite a number which become easy to remember if you can see how true they are and how often they can apply to the many things which you have to do every day of your life. When you are faced with a decision to make, a moment's thought may remind you of a proverb which can turn failure into success, dishonesty into honesty, greed into contentment, extravagance into thrift, impatience into patience—in fact, one could almost say evil into good.

You may be wondering what all this means, so I will give you an example of a proverb and explain its application to you. Have you ever heard anyone say *Look before you leap*? This is a very well-known proverb. If you are running across a field and there is a small wall at the end with a deep ditch on the other side hidden from your view, a jump which you know will take you comfortably over the wall may land you in no end of trouble, whereas a little caution combined with the proverb mentioned would have prompted you to look first and make a bigger jump, to carry you clear of the ditch and so to safety. The knowledge and application of the proverb turns failure into success.

It is not the intention, however, that this proverb should only teach you to look and see where you are going to jump. It goes much farther than that. It tells you that, whatever you are intending to do, you should be sure that you are acting in a way which is generally considered to be right and sensible, kind and helpful. It is too easy in life to do something on the spur of the moment and then regret it afterwards, because a little thought was lacking. *Look before you leap*—a short sentence based on long experience—a proverb. It is easy to remember and it can be so helpful.

With proverbs it is necessary to understand first their literal meanings, and then to think how they can be applied to all the other everyday happenings. The proverb which I have quoted could also be termed "think before you act," and perhaps these words show more clearly its meaning. What are we told to do when we are about to cross the road? "Look right, look left, then look right again." Our proverb tells us this too, and so we avoid unnecessary danger.

Now I am going to tell you about some other proverbs under several headings so that you can see their value. Then, at the end of this chapter, you will find a list of all the proverbs which I have mentioned, together with some others which you can think out for yourself, and which I feel you will easily understand after reading these few pages.

SUCCESS AND FAILURE

From your earliest days to your present age, and from your present age right through life, there will have been many things which you have wanted to do, and there will be many objectives which you will wish to achieve. Your efforts must always result in success or failure. Your parents or your teacher may have told you on more than one occasion "there is no such word as 'can't'." This is not a proverb, but experience tells us that if we fail to do

WHERE THERE'S A WILL —   —THERE'S A WAY.

what we want to do at the first attempt we must not give up. "If at first you don't succeed, try, try, and try again"; and so we try until we do succeed. After all, if someone else can do a thing, we can do it also.

If we cease to try, we shall fail rather than succeed. What is it that makes us succeed? It is our determination to achieve our objective, the strength of our will-power which will not allow us to give in. And so it is a proverb, *Where there's a will there's a way*, combined with the saying I have quoted, that helps to bring success.

This can well be applied to our first attempts to ride a bicycle. After our many efforts to master the art of mounting the saddle, our determination to succeed is rewarded. But our efforts have only taken us so far. They have been rewarded with success without a doubt, but we have a long way to go before we can call ourselves proficient in the art of cycling. Nor can we become proficient by listening to what people tell us to do or by thinking it all out, though both will help of course in a small way. It is practice that we really require. *An ounce of practice is worth a pound of precept* is the proverb which brings this home to us, and the progress which we make could not be achieved without the practice.

We have to tackle many tasks and solve many problems which cause us worry and trouble. We often think we can deal with them on our own, when really they are perhaps a little too much for us and we find that on completion they are not the success which we had hoped. We would be wise in such circumstances to turn back to our old friend, *Look before you leap*, and decide before commencing our task whether we can do it ourselves or whether it would be better to have willing helpers. If thought is required, we should remember the proverb *Two heads are better than one*; if much manual toil is needed, the proverb *Many hands make light work* meets the case.

Here again we have avoided failure and produced success. But supposing instead of tackling a task which needed our attention, we were lazy and neglectful and decided to leave it alone. Perhaps the task in question involved tightening a loose nut on a bicycle, or maybe it was even something which we could not do ourselves, but which could easily be done if we told somebody else about it. So often we are too lazy or too interested in doing other things that we fail either to tighten up the nut or to tell another person, and the necessary repair is overlooked and neglected.

What is the result? The bicycle is used, the nut comes off, and there may be a disastrous accident; or some other simple repair job through neglect becomes a major operation and involves a heavy cost. Had the proverb *A stitch in time saves nine* been followed, these misfortunes could have been avoided.

This proverb, taken literally, refers to the necessity of repairing at once a rent in a garment which, if neglected, will increase. We must learn to make one stitch do where nine may later be needed. It can be seen, however, that the proverb can apply to almost any form of neglect and failure to attend to an urgent task.

There are other proverbs which are similar to this one, and I shall mention two here. They are—*Never put off till to-morrow what may be done to-day*; and that rather attractive one—*By the street of "By-and-by" one arrives at the house of "Never."* I think these are explained by what I have just been telling you.

The picture I have drawn on the next page will show you that it is possible for a great apparent success to turn out in reality to be a failure. The look of triumph on John's face as he leads home his coveted prize, and his mother's expression of horror as she comes out to greet him, tell their own story. *Sometimes the best gain is to lose*, and John's mother must have realised how true that proverb is. There are many things which we think we want, many objectives which we feel we should like to achieve, but we must use our sense of proportion, or we shall find ourselves in the same unhappy situation as John, with our triumph short-lived and rapidly turned to disappointment.

We come now to the proverb *Necessity is the mother of inven-*

tion, and I can illustrate it for you with a case of success actually resulting from laziness, although its aim is really to show you the value of skill and ingenuity. I am going to tell you the story of a boy whose laziness produced an invention which has greatly helped mankind. His name was Potter, and he was employed to work the valves and taps on an engine which pumped water out of a mine.

SOMETIMES THE BEST GAIN IS TO LOSE.

Because he wanted to play, instead of attending to his work, he made the engine operate its own valves and taps by tying these with string to another moving part. In this way the "self-acting" steam engine was introduced.

Although the laziness of Potter led indirectly to success, we must remember that in general laziness will lead to grave troubles. Our picture here shows us the disaster that befell the warrior of old who was too lazy to see that his horse was well shod before he advanced into battle. The proverb runs—*For want of a nail the shoe is lost; for want of a shoe the horse is lost; for want of a horse the rider is lost.*   And probably, without the rider, the battle in the distance is lost too.

One small item of neglect caused through laziness can bring further trouble and lead to a major catastrophe.   The work that must ultimately be done to effect that repair is much greater than

FOR WANT
OF A NAIL—

it would have been to begin with, and thus we shall appreciate the point of the proverb—*Lazy folks take the most pains.*

Even with the help of all these proverbs, and many more besides, we cannot always succeed, and failure to achieve an objective will make its unwelcome entrance.   Sometimes this failure can be attributed to carelessness, sometimes to lack of judgment, and some-times to circumstances quite beyond our control.   In all three cases we shall learn by our experience in some way or another.

Unfortunately, there will nearly always be someone who will

tell us how we could have turned that failure into success. When this occurs we can console ourselves to some extent with the proverb —*It is easy to be wise after the event.* We know all the circumstances; we know where our judgment failed us; nevertheless, we cannot excuse our carelessness or perhaps our neglect.

If we are conscientious, such carelessness or neglect will prey on our minds to an extent that, if we do not shake it off quickly further failures may ensue. Therefore we must remember that *Things done cannot be undone,* that we must put our disappointment behind us. We must, in fact, apply the proverb—*It is no use crying over spilt milk.* Our failure to achieve our objective cannot be rectified any more than the spilt milk can be saved. The failure must be banished from the mind and the milk wiped up, so that a fresh start can be made. To the careless and neglectful, however, there is a well-known proverb to keep in mind, which will help to avoid disappointments. This, like many other proverbs, is descriptive of one careless action, though applicable to many. It says—*It is too late to shut the stable-door when the steed is stolen.* A mistake has been made and it cannot be rectified. The damage is done, and it will not avail us to take action after the loss has occurred.

If you look at the little picture illustrating the proverb—*As*

AS GOOD TO BE OUT OF THE WORLD AS OUT OF FASHION.

good to be out of the world as out of fashion—you may wonder what this has to do with success or failure. But how can this boy be a success among his playmates when, through obstinacy, or conceit, or some other unfortunate trait, he decides that he will be different?

This does not mean that you must invariably follow exactly the modes of others, but it advises against extremes.

There are so many proverbs that can be applied to this heading of " Success and Failure " that I cannot quote them all. I have, however, formed a few into a little sentence and I think that, from what I have already told you, you will easily follow their meaning.

Delays are dangerous, so *Make hay while the sun shines,* and *Strike while the iron is hot,* but remember that *The chain is no stronger than its weakest link,* and it is foolish *To lose the ship for a halfpennyworth of tar.*

When you find you are doing well, you are encouraged to do still better, for *Nothing succeeds like success.* In success we forget all our past trials and disappointments and feel that *All is well that ends well.*

HONESTY AND DISHONESTY

A quiet conscience sleeps in thunder is a proverb which nobody should disregard. We are all conscientious to some degree, and the knowledge that we have done something which we should not have done—probably something dishonest—will introduce a state of guilt into our minds which will give us little or no peace.

Dishonesty can cause suffering to others and suffering to ourselves. To honesty are linked the virtues of courage and kindness, while to dishonesty the vices of cowardice and selfishness are allied. Human experience teaches us that *Honesty is the best policy*, so take heed of this proverb and you are well on the road to a happy and contented life.

I want to show you now how well a proverb can illustrate the disastrous results of dishonesty, and I will start by relating a fable of Æsop from which you will see the sorry outcome of a mischievous untruth.

This fable tells of a shepherd boy who, just for fun, shouted out " Wolf, wolf! " when no wolf was near to hurt his sheep. The silly boy jeered at the friends who hurried to help him on hearing his cry. A few days later a wolf really did come to devour the sheep, and the boy cried out " Wolf, wolf! " in earnest. His friends, thinking that it was another of his pranks, did not trouble to answer his call, and the wolf destroyed the sheep. The disaster can only be attributed to the shepherd boy's dishonesty in the first instance; and his friends, realising this, applied the proverb—*A liar is not believed when he speaks the truth.*

Now dishonest deeds can lead to even greater disaster than dishonest words. To take something belonging to another is a dishonest deed and, however trifling that thing may be, the act of taking it is nothing more nor less than stealing or thieving. These dishonest deeds invariably lead to dishonest words, which may be used in an attempt to hide our guilt and even to cast suspicion on an innocent friend. "Your sins will find you out" the saying goes, and how true it is. One untruth to hide our guilt will lead to another and yet another, and before we know where we are, we shall have contradicted a falsehood already made. A proverb tells us that *Liars have need of good memories*, but no memory is good enough to save the liar from the inevitable humiliation of discovery. This is exactly what our proverb is intended to emphasise.

How often have we been told that it is rude to whisper? Have we ever thought why this should be so? When Jane whispers to Jill she is generally making an unkind or dishonest remark about Jennifer who is fully conscious that she is not meant to hear. Poor

WHISPERING—
A NASTY HABIT.

Jennifer is distressed; Jill maybe is embarrassed; and Jane, in her mischief, has done herself more harm than good. I wonder if Jane would have whispered to Jill had she known the proverb —*There is no whispering but there is lying.* This is invariably true, and we must realise

that it is not only rude to whisper, but it is generally dishonest too.

Dishonest words and dishonest deeds should be banished from

our lives. These two kinds of dishonesty are often linked together, and if we are guilty of one we may be suspected of the other. The proverb—*Show me a liar, and I will show thee a thief*—can be taken most definitely in its literal sense. A person who is known to tell falsehoods can generally be suspected of dishonest deeds.

There is another important aspect of honesty which I would like to stress, and which is so often overlooked. It concerns the necessity of keeping a promise. No promise should be made which it is not intended to keep, for the breaking of promises introduces mistrust, loss of faith and disappointment. A broken promise is often said to be caused by a bad memory, but this is seldom true. A reputation for honesty can be of great value to us when we come to face the problems of our adult life. There is much truth in the proverb—*An honest man's word is as good as his bond*. So let us grow up to be honest men and women, and let it be known that our word can be accepted, that our promises will be kept, and that our outlook on life is based on that most worthy of proverbs—*Do as you would be done by*.

CONTENTMENT AND GREED

Contentment is one of the secrets of happiness; and striving after something we may not have is the root of disappointment. In saying this I am not in any way contradicting the proverb— *Where there's a will there's a way*. Rather, I am now aiming to show you the danger of greed, which you may be sure is very different from ambition.

By contentment I do not mean that we should be satisfied with little when more can be achieved. We should always strive to reach the possible, but to go beyond that will cause us to expend unnecessary energy and will lead us nowhere.

Greed is a word that usually applies to overeating. There are a number of proverbs which display this aspect of it, but we must remember that they apply to other desirable things besides food. *Enough is as good as a feast* is the first that comes to mind. It means in its literal sense that we should know when we have eaten enough. We may eat our fill at a party, but we should not proceed beyond our capacity in an attempt to ensure that those lovely cakes do not remain for others to devour.

We can think of this proverb in connection with many things we do in our everyday life. We should remember that we should not be greedy, but must know when to stop, as failure to do so may cause trouble for ourselves and worry for others.

Our happiness is not increased by having too much knowledge. The gift of imagination can enable us to believe wonderful things about our toys, whereas the actual truth is often very dull and uninteresting. A little girl will regard her doll as if it were her baby. Her imagination endows it with endearing qualities, so that she is able to love and cherish it. She will not thank the rude boy, shown in the picture, who jeers at her and sets out to prove that her darling is a lifeless thing,

WHERE IGNORANCE IS BLISS—

'TIS FOLLY TO BE WISE —

stuffed with straw. She is much happier thinking otherwise and, if she allows the boy to prove his point, she may know more than she did before but she will certainly lose her feeling of contentment. It is our ideals and our hopes that keep us contented. If these are taken from us we shall be miserable, as many a person who is greedy for knowledge has discovered to his cost. This truth is well expressed by the proverb—*Where ignorance is bliss 'tis folly to be wise.*

To demand too much of anyone will cause us to lose all, and if we first remember our proverb—*Look before you leap*—we shall be careful to ensure that our demands are reasonable and not excessive. Excessive demands may bring the retort—*You cannot eat your cake and have it*—which is a widely used proverb, though seldom taken in its literal sense. It conveys that your demands are greater than can reasonably be met, and a reputation for making such demands will ultimately result in your friends giving you nothing.

Sometimes we are uncertain as to how great our demands should be. A kind friend may offer to buy us a particular book. Although we know that we shall treasure this book, our preference is for something else which is far more difficult to obtain. We ask ourselves whether we should be satisfied with what we are going to be given, and whether we should request the other object which we covet more. It is invariably wise to follow

A BIRD IN THE HAND IS WORTH TWO IN THE BUSH.

the proverb—*A bird in the hand is worth two in the bush*—and so be content with the book which we are to be given. If we do otherwise our greed may lead to our losing our treasure and gaining nothing, thus emphasising the truth of the proverb—*Grasp all, lose all.*

John was to have a birthday in two weeks' time, and as the great day drew nearer his excitement increased in anticipation of the presents which he hoped to get. This was only natural; but he made one disastrous mistake. Instead of resting content that all his kind friends and relations would give him presents which would please him, he lay awake at nights picturing an electric train from his fond parents, a bicycle from his Uncle George, a stamp album from brother Jim, and many other wonderful gifts. He even planned how he was going to spend his day with all these new things around him.

The great day came, his imagination had won over all his other senses, and his excitement had reached its highest pitch. The inevitable happened. There were many beautiful presents; but there was no electric train, no bicycle, no stamp album from brother Jim, and John's disappointment ruined for him what could have been a gloriously happy day.

The moral to this little story can readily be seen in the proverb which advises one not *To count one's chickens before they are hatched.* This is another of those proverbs with a literal meaning and with a general application to so many other occasions.

John's greed led to disappointment, and this will happen to us if our aims are too high. Envy may lead us to think that the possessions of others are more sparkling and attractive than our own; or it may be that familiarity has dulled our appreciation of the things that we have. If we remember that *All is not gold that glitters,* we shall be able to fight the desire for those seemingly sparkling possessions and realise that our own belongings can give equal satisfaction.

If we are content with what we are fortunate enough to have, our gratitude to those who have given us so much will be apparent and will provide happiness to all. *He is rich enough that wants nothing* is a wise proverb and, if we can say this of ourselves, we have indeed reached a state of contentment which can rightly be cherished.

Before leaving the subject of contentment and greed, I want to illustrate to you, through proverbs, how the cause of discontent to one can be the source of pleasure to another. We are not all made alike, and tastes and outlooks differ considerably. We read the books, play the games, eat the food, see the films, which we enjoy and are to our liking. But to another those books, those games, that food, and those films may bring no enjoyment. Here are two proverbs which explain what I mean: *One man's meat is another man's poison*, and *It is an ill wind that blows nobody good*.

The first of these should not be taken in its literal sense, as it is hardly likely that food which will be edible to one man will actually poison another. This proverb is only intended to apply to general

ONE MAN'S MEAT IS ANOTHER MAN'S POISON.

likes and dislikes. The second shows that there is seldom an occurrence which does not bring contentment to somebody. Even taking this proverb in its literal sense, it can be seen from our picture that the man on the left is getting enjoyment out of a wind

IT IS AN ILL WIND THAT
BLOWS NOBODY GOOD.

which is causing misery to the man on the right.

Discontent and unnecessary anxiety will come to us if we start to worry about a possibility which may never occur. If we can prevent it happening, or guard against it, we must take what steps we can to do so.

But if it is something beyond our control, we must wait and hope for the best.

There is a proverb which warns us—*Don't cross the bridge till you get to it*; and another which says—*Sufficient unto the day is the evil thereof.* These two, I feel, explain themselves, as long as you remember that the first is not intended to be taken in its literal sense, for it is obviously something which you cannot do. They both tell you quite simply not to worry about something which may never happen. Remember that contentment is essential to happiness, so take notice of these proverbs, for they can help you almost every day.

THRIFT AND EXTRAVAGANCE

To spend money just because we have it, and do not know what else to do with it, is called "extravagance." To save it until we really have need of something which that money can buy, is known as "thrift." The unwise practise the one, and the wise the other.

You may have weekly pocket-money, and you may from time to time be given a little extra for some special occasion—your birthday, or at Christmas, or when you are going back to school. Your immediate reaction may be to go to the shops and to look for something to buy, determined to spend it before you have time to think what you really need. This is extravagance, while thrift can be exercised by tempering your enthusiasm and using some thought.

Some of us learn the value of money through not possessing very much, while others who have plenty can and do use it unsparingly. We, with limited resources, will prosper if we follow the proverb—*A penny saved is a penny gained*. But to those of us whose resources are almost unlimited, and who spend extravagantly, the proverb—*Easy come, easy go*—applies.

George was a thrifty boy, and he saved his pocket-money week by week to buy something which he had wanted for some long time. But he was careless. Rather than use a money-box, or place his savings in the safe hands of his parents or the Post Office, he kept it all in a purse in his pocket. He was proud of what he had saved, and was constantly taking it out of his purse and counting it.

One day he was playing with some friends in the meadow, and, while sitting on the grass, he decided that he would count his

EASY COME EASY GO.

money just once more. Out came the purse, and quickly the contents were spread at his feet. Before he had time to complete his calculations, his friends had called him to join their game; and his careless outlook prompted him to jump up and run towards them, leaving the money and purse where he had been sitting.

In the excitement of the game he forgot all about his money, and it was not until he was safely tucked up in his bed that night that he remembered it. He searched his pockets, but to no avail; and then, realising that he had left it in the meadow, he fell asleep confident that it would be there next morning. But, alas! His visit to the place where he had had such fun the previous day brought only disappointment. His money was nowhere to be found, and his savings were all gone.

This is a sad little story, because George was virtuous in his

A FOOL AND HIS MONEY ARE SOON PARTED.

thrift, though careless in his outlook. And so he fits the proverb —*A fool and his money are soon parted*. There are very many ways in which this proverb can be illustrated, and whilst remembering that it is to our advantage to be thrifty, we must realise that thrift should be combined with care.

Thrift is an excellent quality in moderation, but in excess it may prompt us to be miserly or to hoard. It is worth remembering that money can be turned into more money, if it is invested in stocks or shares which bear interest, or if it is spent on something which can multiply and so sell for more than it cost. There is always a risk attached to either of these methods of using our money, but without being foolhardy, we ought to venture in this manner, remembering the proverb—*Nothing venture, nothing win.* If we are too miserly, we shall miss opportunities for increasing our treasure.

The proverb—*Forbear not sowing because of birds*—is meant to encourage us to face the risks which we shall be taking with our venture. It implies that although certain losses may be experienced, the actual outcome can still be gain. Take a look at our little picture, and you will see the farmer sowing wheat which he could have made into bread. His decision to sow, however, was prompted

FORBEAR NOT SOWING
BECAUSE OF BIRDS.

by his desire to turn his wheat into more wheat. He knew, of course, that not all the wheat which he sowed would be productive, and he knew too that the birds would follow in his wake, and eagerly take what seeds they could. But these drawbacks did not stop him; he knew that he would gain far more than he would lose. You can easily see the reason for this. The birds are missing more of the seeds than they can take, and there will be plenty left to produce the good crop which the farmer hopes to reap. This proverb can be applied to any risks which we take, and really must take, if we are to progress.

Thrift is a virtue, when it means sensible saving and sensible spending. Extravagance can lead only to poverty and worry. I hope that the proverbs which I have mentioned in this section will help you to remember this.

PATIENCE AND IMPATIENCE

When we long for something which we really want, we can hardly wait until we get it, and steadily, as the days go by, it grows and grows in importance. It is our over-anxiety to possess that treasure that upsets our balance, and causes us to think of nothing else. Instead of being happy at the prospect of our gain, we are the reverse. This state of mind, called impatience, takes from us so much enjoyment that we must do our best to overcome it.

This does not mean that we should lessen our eagerness; for anticipation generally brings pleasure, and combined with patience it will be rewarded. To have patience is not easy when we feel eager, but we have to learn self-control.

Almost every day of our lives we have some occasion to exercise patience, and often it is necessary for days, weeks, or even months at a stretch. We may be waiting for something to happen, something that will be to our advantage; but the period of waiting seems so interminable that we feel that what we expected will never come our way. The proverb says that—*It is a long lane that has no turning*, and although this does not tell us for certain that we shall gain our reward, it does enable us to feel that there is every likelihood of our expectations being realised in the end.

Greater confidence in the virtue of patience will come from the proverb—*Everything comes to him who waits*. Although full belief in this may eventually lead to disappointment, patience will itself bring contentment even if it is not destined to be rewarded.

There is a story of a little boy who used to dig up the seeds in his garden every day to see how they were growing, and it was only when they died as a result of his arduous labours that he began to realise the wisdom of waiting patiently. This could be considered as another example of the proverb—*Where ignorance is bliss 'tis folly to be wise*; and so Bill—for that was his name—planted some more seeds and this time he left them to themselves.

These new seeds sprouted nicely and grew into the plants that the picture on the packet had portrayed, and Bill learnt that the proverb—*Make haste slowly*—gives excellent advice.

To be patient is the hardest of all the lessons we have to learn, but we must school ourselves in this art and never doubt in our minds that some pleasant surprise will be forthcoming. The proverb —*Delays are not denials*—can help us to do this, and it is well worth remembering. We must not think that, if the expected does not happen at the appointed time, it will not happen at all. We know only of the delay; there has been no confirmation, no denial. How, then, can we foretell the outcome?

I wonder if you can imagine what patience is being exercised by Mary's friends in the picture on the next page. Mary, quite by chance, has found a four-leafed clover which, as you know, is something very rare. She was not looking for it, and it was luck, not

— THE EXCEPTION PROVES
THE RULE.

patience, that brought her this reward.

Her friends thought that what Mary could do they could do themselves, so down on their hands and knees they went and the great search commenced. It was their desire for their tea that led them to relinquish their almost impossible task, and not their lack of patience; for they did not know that the finding of a four-leafed clover was something they would be most unlikely to achieve. Mary's discovery was an exceptional occurrence and, as it is not expected that a stalk of clover will ever bear more than three leaves, her find was an excellent illustration of the proverb—*The exception proves the rule.* What a thrilling exception this was!

This proverb is really out of place under the heading of "Patience and Impatience," but my story is not; so I hope I may be excused for including it here. It is an interesting proverb, because its intention is to convey to us that a variation to the accepted rule surprises us and only makes the rule itself more apparent.

"Wait and see!" our mother says. "Be patient!" echoes Father. What words of wisdom these are; but I wonder how many of us realise it. You have proverbs to guide you now. Remember to observe them; and you will soon see how much they can help.

FRIENDSHIP

What would life be like without our friends?   Some have many friends, some have few, but it is rare to find a person with no friends at all—almost as rare perhaps as the four-leafed clover.   Yet because we do believe that *The exception proves the rule*, such a rare case must exist.

So much of our life, both in our younger days and when we are grown up, is spent in the company of others, that to have no friends would be unthinkable.   Although we cannot all be friends, it must not be supposed that those who are not our friends must necessarily be our enemies.   We have a feeling of friendship towards some which we cannot have towards others.   That is nature and it cannot be changed.

In our earliest days our friends are chosen for us, because we have no experience to enable us to choose them for ourselves.   But as we grow older we begin to learn the value of friendship; and so a closer friendship springs up with some, while we begin to drift from others with whom we have less in common.

This is quite natural, because genuine friendship must be limited if we are to give to our friends all that friendship implies.   From the proverb *A friend in need is a friend indeed*, we learn that true friends will always help us when we are in distress, and it is only true friends who will.

You must not think from what I have said that you should limit your friends to only a few.   Your circle should be wide and varied, and you must be happy to mix in any company that you are likely to encounter.   To favour those who are smart and important, and to despise those who are perhaps less fortunate, may possibly lead to disaster.   There is a fable of Æsop in which a humble unimportant mouse saved the life of the king of the beasts in the jungle by gnawing through a rope that held him prisoner. *A lion may come to be beholden to a mouse* is our proverb, and this tells us that there is not one of us who is so mighty as to be above the need of humble friends. This lion should now be ever grateful to the little mouse, but unfortunately kind deeds are not always rewarded by kindness in return.

Where a friend has been particularly generous in helping us, we should remember his kindness and be eager to make some return

A LION MAY COME TO BE BEHOLDEN TO A MOUSE.

whenever he has need of help. If, when the time comes, we have only excuses to offer, he will be greatly hurt by our ingratitude and we shall see the truth of the proverb—*Kind hearts are soonest wronged*. This proverb warns us that even if we have been disappointed by the failure of others to help us, we ourselves should always be ready to give that helping hand to those who have assisted us.

We shall meet people who are full of offers of help and who are constantly reminding us that we can depend on them when the occasion arises, but of these we must beware. *A man of words and not of deeds is like a garden full of weeds* is a proverb that may apply here, so we must not place too much reliance on promises made, for they may not materialise.

Friendships sometimes end in quarrels, but if, like the little boy who is sitting on the step, we are slow to take offence, such quarrels can be avoided and friendship can

IT TAKES TWO TO MAKE A QUARREL.

continue. The proverb reminds us that *It takes two to make a quarrel*. By keeping calm when our friend is irate, we will find that we soon hold the advantage, and his wrath will subside.

Nobody likes to be insulted, but if our friend, while his temper is on him, lets slip a contemptuous name, we must not let this prompt us to retaliate. If we do, we shall start that quarrel which care on our part could have avoided. Just remember this little proverb—*Sticks and stones will break my bones, but names will never hurt me*. Our best defence against a contemptuous name is silence, but when it comes to the use of weapons and missiles we may be forced in self-defence to become the second person who is needed to make a quarrel possible.

There is a proverb which says—*While the thunder lasted two bad men were friends*, and here they are, sitting on a log, sheltered from the storm by a sheet of corrugated iron. Although the expressions on their faces do not noticeably portray friendship, there appears to be no quarrel between them.

WHILE THE THUNDER LASTED
TWO BAD MEN WERE FRIENDS.

The picture illustrates the literal meaning of this saying, but its intention is to show that two bad men, who may perhaps be deadly rivals in their criminal activities, will unite together when a common enemy is on their trail. In the picture the common enemy is the storm; but in reality it may perhaps be the police.

People who are always asking favours, or borrowing and perhaps not repaying, are endangering their friendships by exasperating others beyond endurance. There are two proverbs which can be applied here—*The last straw breaks the camel's back*, and *A bow long bent at last waxeth weak*.

The literal meanings of these two proverbs, together with their application, must be understood if they are to be properly appreciated. The camel is loaded to its fullest capacity; the bow has long been bent; and we have endured to the full the requests of our friend. One piece of straw—the last straw—is added to the camel's back; the bow can no longer maintain its strength; and that one extra request from our friend snaps our endurance. The camel's back breaks; the bow becomes weak; and the friendship is at an end.

Another trait that we cannot tolerate from our friends is a continuous outlook of gloom. Look at the foolish boy in the picture, made miserable by his own troubles, while his friends talk gaily on. There is an old saying—" Laugh and the world laughs with you;

weep and you weep alone." Train yourself to follow the first part, and so avoid losing your friends. They will not have their enjoyment spoilt by the troubles of another.

If we value our friends, as of course we must, we should be careful not to lose them. It is thoughtfulness and consideration that can mould friendships, but they can easily fade through quite innocent words or deeds which, though well meant, may be at the same time hurtful.

Amongst our friends we are bound to have our favourites, but to show favouritism by paying more attention to one when another is also present will certainly cause distress to the one who is left in the background. George may say—"I don't want to play with Jack if John will be there"—because, although he is great friends with both, he knows that when the three of them are together he is the "odd man out" and his afternoon is spoilt.

Two is company, but three is none is a proverb that emphasises this unfortunate and all-too-frequent occurrence. It illustrates a state of affairs which can so easily be avoided if Jack and John were to show more consideration and remember that George has an equal

TWO'S COMPANY –

right to the company of either of them when all three are together.

You can see poor George left far behind, while Jack and John enjoy their ride. Neither of them is willing to take turns riding with him, so that he is always left by himself. A considerate Jack and a thoughtful John realise that three can play together just as happily as two.

I will end with a proverb that will apply to all, whether we be boy or girl, young or old. It is—*Handsome is that handsome does.* We will be judged by what we do and how we behave, and on this our friendships will depend. It is the thoughtful and the considerate that make and keep their friends, so be mindful of such virtues, and your future happiness will be well within your reach.

CONCLUSION

These simple, homely sentences, based, as we have been told, on long experience, have been given to you in this chapter to help and guide you through the life that lies ahead. The virtues of honesty and contentment, combined with patience and thrift, can bring friendship in their wake and lead you to happiness and success.

The proverbs I have quoted and the explanations I have given can lead you to these heights and can assist you to avoid those opposites that only make for distress.

It has been difficult to decide which proverbs should be included and which should be left out; but I hope you like my selection. Proverbs are not always worded the same, but I have taken *The Oxford Dictionary of English Proverbs* as my authority. So that you can see quite easily those I have already quoted, I am including a list, showing the page in this chapter where they can be found. Some proverbs which I have not described follow at the end.

THE PROVERBS QUOTED IN THIS CHAPTER

SUCCESS AND FAILURE

HONESTY AND DISHONESTY

CONTENTMENT AND GREED

THRIFT AND EXTRAVAGANCE

PATIENCE AND IMPATIENCE

FRIENDSHIP

A SELECTION OF OTHER PROVERBS

Beauty is but skin deep.
Beggars must be no choosers.
A new broom sweeps clean.
Make the best of a bad bargain.
Better be alone than in bad company.
Between two stools one goes to the ground.
Better bend than break.
Let bygones be bygones.
Charity begins at home.
Comparisons are odious.
Better give than take.
Birds of a feather flock together.
The child is father to the man.
Better late than never.
A rolling stone gathers no moss.
Everybody's business is nobody's business.
What is worth doing at all, is worth doing well.
Well begun is half done.
A place for everything, and everything in its place.
A bad workman quarrels with his tools.
A miss is as good as a mile.
Discretion is the better part of valour.
He laughs best who laughs last.

Virtue is her own reward.
Once bitten, twice shy.
Never judge from appearances.
In for a penny, in for a pound.
Too many cooks spoil the broth.
A word spoken is past recalling.
Practise what you preach.
Use (practice) makes perfect.
The noblest vengeance is to forgive.
Let sleeping dogs lie.
Live and learn.
Live and let live.
Look at the bright side.
Look not a gift horse in the mouth.
Two dogs strive for a bone, and a third runs away with it.
Out of the frying pan into the fire.
Familiarity breeds contempt.
Exchange is no robbery.
Failure teaches success.
Truth will prevail.
Content is happiness.
He who pays the piper may call the tune.
A friend is never known till a man have need.
A good beginning makes a good ending.

C. —13*

Chapter 11

HELPING CHILDREN TO
ENJOY MUSIC

THE companionship of children has been of infinite delight to the greatest men of every nation at all times, and many tales are told of famous philosophers, writers and men of science passing hours of their leisure with small friends. A great many adult pleasures are the more enjoyable for being shared with someone to whom they are fresh and exciting; this applies particularly to country rambles, visits to zoological gardens and museums and so on. Novelty appeals to children, and much of the world that is commonplace to us is novel to them.

Sooner or later the child lover will try to share with his young friend the pleasures of looking at pictures and listening to music. Here he may find himself disappointed, for not all children can share with the adult an appreciation of fine paintings and a liking for beautiful music. Indeed, the child who can is something of a rarity. We may take Tom or Dick with us on most of our travels and excursions, certain that he will remain willingly at our side, but if we take him to a picture gallery or a concert hall the chances are that he will become restless or even openly rebellious. Why is this?

The facile explanation would be to say that children have limitations, and that child lovers sometimes over-estimate the childish capacity for appreciation, taking them to see or hear things that are beyond them. A case in point would be taking children to see films or hear vocal music in which the love interest was predominant.

This cannot be the whole explanation, however, because many lovely things in art are significant in non-sexual ways. Moreover, there have at all times been gifted children capable of appreciating such things. More rarely still there have been even more gifted children capable of actually creating such things. The youthful composer of music is met with again and again in the annals of this art.

The reason why beautiful music so frequently fails to hold the attention of children is not far to see. The world is new to children in many ways, so that in the concert hall there may be half a dozen other engaging distractions or bids for their attention that entirely escape our notice. For instance, the design of the windows, the movement of the ushers, the decorations and lighting—any or all of these may count for so much to the child as to divert his attention from the music.

It may not have ever occurred to the child that the music was meant to be attended to. So much " music " is provided in these days as a background to cinematograph entertainment, restaurant feeding, domestic small talk at home and so on, that the small child could quite easily be excused for hearing real music yet wondering all the time when the main fun was to commence. The example we set the child in this respect is rarely a good one. In many a home where the radio is turned on for long periods, close attention is given to it only when somebody begins to lecture or to make jokes. The musical items seem to be a signal for everybody in the room to fidget and talk. The child who automatically composes himself to listen to music is the child who has already seen his elders do this at home.

Listening to music is enjoyable only when the listener is conscious of active participation in the performance. Though our bodies may be quiescent, our minds and our emotions are greatly exercised by enjoyable music. Some people react to music by bodily movement. They feel the urge to move their arms like the conductor of the orchestra. They sway to and fro, or tap their feet on the ground. This bodily response to music may be deemed primitive and uncultured by less demonstrative listeners, but it may give us the clue to the child's discontent with concert going. To sit still for any reason whatsoever is not natural in children, and to sit still when music is being played may be tantamount to torture. Music is often a positive invitation to dance, and it may be an invitation to sing too. The disciplined adult can do these things in his imagination without moving a muscle, but the child requires to give physical expression to his feelings. This means that the concert hall may be the wrong place for hearing music, so far as children are concerned. It is probably better to bring music to them in their own private domains where they can react to it as they will.

If, however, the children are taken to a public concert it should be one in which the music consists of short and lively items that do not demand too long a straining of the attention. Children cannot listen for long but need frequent brief intervals for questions and looking around. Of very long pieces of music hardly any are able to hold the children's attention throughout. Any theme that there may be is too long drawn-out and the tone is monotonous. The music children like is full of climaxes and full also of quick changes in tone and tempo. Some of the acknowledged classics offer what is needed, particularly if they are condensed in the form of a selection of the best bits, but in general a programme for children will have to consist of marches and operatic tunes of simple construction and emphatic address.

Children can hear too much of the piano and the violin; consequently there should be liberal use of the lively piccolo, the brassy trombone and the deep bass drum. A single example of the kind of music that might be used to draw the young child's attention away from jazz and swing to something a little better is the overture to *Zampa* by Hérold. This overture, hackneyed though it may be to us, is full of contrast and quick change and is therefore thoroughly exciting to the child. There are plenty of other equally compelling concert pieces that might go into a children's programme.

The bringing of music by radio to children in school is a development of comparatively recent times, and it affords us with a splendid opportunity for discovering the natural response of children to music of different kinds. In the beginning children should not be expected to listen passively to music for more than a few moments. Arrangements should be made for them to play to music or dance to it. I do not mean that music should be used as a background for unrelated activities; what I mean is that it should provide the rhythm and set the pace for concerted and individual occupations. The old-fashioned singing games are of splendid value in relating music to life's principal interest which, for the child, is play.

Music should always be thought of as related to life, though too often it comes to be regarded as something apart—something divorced from the earnest business of getting a living, something of secondary importance.

Children could very well be reminded what a large part music plays in the life of the bird and in the lives of primitive peoples. They could be told of the part military or martial music has played in human history.

I am not sure that it is ever right or natural for children to remain quiescent while enjoying music, but possibly the highly imaginative child can enjoy music in this way just as an adult can. The suggestion made to music teachers by those most competent to speak on this matter is that children should be encouraged to make movements when listening. They can at least "trace the 'shape' of the tune in the air with a finger." (See also *Musical Appreciation in Schools*, by G. Kirkham Jones, M.B.E., F.R.S.A., Macmillan & Co., Ltd.)

MUSIC AND DANCING

Children delight in dancing, and they are often provided with very inferior music for the purpose, but there is no reason why dancing teachers should not be encouraged to use first-rate music for the inspiration of their pupils. It might give more natural life and grace to the children's movements if the music were of a fundamentally stirring kind. Indeed, the teacher might well find her constant exhortations to do better become unnecessary were she to provide adequate music. To use music *merely* as a pace-maker is to misunderstand the true relation between music and dancing. Real dancing is not just a mechanical exercise, but the result of being possessed by joy, exhilaration or some other internal feeling: the proper function of the music is to arouse the requisite feeling. A badly vamped piano may provide the rhythm and speed, but it can hardly be expected to excite the essential will to dance.

SINGING

To sing "in cold blood" before a critical teacher or audience is an ordeal for anybody. Here again the best results will be obtained from children if their feelings are suitably worked up as a preliminary. The music should be used to induce in them a carefree spirit before they are required to sing. They should be encouraged to dance and play first of all; singing should be a further activity superimposed on the others. It should be the ultimate and not the initial outlet for feeling. In a school the time for singing must often be squeezed in where it will fit the time-table and without regard to what has gone before. Thus children may have been reduced to the lowest ebb of vitality before they are asked to stand up and sing. It is in ways like this that the young may be given an everlasting distaste for music.

People who cater for children's enjoyment, notably hosts and hostesses who organise parties, know very well that there is a right time for singing and half a dozen wrong ones. The right time comes nearer to the end of the party than to the beginning. The worst possible time would be immediately after the arrival of the children, when they are still fresh from diverse and unshared experiences. There have been, and doubtless still are, schools in which the children are expected to start the day with a song. A more appropriate time would be at the end of an interval for play, after the more irksome part of the day is over and when the future can be viewed once again with confidence and optimism.

INSTRUMENTAL MUSIC

If anybody is so bold as to venture among children playing an accordion or other instrument, the result will not usually be to his liking. The children will not sit down and listen; instead they will crowd round and ask to be allowed to try the instrument. They want to make the music themselves, for at this stage other people's music is not of much value to them. Yet, if in a weak moment the instrumentalist gives his instrument to the children, they will do nothing effective with it. They will attempt to play, and after making some unsatisfactory noises they will put down the instrument and show no further interest in it.

To arouse a real interest in his instrument the player should refuse to part with it until the children really appreciate what it can do. He should invite them to help him make music. "What do you know?" he should say; "I will play it for you and you can join in if you like." If he can get the children singing, it will not be long before he has them learning new things under his direction and inspiration. They will learn new and likeable melodies from his playing, and ultimately they will appreciate the instrument for itself.

Children should have a long and agreeable introduction to the piano or violin before they are made to study it seriously. Without this introduction they cannot know "what it is all about." A part of the introduction should take the form of merely watching a skilled performer play. The nimbleness of the player's fingers will fascinate any normal child and induce a spirit of emulation. (See the story on page 393.) Then and only then does it become right and proper to suggest exercises in fingering to the child.

To obtain any benefit from instruction or practice, the child must be willing to learn; he must be co-operative and not sullenly resentful. It seems elementary common sense to give children a real zest for music before putting them to musical studies, yet this was not often done in days past, and it is not always done to-day.

CONCERT GOING

When children are invited to watch musicians at work they should be given the benefit of the best possible examples and not be treated to stodgy or inaccurate performances. The difference between good music indifferently played and good music well played is the difference between butterflies and flowers seen on a dull day and the same seen on a brilliantly fine day. Children are too often given music that lacks sunshine. In this connection another point may occur to the reader. Good music is generally presented to children by gramophone or radio, thus lacking the sparkle and visual appeal of the seen performance, whereas dance music and song hits of the day, dreadful though they may be in themselves, are brought to every town and every village by live performers. Bringing music to children by gramophone and radio is excellent in its way, especially if modern high-fidelity equipment be used, but perhaps more should be done in the way of bringing real orchestras and vocalists to them. In the long run it might pay our best interpreters of good music to offer school children the benefit of free concerts in their own school halls, inviting the youngsters to talk with them and even examine their instruments.

If good music is to be "brought home" to children (and in no other way can audiences be ensured for the future), a certain aloofness on the part of its exponents must give way to sociability. The manner of platform or pedestal does not appeal to children.

THE RÔLE OF THE AMATEUR

From what has been said here it might seem that tyros have no business to make music; that if they do so within the hearing of children they may positively turn some children against music. It is, of course, true that no performers have any excuse for trying to play or sing in public music that is completely beyond their ability to render tolerably well. It is, however, not true to say that this rules out amateur playing completely. Much excellent music is fundamentally simple and easy to play well. The amateur should study to do easier works as well as he can. He should not essay to perform difficult things except by way of exercise in the privacy of his own home or studio. All public performances by anybody should be excellent of their kind. In a story I have told elsewhere (page 384) I have shown that there is room for everyone in music—even for unskilled child performers—provided that too much ambition is not displayed at the outset.

Music is not music when the performers must still torture themselves to make it. They can put effort into it certainly, but the effort must be successful effort. And effort is different from strain. Anything that sounds forced in music suggests the imminence of breakdown and distresses the listener. If a listener is continually wondering whether a singer will reach her top note, he cannot really be enjoying her music very much. It is a common custom to try to impress audiences by struggling through very advanced music, but it is a mistaken one. The object of a concert should be to provide genuine entertainment and not to " show off."

When children are made to perform in public, they should not be permitted to display their newest and most advanced accomplishments; they should be required to do only what is well within their powers.

Chapter 12

HOW MUSIC BEGAN

Nobody can tell us when people first began to make music. We know from the carvings and paintings of bygone times that singing and dancing and playing of instruments goes back before the dawn of history. Explorers have encountered people of many races, some cultured and polite, others primitive and savage, but never yet have they discovered a race of people that did not make music.

The reasons why people first began to make music must have been many and various. A shepherd boy might have amused himself with making strange noises merely to pass away the time. In this he would be aided by a twanging stick or a bow-string or some hollow object on which tapping or blowing would make an unusual sound. He might be tempted to imitate the song of birds or the cries of wild animals.

Primitive peoples lived in fear of unseen spirits whom they sought to please with gifts or to frighten away with hideous masks or horrible noises. The unearthly sounds that could be made with hollow pipes and big drums must have had uses such as these.

Much early speech may have conveyed the meaning of the speaker more by the intonation of the voice than by the device of words. Some early music may have had linguistic beginnings. To this day a favourite comic act on the variety stage is speech imitation

by the use of a musical instrument. More than we realise, our
conversation with those we know really well is carried on in mono-
syllables and grunts, and an observant player of trumpet or fiddle
can reproduce much of its sense with his instrument. We laugh to
hear ourselves guyed in this way but, of course, such a performance
is intended to be funny. Done with a different intention it might
impress us in other ways, and we are often stirred in listening to
good music by the almost human sound of some clever instrumental
effect.

We are all able to convey or receive through the medium of
sound waves the different moods of the spirit. No words are needed
to communicate fear or anger or tenderness or boredom. A shriek
serves for fear, a roar for anger, a cooing for tenderness and a yawn
for boredom. Early music was probably an elaboration of such
sounds, and no doubt it was improvised on the spot rather than
self-consciously contrived and written down on paper.

Early dancing was probably the enactment of similar feelings.
Modern ballet dancing consists of a series of movements and attitudes all of which are intended to signify something that could be
put into words.

At some time in the remote past there must have been taken the
decision to separate music and dancing from the mood of the
moment and give them a life of their own. After this the sounds
and gestures could be performed by people who did not really feel
the sensations to which they were giving expression. This would be
the beginning of acting. From very early times there have been
singers and dancers and actors who could produce all the sounds
and appearances of humanity to order, simply for the enjoyment of
those who liked to watch. In this way much that was originally
spontaneous became codified and professional.

The advancement of music since those times has been partly the result of spontaneous creation by peasants or other labouring people, who have given us folk songs and work songs (such as sea shanties) and partly the result of conscious workmanship by learned composers. In the last few hundred years a new factor has entered into the situation and that is science. The combinations and sequences of sounds have been studied so that it is possible to distinguish between harmonious or pleasurable ones and discordant or jarring ones. Some successful makers of music have based their compositions on systems or theories that have very little to do with primary human emotions.

The oldest positive information we have about the making of music and its uses is in the carvings left by the Assyrians. A conqueror returning from battle is shown being greeted by people playing instruments; they no doubt sang and danced as well. From their wall paintings it is clear that the Egyptians used music to please their gods. The Greeks left behind them some wonderful poetry and stage plays, and it is known from their writings that they used music to heighten the effect of dramatic performances. The early Romans were conquering barbarians with little taste for the fine arts, but they approved of military music. From remotest antiquity warriors advanced against the enemy in step to make their tread sound heavier and more fearsome. The drum was used to reinforce the sound and also to keep time for the marching men. The blaring of mighty trumpets was a later addition, but the Romans had trumpets. That the trumpet is a very old invention indeed we know from Biblical records: we read that the walls of Jericho were overturned by the sound of trumpets.

At the commencement of the Christian era we can be sure that music was already being used to intimidate enemies, soothe babies, placate angry tyrants, and charm snakes.   We can feel sure that it was also used by boy to gain the favourable attention of girl.   Needless to say, the music for all these different occasions would be of widely contrasting kinds.

With the beginning of Christian worship yet another human mood began to seek musical expression and we read that towards the end of the fourth century A.D. St. Ambrose, Bishop of Milan, made a collection of the tunes used in singing the Psalms and published an edited edition; this is still used in Milan.   About 200 years later Pope Gregory felt that there was again a need to overhaul church music and impose a properly edited system on worshippers throughout the Christian world.   The system of St. Ambrose had not been followed everywhere: sometimes it had suffered changes for the worse, but elsewhere it had been improved.   The new Gregorian system admitted the real improvements, and it still forms the basis of liturgical music.

From about this time there came into being a clear distinction between secular music—the music of fun and·games and other purely human affairs—and sacred music.   Also, from the tenth to the twelfth century, there developed the system we know to-day for setting down notes in writing on parallel straight lines.   Until such a system came into being it was difficult to make a permanent record of music that had been sung or played, and much music had to be reproduced from memory.   Not that there was any shortage of people to keep alive the memory of popular songs and airs, for this was the age of the wandering minstrels, the troubadours, the bards and the meistersingers.   Such people went from place to place entertaining the nobility and anybody else who would pay them for their performance.   They went alone or as a company, and sometimes they were assisted by jugglers, acrobats or actors.   Music was made for its own sake or to be an accompaniment for a dance, a dramatic story, or a recital of love. Princes or kings might give permanent employment to a clever minstrel or instrumentalist.

Through the greater part of recorded history the musician has had to depend for his livelihood either on a princely patron or on the church. In the service of the church he would be organist and choir-master. Some very great musicians moved about from one kind of employment to the other, and to these we owe much wonderful music both secular and sacred.

In princely palaces the musicians were often treated as inferiors and made to eat with the humblest of the retainers. It was not always like this, however. A special favourite might be welcomed by his patron as friend and equal and be shown many favours.

In the story which follows this chapter I have tried to give you some idea of what it might have been like to depend for a living on one's talent for making music. It is a made-up story and not a true one.

Chapter 13

THE KING WHO LOVED MUSIC

ONCE upon a time there lived a king who was very fond of pretty music, and in the spring-time he used to listen with great joy to the singing of the birds. All round the king's palace there were beautiful trees, where the birds made love and built their nests. From early in the morning the air was full of their happy flutings and trillings.

One day the king heard the voice of a bird he had never heard before. It was louder and happier than any of the other bird voices.

"Catch me that bird," the king said to his soldiers; "it may go away and never come back any more. I want to have it so that I can keep it for always."

The soldiers of the king caught the bird and put it in a cage; the king kept the cage

"SING NICELY, STUPID BIRD!"
BELLOWED THE ANGRY KING.

354

in his palace quite close to his favourite throne. But once it was inside the cage the bird did not sing so gaily. It sang only sad complaining songs, because it wanted to be free again.

" Sing nicely, stupid bird! " the king bellowed in a rage one day. The bird was so frightened then that it stopped singing altogether.

"Very well, then," roared the king, angrier than ever, "I will have your head chopped off and you shall be put in a pie." Saying these words, he ran from the room to find the butcher and the cook.

While the king was out of the room, the king's son, a handsome little prince ten years old, crept from behind some curtains where he had been hiding and went to the cage of the imprisoned bird. "Poor bird," he said, " I will let you go, and then you can sing happily again." The little prince opened the door of the cage and the bird flew away. Then the little prince shut the cage again and went out into the royal grounds to play.

When the king came back with his butcher and his cook he found that the bird had escaped, and he was nearly mad with rage. He threw the cage on the floor and jumped on it until it was squashed flat. He never guessed that anybody had let the bird escape.

Next day the king's temper was better again, and he hoped that the golden-voiced bird might return to the royal trees and sing as it had sung in the days before his soldiers had taken it prisoner. But the bird was afraid of being caught again, so it flew hundreds and hundreds of miles away, and it never came back.

You would think that after this the king would have learnt his lesson, and would have treated music-makers kindly, but he was a silly king and a cruel one, and he went on behaving badly to everybody.

One day a young man called at the back door of the royal

palace and said, "Does His Majesty want any music to-day? I make up pretty songs and sing them to my guitar."

The servant who had opened the door to the young man said, "Wait here while I go and ask the king."

When the king heard that a young music-maker was at the door, he jumped with joy and shouted, "Certainly I want music—bring him here!"

So the servant went to fetch the young man, who was still patiently waiting at the back door of the palace. Very soon the young man was making his bow before the king.

THE YOUNG MAN SANG SOME OF HIS BEST SONGS.

"Sing a happy song," the king commanded, "and if you do it well I will make you the court musician."

The young man sang some of his best songs, and the king was very pleased with him. "Find yourself a house near here," he commanded, "and come to sing three new songs to me every day at ten o'clock in the morning."

"Very well, Your Majesty," the young man answered, and away he went to look for a house. That same afternoon he found a house big enough for himself and his wife and ten small children, so they all moved in, and the very next day the young man went to the palace at ten o'clock and sang three more songs to the king.

Now the king was wondering what he ought to pay the young man for singing to him so nicely. Being a mean king, as well as a silly king and a cruel king, he did not want to pay much, so when the young man came to sing songs for the third time the king

HE FOUND A HOUSE BIG ENOUGH FOR HIM- SELF, HIS WIFE AND TEN SMALL CHILDREN.

pretended that he did not enjoy them very much. They were very beautiful songs, and they made the king feel very happy inside, but the king's face wore a frown.

Every day the king listened with a frown to the young man's singing. The young man was very worried, because he thought the king was displeased with him. "I shall not get much money for my wages at the end of the week," he thought.

On Saturday the king handed the young music-maker an envelope containing his first week's wages. Really, the music had been worth quite ten pounds, but the king put only five pounds in the envelope. The young man felt that the king had not been pleased with him, so when he saw five pounds in the envelope he was overjoyed, and he not only thanked the king very warmly, but kissed his hand.

All next week the young man sang as beautifully as ever, but the mean old king pretended that the songs were bad and, at the end of the week, he put only three pounds into the pay envelope of the music-maker. This was not nearly enough money to pay the rent of the music-maker's house and the bills of his baker and his butcher and his grocer and his milkman.

At the end of the third week the cunning old king put only one pound into the music-maker's pay envelope, and so the young man went down on his knees in front of him and said, "Pardon my impertinence, Your Majesty, but I cannot feed my wife and children, nor yet keep a roof over their heads, if you do not give me more money."

"Fool!" said the king. "Do you think I mind about your wife and children? You ought not to have any. Your business is to make music. How can you make music if you keep a grumbling wife and a lot of whining brats? Get rid of them all. I pay you to serve me. To make good music you must be happy. How can you be happy if you give to other worthless creatures all the money I give to you?"

The young man bowed even lower. "Pardon me again, Your Majesty," he said; "but it makes me happy to see others happy. I must have the happy faces of my wife and children round me, else I cannot make good music."

"You are even a worse fool than I took you to be at first," the king answered. "Do you not know that the bird which sings loudest and sweetest is the one that uses other birds' wives and other birds' nests? It puts its eggs in the nests of its neighbours, and they must hatch the fledglings and go to the trouble of feeding them."

The young music-maker bowed so low at last that his head touched the ground at the king's feet. "A thousand million pardons, Your Majesty," he said humbly; "but I think Your Majesty is wrong. The bird you mention does not sing sweetly at all; it is called the Cuckoo, and it has a silly monotonous song that just goes 'Cuck-oo, Cuck-oo, Cuck-oo' all the time. And in June its voice breaks so that it cannot even say 'Cuck-oo.' Instead it says, 'Cuck-gurgle, Cuck-gurgle, Cuck-gurgle' or only 'Cuck, Cuck, Cuck.' It is the good mother birds and the good father birds that sing best, if it please Your Majesty."

WAY OUT FROM ROYAL PALACE

"GET UP AND GET OUT !"
ROARED THE KING.

"It doesn't please me at all, and I won't be lectured to by a young popinjay," the king roared. "I pay you to cheer me up with song, and you have the impudence to come here with your moaning whine about a starving wife and family. Get up and get out!"

The angry king actually kicked the young man, who was still bowing in front of him. Then the young man knew that he would

"SING ME A SONG
MR MUSIC-MAKER" SAID THE PRINCE.

never be wanted to sing again, so he ran out of the palace, nearly crying. On the way to his home he passed the young prince who was playing in the palace grounds.

"Sing me a song, Mr. Music-Maker," called out the little prince.

"Alas!" answered the music-maker. "I cannot sing to-day. I have been told by the king, your father, that I am dull company, so I am going away never to return."

"Oh, goodness me," the young prince exclaimed, stamping his foot. "Has the king been spoiling his own fun again by being mean and cruel? Listen! When I am king everything will be different. I am going to pay for my fun by being nice to the people who help me to enjoy myself. But enough of all this: I want you to sing for me now."

The little prince went to a hole in the trunk of a big tree and pulled out his money-box. "I hide it there," he said, "so that the king cannot help himself to what the Queen and the Prime Minister give me. He is mean enough even to rob his own child's money-box; think of that! Well, now I am giving a concert in the royal nursery. All the children in the palace—the children of the nobles and of the ladies-in-waiting—are going to be in my concert, but I haven't any music for them, not any *new* music, I mean. I want a children's opera with band music and dozens of lively songs. Do you think you could make some up?"

While he was speaking, the young prince shook coin after coin out of his money-box until there were twenty big gold pieces, which he arranged in a row. They were worth quite one hundred pounds. "I will pay you that for your trouble," the young prince went on. "Will it be enough?"

"Your Highness!" gasped the poor music-

THE YOUNG PRINCE SHOOK 20 GOLD PIECES OUT OF HIS MONEY BOX.

maker in great surprise, "I could never take all that money from you!"

"Why not?" the young prince countered, shaking his money-box. "There's plenty more where that came from. Listen!"

The poor music-maker heard the cheerful tinkle of some more gold coins in the little prince's money-box. "Very well, Your Highness," the poor music-maker said at last, putting the gold coins in his pocket, "you shall have the best music that was ever written in the whole world. You shall have music fit for angels."

"How can you give it to me and show me how it ought to go?" the young prince asked.

"I will teach the parts to my own children and to my children's

THE MUSIC-MAKER'S
CHILDREN PRACTICE
FOR THE PRINCE'S CONCERT.

friends, and I will make all the poor musicians I can find into a band. Then, when I have made my children's opera a success, I will find a big barn where Your Highness can come with your friends to hear it performed."

"That is splendid!" the little prince exclaimed; "and if it pleases me you shall have twenty more gold pieces. A good workman is worth his hire; I learnt that in my first reading book, and it is something everyone with a lot of money ought to remember."

So the young music-maker, who was one of the best music-makers ever heard, became a secret follower of the little prince, and the king, who was much richer than his son, had to go without a music-maker because he was so mean. The king tried one or two music-makers of the kind who enjoyed themselves at other people's expense, like the Cuckoo, but these wicked men made only wicked music, and it filled the king's head with wicked thoughts, so that he did more and more wicked things. At last he grew frightened of his own wickedness, so he stopped listening to any more music-makers.

When the king became very old he sent for his son, who was now a strong and handsome young man.

"Listen, Son," he said, "I am old and miserable. I want good music to cheer me up. A long time ago I had a singer here who gave me wonderful music, but I was mean to him. I paid him too little money. Worse still I gave him some bad advice. I told him that the way to be happy was to spend his money on himself. He had a wife and family; I told him to turn them out of doors so that they should not be always bothering him for food and new clothes. I want you to find that man for me if you can, and I want you to tell him that I need his music again. Tell him that I will let him ask his own price this time. And if any butchers and bakers and landlords have been so cruel to him as to let him starve or suffer from the cold, just because he did not pay their bills, bring them to me too, for they deserve punishing. His music was so wonderful that they should have been glad to let him have food and drink in exchange for his songs."

"Forget about the butchers and bakers and people, Father," answered the young prince, "many of them are dull, stupid folk who do not have any use for music. Others again would rather be paid in money by the good poets and musicians so that they can buy the rubbish written by bad poets and musicians; you cannot punish them for being dull. I will find your music-maker for you if he is not dead by now."

"Oh, I pray that it

THE KING ASKS
THE MUSIC-MAKER
TO FORGIVE HIM.

may not be so," the old king cried, clasping his hands earnestly together; "I should never forgive myself if that poor man died, or if he took my advice and let his family die. He was quite right to want to be happy in his own way, for his way was a better one than mine."

The prince was still having music made for him by the man who had once written a children's opera for him, so he knew all the time that this man was not dead or even poor. After pretending to search for him for a week, and keeping his old father in a state of great anxiety, he at last brought him into the royal presence. The repentant old man fell on his knees at the feet of the music-maker and said, "Forgive me. You were right and I was wrong."

The music-maker forgave the king, and for the few remaining years of the old man's life he sang and played wonderful music for him. But the best music of all he saved for the prince, who had for so long been his true friend.

Chapter 14

SOME GREAT COMPOSERS

THE music we hear to-day comes from so many different music-makers—or composers as they are called—that I could not possibly tell you about every one. These composers were not equally famous in their own time; nor are they all remembered with equal affection by the music-loving public. Some composers stand out among their fellow composers in the way that bright stars stand out among a lot of less bright ones.

The most memorable composers are comparatively few in number so perhaps it would be a good idea to tell you about these great ones first of all, leaving the less famous ones to be mentioned in a later chapter.

Johann Sebastian Bach, who was a German and lived all his life in Germany, was born in 1685 and died in 1750. He is known chiefly for his love of weaving several tunes together, and it is not usually difficult to distinguish his music from that of other composers, though a few composers, notably Handel and Scarlatti, have written some music that could be mistaken for Bach's. Bach believed that "the ultimate end and aim of music should be only to the Glory of God and the recreation of the mind." He was a good and deeply religious man, who managed to follow his vocation of organist and composer without becoming unduly poor or unduly eccentric in his behaviour. He did lose one post as organist "for harbouring a strange maiden" in his church, but he was not wasting his time with her, for, in reality, he was only teaching her to sing. He married her eventually. After her death he married again. Altogether he had twenty children, and the surprising thing is not that he was poor, but that he was not altogether distracted with worry. In his own time he was not much appreciated, except by fellow musicians. At sixty-five he fell ill, went blind and died. He was put in an inconspicuous grave and forgotten, his poor wife meanwhile having been left destitute. Very little of Bach's noble music was printed, and consequently much of it has been lost. The famous *Brandenburg Concertos*, among the loveliest and liveliest music ever written, were reckoned to be worth fivepence each when valued with other goods belonging to the Markgraf of Brandenburg. These, however, were saved, and altogether there is a good deal of Bach's music treasured up to to-day. The Markgraf had been an understanding man with a liking for fine music. He goes down in history as one of those who helped a great genius to flower and give of its best. He paid Bach to provide music for the delight of himself and his friends. We do not know the name of the valuer who believed Bach's manuscripts to be worth only fivepence apiece. He is much to be pitied for having been so insensitive to the master's wonderful compositions.

Handel, who was born in Germany in the same year as Bach and lived to 1759, experienced his most serious troubles in his youth. His father disapproved of music and is said to have burnt his son's toy instruments. Thereupon Handel, still only a little boy, smuggled a clavier (a keyboard instrument something like a piano) into an attic, and went on with his studies and practising in secret. Eventually his father let him have his way, and he became known as an infant prodigy. After beginning his career as an organist in Hamburg, he went to Italy, where he met Domenico Scarlatti, who was very impressed by his playing of the harpsichord. Scarlatti himself had written some wonderful music for the harpsichord, very quick and elaborate music, rather like Bach's. Handel eventually obtained another post in Germany, but was able to enjoy long holidays, during which he visited England. Here he wrote a successful opera, and eventually he came to live in London. He made an enemy of a rival musician whose operas were being sung by a very popular lady called Faustina. Handel found a lady called Cuzzoni who could do justice to his own great works, and he was unwise enough to write an opera for both ladies. I am sorry to say that on the stage they fought one another and tore out each other's hair. The audience was highly delighted! Handel ventured to stage his own works, hiring a theatre for the purpose, but he lost all his savings. Several times he was to lose all his money in attempting to find favour with the public, and some of his best work was sold to pay off his debts. One of the best and most famous compositions that has ever been written to meet the demands of creditors was Handel's *Messiah*—an immense oratorio. It was written in twenty-three days. Handel continued to write oratorios, and was eventually immensely successful, even financially. But like other musicians who have overstrained their eyes by writing music, he eventually became ill and blind. In a comparatively short while he died, and was buried with much honour and great public mourning at Westminster Abbey in London.

Joseph Haydn, an Austrian, lived from 1732 to 1809 and became known as the "Father of Symphony," because, unlike his predecessors, he wrote for the orchestra rather than for human voices, and favoured the long three-movement form of composition known to-day as the symphony. Generally a symphony begins with a bold, lively movement, goes on to a slow one, and ends with another noisy and cheerful one, but Haydn allowed himself to vary the pattern at times. Also he favoured simple melodies instead of the elaborate weaving of several tunes into a single whole, which was Bach's favourite method of composition. Haydn was happy and successful and full of fun. Once, to remind his employer that neither he nor his orchestra had had any holiday, he wrote a symphony in which the players became fewer and fewer until only two violins were left. As the musicians finished their part of the performance they blew out their lamps, rolled up their music and walked off the stage. The audience was very surprised, but Haydn's employer saw the point and good-naturedly granted everyone a holiday.

Haydn also noticed that over-fed members of his audience were apt to doze off and snore during the slow quiet movement of the symphony, so he composed the "Surprise" symphony, in which there is a sudden change from *pianissimo* (or very soft) in the slow movement to *fortissimo* (or very loud). The full blast of the orchestra came as a huge surprise, waking all the snorers up, and one man is said to have awakened from his dreams shouting, "Don't come in!"

Haydn visited England, where he was a great success. He returned to Vienna, however, and there he wrote his last work, an oratorio for orchestra and voices, called *The Creation*. He died at a ripe old age, much loved by all.

Mozart, like Handel, was an infant prodigy, and all his life he was acclaimed with joy by every kind of audience and richly applauded; but everyone seems to have taken what pleasure they could from him without ever thinking of rewarding him. His loyalty to his Emperor and to his family cost him the loss of several good opportunities. **Born in Austria** in 1756, he died in 1791, and was buried with two other people in a pauper's grave. None of the people he had pleased cared whether he was happy in his life or honoured in his death, though he was not without friends and admirers among other musicians.

Mozart's music is tuneful and lively, and it was written to give every kind of instrument a chance to display its charms. His operas, moreover, provide some of the loveliest opportunities for good singing. Much of his music is easily recognisable for a peculiar mannerism of its own, just as the music of Bach is recognisable for its own individual qualities.

Those who have written about Mozart seem to think that his failure to earn a living was a matter of deficient personality. It was not in his nature to drive hard bargains with people. He might have demanded his rights but, instead, he wrote begging letters, asking for financial assistance as though for a favour. The more men smile upon some kinds of employer the more they are regarded as simpletons and cheated behind their backs.

Beethoven, who lived from 1770 to 1827, was another German, but of an altogether different character from Mozart. He was a real "bear" of a man, and was treated very much better than the genial Mozart, possibly for this reason that he made people a little afraid of him. In one royal house where he was employed the prince actually ordered the servants to answer the bell of Beethoven's room before anyone else's because his temper was so bad.

He taught pupils, and they loved him, although he often smacked them and tore up their music. At one time he lived in lodgings, but he was such an awkward lodger that landladies were glad to be rid of him. He would think of an idea for a tune in the bathroom and run off to write it down, leaving the water to pour all over the floor and even down the stairs.   At one place he threw eggs at the head of the cook to teach her to give him better ones.   He would start playing and roaring before dawn, to the annoyance of everyone.   He swore horribly when interrupted, and he told rude stories.   But with all his eccentricities, he wrote the grandest music that has ever been heard.   He carried on the composition of symphonies where Haydn left off, and he wrote nine that have never been surpassed and are never likely to be.   He called himself a poet in sound.   Many ideas he thought were too great to be expressed in words, even in the words of a genius like Shakespeare, but nothing seemed to him too sublime to be expressed in music.

Beethoven's bad temper can be attributed partly to the fact that he became totally deaf at an early age.   This was a dreadful misfortune for a musician, but, fortunately, he could hear his music in his mind and did not need to hear it with his ears in order to make it come right as he wrote it down.   Most composers can do this, but Meyerbeer was an exception.   He had to write his music while sitting at a piano.   He rented three flats, occupying the middle one and keeping the other two empty so that nobody should be disturbed!

Beethoven's other contribution to music was a great quantity of works for the piano, then a new and relatively unpopular instrument, criticised by Mozart as "rather noisy."   It is proper to play Beethoven's music on the piano of to-day, but for the music of Bach, Mozart, Scarlatti and other early composers it has not a sufficiently piercing tone.   Nor is it lively enough.   Music, like poetry, has punctuation, and compared with the harpsichord's sharp, clear rendering of the intervals piano renderings are blurred.

Schubert, a Viennese, lived from 1797 to 1828, dying at the age

of only thirty-one.   He was a gay and irresponsible creature who
should have had a kindly protector or agent to see that people did
not cheat him or impose on him.   It is said that in his whole life he
earned only £575 for his work.   One publisher made a fortune out
of his work (mainly songs), and yet refused to give him any money
when he was destitute.   He was paid only 17s. 6d. for one of his
well-known compositions.   Shortly before he died he wrote his lovely
Unfinished Symphony and the *C Major Symphony*, which is
considered to rank with the work of Beethoven.   Here indeed was a
man who was killed in his prime by the wolfish greed of dull business
men.   He was not the first to meet with such a fate, and neither was
he the last.   He lived wildly, and was partly to blame for his unhappy end, but a few steady friends might have saved him.

Felix Mendelssohn, a German Jew who lived from 1809 to 1847,
was born with every advantage a young musician could have.   His
mother gave him music lessons from an early age, and his little sister
Fanny promised to be even more brilliant than he.   At the age of
nine young Felix was performing in public, and at twelve he was
composing his own music.   He visited London and played Bach
fugues on the organ at St. Paul's Cathedral.   He received so many
encores that at last the vergers had to disconnect the blower from
the organ to stop the music and make the people go away.   Mendelssohn should have lived long and successfully, but he overworked
himself and died before he was forty.   His best-known work is the
oratorio *Elijah*.   Some people think that he owed his success to
the fact that he did nothing new.   What he composed was in a
general way like work that already found favour with the public.

Robert Schumann, yet another German composer, lived from
1810 to 1856.   Unlike Mendelssohn he originated much that was
new in music, consequently he was much misunderstood and had a

hard struggle to find favour, even with those who knew him well. His teacher had a wonderful little daughter, only nine years old, named Clara, who was already giving public performances on the piano. Eventually Schumann fell in love with her, and her father whisked her away to every European capital in turn to keep her from her persistent suitor. At last the girl was old enough to know her own mind; she wanted to be with her lover and so her father turned her out of doors in disgust. She married Schumann, and the two musicians were exceedingly happy together for many years. Then a habit of melancholy, to which Schumann was prone, overcame him, and he tried to drown himself in the Rhine. For his own safety he asked to be taken to an asylum and here he died, not without friends, and still enjoying the devotion of his beloved wife Clara. As might be expected, Schumann's music is rather sad, although he wrote some songs specially for children.

Berlioz.—Mention must be made of Berlioz, if only because it is a change to mention a composer who was not German or Austrian in origin. Berlioz was French, and lived from 1803 to 1869. Opinion differed as to his merits. He was compared with Chopin, the Polish composer of sweet piano music, by a critic who said that Chopin was to Berlioz as a sentimental flea to a roaring lion. Heine, a very great German admirer of Berlioz, said that his music made him "think of vast mammoths and other extinct animals, and fabulous empires filled with fabulous crimes and other enormous possibilities." This is high praise. Berlioz did all sorts of mad things besides writing weird music. He did not like the music of Handel and he detested that of Bach, but he made the unfriendly Parisians listen to, and enjoy, the symphonies of Beethoven, in itself a great and useful achievement.

Richard Wagner, a great German composer of opera, lived from

1813 to 1883. In his own way he was as great as Bach, but his way was the way of a pagan, whereas Bach was a devout Christian. Wagner loved the old German folk legends, dating from the days when men worshipped many gods. He wrote the sort of music that might be expected to accompany the end of the world as prophesied in Revelations. It would go very well with earthquakes and tidal waves and collisions between planets. It is grand and gloomy, though sometimes softly tuneful, as if in memory of pleasant things that have passed away.

As a man Wagner was utterly selfish and ruthless. So that he should be in the mood to write his great music, he took his pleasure wherever he found it. He neglected his devoted wife Minna in order to love younger and prettier women, and under their spell he did work that has ever since divided the whole world. He cared not one rap what audiences thought of him, and one of his operas, *Rienzi*, took no less than six hours to perform. His answer to all criticism was more or less to the effect that if people did not like it " they could put up with it." He wrote unkindly of Jews and of many people who had befriended him. He was one of the first of the Germans to form the big German idea that what a German wanted it was right for him to have. Not unnaturally he was an idol of Hitler's. Not only in 1914 to 1918, but again in 1939 to 1945, the Germans went to war with Wagnerian indifference to everything but their own dreams. They used the world for their stage, and started tragedies that for scenic beauty and dramatic noise effects would surely have rejoiced the spirit of Wagner could he have been an onlooker. Wagner would have revelled in the nights of horror in London, when flying bombs, rockets and parachute mines were threatening the very foundations of civilisation. The atomic bomb would doubtless have been a fresh inspiration to him.

It is not possible to like such a man, but it is impossible to help admiring him. Our feeling for his music is something like our feeling for anything else that is too tremendous for us to resist or understand. He almost makes us believe that the German heel is more noble than the harmless things it would seek to crush. We are as sparrows hypnotised by a snake, ready to sacrifice ourselves to a lust that exceeds our own desire for separate life.

Some people think that Wagner's music helped to bring a great sickness into the world by giving the Germans too much pride. This pride is supposed to have been the cause of the unprovoked aggression by the Germans in 1914 and again in 1939. Personally, I think that some of Germany's writers and philosophers were just as much to blame as Wagner for spreading among the German people of twenty and more years ago the complaint which is popularly known to-day as BIG HEAD.

Chapter 15

OTHER COMPOSERS

In the last chapter we learnt about the composers of dazzling and overwhelming brilliance but, of course, they were not the only stars in the firmament.

Until the music of Bach burst upon the world some quite excellent work was being done by other composers, now largely forgotten by all except those people who study music.

Bach is known to have profited from a knowledge of the work of such early Continental composers as Palestrina, Frescobaldi, Monteverdi, Buxtehude and Schütz, and it is highly probable that the musicians of England were also helping to set the pattern on which he built his success.

Fully a hundred years before the triumph of Bach there was, at Lincoln Cathedral, an organist named William Byrd, who was to enjoy the encouragement of the first Queen Elizabeth on account of his great talent. He is said to have originated the madrigal form of unaccompanied part song.

John Dowland lived at about the same time, and he wrote beautiful songs for lute accompaniment. A lute is something like a guitar. Dowland also was employed by royalty and his songs are still frequently sung.

At Hereford, serving in the capacity of cathedral organist, was

yet another competent musician, John Bull. He composed keyboard
music for organ and virginal (a forerunner of the piano), and he spent
part of his life working in Brussels and Antwerp.

The temporary overthrow of the Stuarts by the puritanical Cromwell put an end to English music for a brief interlude, as the Puritans
considered joyful music to be unholy.   However, under Charles II,
a new opportunity was created and this was seized by three clever
men who started their careers as choirboys at the Chapel Royal.   All
of them were composing excellent music before Bach had grown to
be a man—their names were John Blow, Jeremiah Clarke and Henry
Purcell.   We know Clarke to-day for his *Trumpet Voluntary*, signature tune to the B.B.C. overseas broadcasts.   Purcell you may know
for his children's song *Nymphs and Shepherds*.

The promising stream of English music was destined to be overwhelmed by the much greater volume and variety of music from
Europe.   Bach and Handel were not the only giants to appear there.
In Italy there were the two Scarlattis, father and son; in France
there were Rameau and Couperin; and in Germany Bach himself
had a rival in the person of Telemann.   Any one of these men, in
the absence of Bach and Handel, might have taken the lead.

Bach and Handel were particularly successful with sacred music,
but folk-tales and legends were destined to be clothed in beautiful
music too.   Christoph Willibald Gluck, another German composer,
took the old Greek story of *Orpheus and Euridyce* and made it into
what we would now call an opera.   It was a play in which the actors
sang their lines.   The romantic flavour of such a work made it
popular and inspired imitation.

Mozart wrote some solemn or romantic operas with success, but
his comic operas (especially *Il Seraglio*, *Le Nozze de Figaro*, *Don
Giovanni* and *Cosi fan tutte*) are those most often performed to-day.

Equally successful with comic opera were the Italian composers Rossini and Donizetti. Rossini's *Barber of Seville* and Donizetti's *Don Pasquale* are still great favourites both in Britain and overseas.

Beethoven attempted opera too, and his *Fidelio* is sometimes performed but, together with Haydn, he is remembered chiefly for vast orchestral and instrumental works of surpassing beauty and competence.

After Beethoven there came Johannes Brahms (German) and Tchaikovsky (Russian), but neither really succeeded in maintaining the exalted tone and unfailing assurance of Beethoven, though both enjoy to this day a great following of appreciative listeners. You probably know already the music of Tchaikovsky's *Swan Lake* ballet and also his *Nutcracker Suite*.

With the opera *Nabucco* of Verdi, first performed in 1842, there began in Italy a new fashion in more serious musical dramatisation. Passionate and tragic tales took the place of such comic ones as had pleased the public of Mozart and Rossini. Verdi, an Italian, lived through most of the nineteenth century and he wrote many more extremely successful operas. Other operatic composers of the century were Gounod, Leoncavallo, Bizet and Puccini. Puccini produced his most famous work, *Madame Butterfly*, after the commencement of the twentieth century.

In most great cultural centres—London, Paris, Milan, New York —the Italian or Italian-style operas are still frequently performed.

Comic opera was enriched in the last half of the nineteenth century by the productions of Arthur Sullivan and William S. Gilbert, both Englishmen. Sullivan was a writer of serious music, but he was persuaded to collaborate with Gilbert in the production of witty and farcical stage shows of a kind never seen before or successfully imitated since. The music from some of these you must have heard

many times, as selections from *The Mikado, H.M.S. Pinafore,*
Iolanthe, The Pirates of Penzance and other Gilbert and Sullivan
operas are popular with every concert orchestra.

In Vienna the two Strausses, Johann the father and Johann the
son, were making another kind of music popular. All Europe and
America waltzed to the *Blue Danube* and *Tales from the Vienna*
Woods and other still loved tunes. During the prosperous and comparatively peaceful years of Queen Victoria's reign, nearly everybody
danced to the strains of the Strauss waltzes, though it is likely that
the Irish and the Scottish still preferred to hop, skip and jump to
their own delightful rhythms—as indeed they do to this day!

Other nineteenth-century composers who deserve to be remembered for music that is still played are Weber, with his *Invitation to*
the Waltz, and Offenbach, with his tuneful *Tales of Hoffman*, an
opera. The *Barcarolle* from Offenbach's opera must be one of the
most frequently played concert items in the whole world. Remembered chiefly for but a single great work are two other composers of
this period, Smetana, for an opera called *The Bartered Bride*, and
Mascagni, for an opera called *Cavalleria Rusticana.*

Some time during the latter half of the nineteenth century all the
arts became afflicted with revolutionaries who wanted to stop creating
things that bore any resemblance to what had gone before and give
the world a new sensation. Sculpture became blobby and half-
finished-looking, painting assumed an aspect of cheeky incompetence
and music started sounding like accidents in an ironmongery.

Not everybody in the business gave way to the temptation to be
outrageously different. In the world of music a praiseworthy degree
of restraint was still being exercised by Greig, the Norwegian; Saint-
Saëns, the Frenchman; Edward Elgar, the Englishman; Dvořák, the
Bohemian, and several more. Music that almost everybody liked

continued to be composed until well on into the twentieth century by the great pianist Rachmaninov, by Franz Lehar, Edward German, Coleridge Taylor and, down to the present time, by Ralph Vaughan Williams. Also, much new but quite delightful music was coming from civilisations somewhat cut off from European influences by reason of natural or political barriers.

Operas and concert pieces of barbaric splendour came from Borodin, Mussorgsky and Rimsky Korsakov in Russia, and from such Spanish composers as de Falla, Albeniz and Granados came music of yet another flavour—sometimes Moorish.

It must be admitted also that a few of the revolutionaries of the nineteenth century really succeeded in creating acceptable novelties. Most people would agree that Ravel, César Franck, Debussy, Holst and Sibelius deserve what entertainers call " the big hand " for some of their works. Less general is the approval of Mahler, Stravinsky or Bax, though they all have a limited following of devotees.

The twentieth century has given us Walton, Prokofieff, Poulenc, Bartok and Benjamin Britten. Each of these composers enjoys a following of appreciative listeners, but it is not their good fortune to be popular even in the restricted sense that Bach and Beethoven are popular.

Some of the old-time music of Bach's day was scientifically put together in accordance with the rules relating to harmony, rhythm and so forth, but the music of many modern or relatively modern composers is constructed with a deliberate disregard of such rules. We are treated to jarring discords and surprising avoidances of the expected, both in melody and rhythm. Such music can be enjoyable only to those who know the new rules of composition since it strikes no naturally responsive chord in any human breast. The taste for it must be acquired by study.

Chapter 16

EVERYBODY'S MUSIC

OUGHT all people to like the same kinds of music? Sometimes people tell you that certain pieces of music are very good and that you should learn to like them. They think you are wanting in good taste if you say you think their favourite music is dull. You need not feel very worried by their remarks, however. If you lived in China or India or Abyssinia, you would be expected to like music that sounds completely different from anything you can hear in Europe or America. The coloured races have different tastes in music, and what we think good they would think terribly noisy and stupid, and vice versa.

Though people will try to force their standards of musical appreciation on you, there is really no absolute or world-wide standard. Different people enjoy different things, and it is mainly a matter of what they have grown accustomed to. You like best the kind of thing that has been played or sung to you from your earliest years.

Even in the British Isles the standard does not remain the same. Music once thought good is now thought very tame and uninteresting, while music once thought revolutionary and impudently bad is now thought very pleasant. It is really rather silly to be argumentative about what is good and what is bad in music, because there are fashions in music just as there are in clothes. What is good at one time and in one place becomes unpleasing at another time and in another place.

It is, however, possible to say this about music. Some compositions give pleasure for a much longer time than others and to a much greater diversity of people. The work of Handel, Bach, Beethoven and many more composers has given pleasure to people more than a hundred years after it was written. Moreover, it has given pleasure to people in many different lands speaking a great diversity of languages. There must be something in this music that everyone can enjoy, just as everyone can enjoy sunshine, recovering from pain or sorrow, and so on. There is an older language than any of those we speak or write, the language of sighs and groans and cheers and laughter, and music is language of this kind. Everyone who is made in the same way as ourselves can understand these very old languages. Coloured people do not show their feelings in the same way as white people do, and it is for this reason that they need and make another kind of music.

Different people show their feelings differently even in the British Isles, and that is why they care for different sorts of music. There are some people who really like swing music and crooning, and others who dislike it. The two sorts of people can never agree about what is good in music.

When music is being enjoyed, it usually satisfies some inner longing. Simple people with simple longings like simple music. People who are bursting with thankfulness for God's gifts like hymns of praise and gratitude. Very simple hymns will suit some people, but others want the immense musical tributes to God that were composed by Handel, Bach or Mendelssohn. People who live dull tame lives like lively stirring music, even military music, whereas people whose lives are exciting enough prefer peaceful music. A composer of music can be called great when he knows how to give people music of all these different kinds, music that they can bear to hear again and again and that never fails to satisfy.

From what I have said you can see that there is not really any such thing as "Everybody's Music." There is, however, music that it is fair to call "Nobody's Music." This is the music that is popular for a few weeks or a few months until it makes people weary and is then never heard again. Most of the music being played to-day is of this badly wearing kind that is destined to be utterly forgotten in a few months' time. I call it "nobody's music" because nobody will take it to his heart for all time. It serves the purpose of the day, like a cheap hat or a cheap book, and then it is thrown away. It is rather dreadful to think how much time is being spent in composing things or in listening to things that will give pleasure for only a brief spell of weeks.

Swing-music fans and those that like crooning will tell you that their kind of music is the only music that is worth hearing, but you will notice that even they must have a continual supply of new music if they are to remain satisfied. They would feel you were trying to put back the clock if you were to play to them the popular hits of a year or two back. The truth is that music of this kind means no more to those who like it than does their chewing-gum. When they have once sucked the sweetness out of it they have done with it and want to throw it away. People who love the classical music of the great composers are more loyal in their love; they want to hear their favourite compositions again and again; they never grow tired of them. The well of sweetness in good music can never be sucked completely dry.

So you see, the real test of a piece of music is whether it will remain a favourite. There is hardly a soul who would stand up and ask for a repeat performance of the dance tunes of five, ten or fifteen years ago, but there are thousands who still ask for the compositions of Handel, Bach, Mozart and others to be played. These compositions therefore deserve to be called great.

Some very strange new music is played to us to-day by the great symphony orchestras. We are told that this music is great and will live, but nobody can really tell, and we must reserve our judgment of such music. Some of the music that is ten and twenty years old still sounds strange to our ears, but the orchestras are giving it a chance to win our hearts by repeatedly playing it. A few people think it is splendid music, and ask for it to be performed, but many more have already decided that it should be forgotten. People argue fiercely about music just as they do about painting and poetry, but there is no need to be fierce. Time alone will decide who has the right end of such arguments.

Many old people dislike most of the "pop" music—the glutinous sentimentality of the words especially—but, without a doubt the more successful "groups" are becoming less crude and are employing more competent musicians to "arrange" and orchestrate their tunes. Sometimes the better music is only a thinly disguised revival of an item by Bach or Mozart or Haydn, but not always. Out of the welter of sound created to assuage in teenagers their perpetual craving for aural stimulation there is the possibility that truly new but enduringly valuable works may emerge—works never to be wholly lost or forgotten but preserved as part of our folk tradition. Inspiration is as important in music as education so that peasants, gipsies and other relatively primitive people have made valuable contributions. This could still be happening today.

Chapter 17

THE SCHOOL CONCERT

JOAN had been practising on her violin for weeks and weeks, and now the day of the school concert had arrived. The children were to give their performance to parents and friends at three o'clock in the afternoon. Joan awoke very early, and at six o'clock she became impatient with lying in bed, so she decided to dress. She ran to the bathroom to freshen herself up with douches of cold water on her face, neck and arms; and then she put on her clothes. "Now for a last practice!" she said to herself. She fetched her violin in its long black case from under her bed and crept downstairs with it. She moved as silently as she could, because it would be another half an hour at least before the other members of her family began to stir.

So as not to disturb anybody with her playing, Joan took her violin into the big empty shed at the bottom of the garden. Her piece at the concert was to be the old favourite *Home Sweet Home*. If people liked her perform-

EARLY PRACTICE.

384

ance well enough to clap for an encore, she was to play *Early One Morning*, and some of the girls were going to sing to her playing. Joan practised her two pieces until she had performed them perfectly three times each. Then she heard her mother calling to her to come and help lay the breakfast. She put her violin away carefully in its case and went back with it to the house.

At school that morning Joan's teacher said to the class, "I have an important announcement for you, girls. I am sure you will be pleased to hear that someone is coming to help us with our concert this afternoon; a very famous person, none other than Udolpho Upstarto, the famous violinist. He has consented to open our concert by playing one of his most sensational pieces. Our little Joan here is the only other violinist on the programme, and she will have to look to her laurels."

Joan was not at all pleased to hear her teacher's news: "Oh dear!" she thought; "nobody is in the least bit likely to enjoy hearing me playing after listening to the celebrated Udolpho."

Her melancholy thoughts were interrupted by her teacher, who was speaking again. "My second piece of news may interest you even more," she said; "we are to be honoured by the presence of Lady Gwendolen Gwilliam in the audience. As you know, Lady Gwendolen is one of our Governors, and it was she who gave us those nice new hockey balls with which we started our games last autumn."

"Worse and worse," groaned Joan inwardly; "Lady Gwendolen is a fussy old thing, and she will not like me at all for playing my miserably easy little piece after she has heard Udolpho."

All that morning, and right up to the hour of the concert, Joan went about with a face as long as her own fiddle. Her friends guessed what was worrying her, and they were sympathetic. Her teacher had something else to worry about, however, and she never noticed how miserable Joan was looking. What concerned the teacher most was the fact that no programmes had yet arrived from the printer. At three o'clock everybody was ready to begin the concert and the concert hall was packed with people, but still there were no programmes to sell, so Joan's teacher had to appear on the stage and announce the first items herself. She announced the celebrated Udolpho Upstarto, and said that his piece was to be a surprise. And it was a surprise indeed! Udolpho played one of the most difficult and tricky pieces ever composed for a violin, while Lady Gwendolen sat in the front row and watched him intently.

UDOLPHO MAKES A GREAT SENSATION.

In the middle of Udolpho's playing, a messenger boy arrived with the brown-paper parcel from the printer. Joan's teacher hastily tore off the outer wrapping and thrust the programmes into the arms of Mavis, Joan's best friend, who had been chosen to sell them.

"Oh, Mavis," poor Joan almost wept, "what *will* Lady Gwendolen say when she sees that I am down on the programme to

LADY GWENDOLEN SAT IN THE FRONT
ROW AND WATCHED UDOLPHO INTENTLY.

play *Home Sweet Home.* Just listen to Udolpho; she must think him simply marvellous."

Mavis went out into the hall at once and started selling her programmes. She reached Lady Gwendolen just as Udolpho, with a final flourish, finished his sensational piece.

"Thank goodness *that's* over," Lady Gwendolen said grimly, looking in Mavis's direction; "it

AT LAST THE PROGRAMMES WERE
BROUGHT BY A BOY FROM THE PRINTER.

may have been very good but I really came to hear the children. Here, child, have you a programme to give me? Let me see what there is to come."

Mavis timidly gave the angry lady a programme. She hadn't the courage to say it cost threepence. Lady Gwendolen examined the programme through her lorgnette. "Ah," she said, "I thought so. Upstarto's piece was called *Scherzo in E major Op. 72*, by Pipsqueeki. Now here's something I shall enjoy. Another violin piece—a nice simple thing not beyond the range of the instrument —*Home Sweet Home*—I know it well."

Mavis started to bubble inside with joy and laughter. She hurried through the business of selling programmes, as she was all eagerness to get back behind the stage to tell Joan about what Lady Gwendolen had said. "I *must* see Joan before her turn comes on," she thought. "It will cheer her up and give her courage if I can say that Lady Gwendolen is looking forward to hearing *Home Sweet Home*."

Mavis managed to get to Joan a few minutes before she was due to appear with her violin on the stage. Joan did a little dance of joy and relief when Mavis gave her the news.

"Why, Joan!" said her teacher, who had overheard the conversation of the two girls; "I had no idea you were feeling so nervous."

"Oh, Miss Green!" Joan burst out, "who *wouldn't* be! Fancy being asked to play the violin after Udolpho Upstarto! The great news you gave us this morning didn't please me one tiny bit. I've been feeling quite ill all day. Just now I was nearly sick."

"Poor child," said Miss Green, "I think I understand. But you needn't have worried, you know. The violin is intended to make simple music as well as difficult music, and a child can make the simple music just as well as the great professional—perhaps better.

All your practising has been well worth while, for what you *can* play you play with true feeling and very sweetly. You might have known that I should not have permitted you to play after Udolpho had I not thought you really good."

Joan was now all excitement, but she was cool and collected again when the time came for her to play. She went on the stage with a firm tread, and commenced her playing at once. Yes, it was true what her teacher had said. Her little slim arm was not very nimble yet, but it could coax her violin into giving forth the purest and clearest of notes, almost flute-like. If people shut their eyes while she was playing they could forget that the sounds

WHEN JOAN PLAYS "HOME SWEET HOME" THE GREAT LADY SHUTS HER EYES AND DREAMS OF HER OWN HAPPY CHILDHOOD.

came from someone sawing at a string with a bow. The secret of their loveliness was never given away by the slightest slip or roughness. Lady Gwendolen did shut her eyes, and her face took on a most blissful expression. Then she found herself wanting very much to study the personality of the young person who could delight her so much. Consequently she opened one eye, and afterwards both eyes. Joan's gleaming arm fascinated her, and so did her slightly swaying figure. "The child's bewitched," Lady Gwendolen said to herself; "she's no child at all, but a witch or a fairy."

The clapping that greeted Joan when she finished playing was thunderous—even louder than the clapping that had greeted Udolpho. If Udolpho could have heard it he would have been jealous indeed, but he was already rushing off in his high-powered car to keep his next engagement.

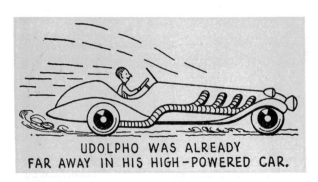

UDOLPHO WAS ALREADY FAR AWAY IN HIS HIGH-POWERED CAR.

All Joan's friends stamped and cheered with joy. The teacher had tears in her eyes.

Then Joan started playing *Early One Morning*, and a score of fresh young voices chimed in to ask the old questions, "How could you leave me?" and "How could you treat a poor maiden so?" One or two ladies took out their handkerchiefs, and some of the gentlemen trumpeted loudly with their noses. Everyone knew that Joan had been a great success, and the applause that followed *Early One Morning* was even greater than that which had followed *Home Sweet Home*.

"Oh, Joan," the rest of the performers said in chorus, as she bowed her way among them to the room behind the stage; "how can we play and sing our pieces after this? Nobody will be a bit interested in us now."

But all the same the people *were* interested in them, Lady Gwendolen as much as anybody. Joan's beautiful playing had awakened them all and made them specially observant. When they had first come into the hall the people had been prepared to listen in a patronising way, and some of them had said, among themselves, "Of course, it's only little schoolgirls; we cannot expect to hear anything very good; but one comes just to give them encouragement." These same people now were really enjoying themselves. The child performers were happy and confident, and since they sang or played music that was well within their powers to render properly, they gave a first-rate performance.

At the end of the concert there was a general move to put on hats and coats, and a loud buzz of conversation. Everyone was saying how good the concert had been. Lady Gwendolen went to the back of the stage and shook Joan's teacher by the hand.

JOAN RECEIVES A PINCH FROM LADY GWENDOLEN THAT MAKES HER SQUEAK.

"I congratulate you on the whole performance," she said; "it was splendid. You must have worked hard to turn all these little imps of mischief into such angelic performers." Here Lady Gwendolen gave Joan such a pinch that she could not help letting out a squeak. "As for you, you young witch," the great lady went on, addressing Joan; "I've a good mind to spank you for upsetting me so. I nearly cried, and that is a thing I have never done in public yet. You reminded me of the happy home of my own childhood —it's all gone now and all those I loved are dead and gone too, but you made me see them again by your playing. You took my mind back fifty long years, you little demon. You made me feel like being ten years old again.   Can't you keep your spell over me for always, eh?   Can't you put back the clock for an old woman like me if she goes down on her bended knee to entreat you?"

Joan was not used to jokes of this kind, and she turned very pink.

"I'll play to you whenever you are pleased to ask me, Lady Gwendolen," she answered very nicely.

"Then you can come and play for me this day week at my house," Lady Gwendolen went on.   "It's my birthday.   I had thought of trying to forget my sixty-first birthday, but you've made me change my mind.   I'll give a party, and you shall be my principal guest."

Saying these words, Lady Gwendolen prepared to depart.   "I will send out my invitations to-morrow," she concluded, waving vaguely round the room at everybody.   "Good-bye."

Chapter 18

THE MUSIC WIZARD

It was two o'clock on a sunny Saturday afternoon, and Michael wanted to go out and play with his friends. "Can't I go, Mummy?" he pleaded.

"No, dear," answered his mother firmly; "you know very well that this is the hour when you always do your piano practice."

"Oh, I hate the old music," Michael said in a temper, stamping his foot. "It is horribly dull spending the afternoon all alone in the front room. Besides, it smells of moth balls, and there is never any sun."

"But, Michael," his mother persisted, "you want to be able to play like Auntie Agatha, don't you? You never will, you know, unless you practise."

"I don't care whether I ever play or not," Michael answered shortly.

"Well, I do, then," his mother snapped; "and I am going to put an end to this argument." Saying these words she took Michael firmly by the arm and led him into the front sitting-room. She put him on the music stool in front of the piano and then she left the room. Michael heard her close the door and turn the key so that he should not escape.

"I could easily get out of the window," he thought; "it is wide open." But he dismissed this naughty idea from his mind and started to practise. "One, two, three, four, five" up the scale; "one, two, three, four, five" down the scale.

After he had been practising for half an hour, without enjoying it at all, Michael heard the front door shut with a bang, and he knew that his mother had gone down to the shops. He stopped playing and gazed with longing out of the window. Just opposite was a dull-green privet hedge, but on the other side of the road he could see the house tops glowing warmly in the summer sunshine, and over them shone the deep, deep blue sky. Michael heaved a sigh; he felt very sorry for himself. Then a strange thing happened. He suddenly found he was gazing into the face of a queer old man,

A DULL SATURDAY.

who was looking over the top of the hedge straight into the room where he sat.

"Hullo," said the old man; "how do you like music?"

"I *hate* it!" Michael burst out, on the point of tears.

"Tut tut, that can't be true, surely," the old man said softly; "think again."

"Oh yes, it is true," Michael went on; "I have to sit at this miserable old piano while my friends are out playing cricket in the sunshine. Mummy says I am musical, but I'm not. She says there's music in our family, because I have an auntie who can play, and she wants me to play like my auntie. I am supposed to be like her. But I hate music—I hate it—I——"

Michael stopped speaking just as he was going to say again how much he hated music. He stopped because the old man made a sudden spring into the air and jumped right over the hedge into the front garden. Then he bounded through the window and came to where Michael sat on his stool. Michael knew then that he was

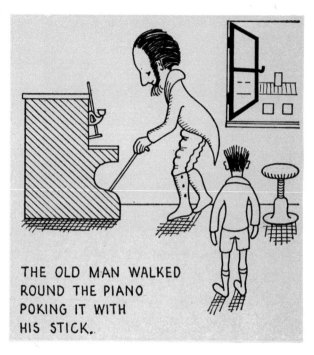

THE OLD MAN WALKED ROUND THE PIANO POKING IT WITH HIS STICK.

no ordinary old man, but a kind of wizard. He was rather frightened.

But the old man looked just like any ordinary old man, and he walked round the piano, poking it with his stick. "Is it a nice piano?" he asked at last.

"No," replied Michael. "It's a stupid old piano; but Mummy says it is good enough to practise on. It's a silly shape, and it makes a silly tinkling sound."

The old man made a clicking sound with his tongue. He did not like Michael's description of the piano at all.

"It may not be so bad as you think," he said at last. "However, they say that a bad workman always blames his tools. I will try

THE MUSIC BEGINS.

your piano." So saying he lifted Michael up and sat him on the top of the piano. "Hold tight, young man," he said, taking Michael's place on the stool; "I am going to give you a ride."

The old man struck the keys a few mighty blows and Michael felt a tingling sensation travel up his spine. After trying a few more chords the old man let himself go. The piece he played opened with some tremendous low notes that made the room shake, but suddenly the old man's hands flew with lightning speed up the keys to the high notes, where they moved so fast that Michael could hardly see them. The sound was like a million bells all chiming at once. After this Michael could not have described what the old man did; he only knew that the music became wilder and wilder. There was a roaring sound like thunder and a great wind competing to see which could make the most noise. On top of this was a furious tinkling like hailstones on an iron roof. Every second or so a sharp clear sound stabbed like lightning through Michael's brain. The piano seemed to rock like a mountain in an earthquake; the room became darker and darker. Michael clenched his teeth and held on with all his might. Wilder and wilder became the old man's playing —now there was a battle raging as well as a storm.

"Stop! stop!" Michael called out, but his voice was drowned by the fearful noise of the music. It was pitch-dark at last, and the piano tossed about like a ship at sea. Michael clung desperately to the woodwork, fearing every minute that he would be thrown overboard. He was calling and crying with all his might, but it made no difference. He knew that this was the most terrific nightmare he had ever had in all his life, and yet, strange to

THE PIANO SEEMED TO ROCK LIKE
A MOUNTAIN IN AN EARTHQUAKE.

say, he was enjoying it. "If I come through this alive," he screamed to himself, "I shall have something to remember for ever and ever."

Bang, crash! Michael lost his hold on the piano and fell to the floor. Coloured lights stabbed the darkness and stars came and went in front of his eyes. For a moment he was too confused to

MICHAEL FINDS HIMSELF
ALONE AGAIN.

remember where he was, or what had been happening. Then he sat up suddenly. The room was quite light now and very still. The piano was where it had always been and so was the music stool. There was no sign of the old man.

Michael rose from the floor and ran to the window. There was the dull old privet hedge, and there were the sun-lit houses across the road. Overhead the sky shone as clear and as blue as before. " I must have gone to sleep on my stool and had a dream," he said; " then, I suppose, I fell off with a bump and woke up. There hasn't been any rain or any wind or any thunder and lightning. And there hasn't been any old man here." He turned from the window, and climbed back thoughtfully on to his stool. He was just about to start practising again when a voice at the window made him jump. " Pardon me," it said; " but I left my stick behind. Would you mind passing it out to me through the window?" Michael turned round at hearing these words, and saw the old man smiling at him. He was so astonished that the old man laughed outright. " Thought I was a dream, didn't you?" he chuckled. " Well, well, perhaps I was. Give me my stick, boy, and I'll be gone before your folk get back. That's a good piano you've got there. She goes fine. Maybe I'll give you another ride on her one day." The old man peered up and down the road, and then, seeing that nobody was watching him, he bounded over the hedge and disappeared.

Michael went back to his stool and stared at the piano. He hardly dared to touch it, for it seemed to him now that it was alive and only waiting for a single touch to awaken it and turn it into a roaring monster. He was still staring at it when he heard the front door open. His mother had come back, and with her was Aunt Agatha. The sitting-room door was opened and Michael's mother looked in. " You've had your practice now, Michael," she said, " but you can stay and listen to your auntie, who will play something nice for you."

" Oh yes, Auntie, do," Michael cried, and he scrambled from the stool to his perch on top of the piano.

"Why ever do you sit up there?" his mother asked in great surprise.

"I always do," Michael answered.

"Indeed!" exclaimed his mother, "I've never known you do such a thing in your life before." She would have said more, but Aunt Agatha started to play. Michael held on to the woodwork, expecting to be taken for another thrilling ride into a world of strange and glorious sounds, but Aunt Agatha's playing was rather tame by comparison with that of the old wizard.

"Come, Auntie, play up!" Michael said suddenly, "put some pep into it!"

AUNT AGATHA'S PLAYING SEEMED
RATHER TAME TO MICHAEL.

"Michael!" gasped his mother, "how dare you speak to your auntie like that! What do you know about music? Your auntie plays very soulfully and beautifully."

Aunt Agatha went on playing, but Michael bounced up and down on the piano with impatience. When she had finished, Michael said, "Perhaps little children don't like learning to play the piano because the things they hear grown-up people playing never seem worth all the trouble of learning."

"You are a very rude boy," said Aunt Agatha, shutting up the piano with a bang; "I don't know what's come over you: you used to like my playing."

"Don't take any notice of him, Agatha," interposed his mother, "he's been like this all day. It's a tummy upset, I expect. I will give him some syrup of figs before he goes to bed to-night. He will be all right in the morning."

Michael wondered whether he should tell his mother about the strange old man, but he decided that he wouldn't. After all, it might have been a dream, and if his mother thought this she would scold him for going to sleep over his practice. The thing that puzzled Michael's mother most of all, however, was the eagerness with which he looked forward to his next piano practice. He actually went to his stool without being told to do so, for, you see, he was hoping that the old music wizard would visit him again. And besides, he knew now that the piano was not so dull and stupid as it had once seemed to be. He was eager to learn the secret of waking it up and making it alive. "I must teach my hands to move as fast as the old wizard's," he said to himself, and he practised so hard in the next few years that at last he succeeded.

Section Nine

PAST, PRESENT AND FUTURE

Chapter 1

THE CHILD AS AN INDIVIDUAL AND A MEMBER OF SOCIETY

We hear a great deal in these days about "progress." Our children learn in their history books something about the past and, while living in the present, they are frequently encouraged to dream about the future. Will it be a future remarkable for warlike preparations, or will it settle for peace and prosperity? Will space travel come into the picture?

Nobody can be quite sure what the future holds, but most of us would be glad if some good fairy could come to offer us two or three wishes for the future. The less mature among us might wish for material advancement of some kind or another—say the construction of successful space ships, but the more thoughtful person would surely hope for some increase in Man's wisdom, enabling him to find the proper formula for earthly peace and goodwill.

I believe that the seed of universal goodwill is sown already in the hearts of our children, and I am sure it can be fostered. With equal facility, however, people can hand on to children their prejudices and grievances, making them into fighters for old causes. In this part of my book I am more interested in fostering the seed of universal goodwill that I regard as a feature of youthful innocence.

Very young children take kindly to animals and come to feel a sort of kinship with their pets. Among themselves there may develop jealousies and rivalries, but their pets rarely experience anything other than their affectionate regard. Sometimes a child's regard for a pet is intermittent and unreliable, but constancy in love and a measure of self-sacrifice are easily inculcated in children who accept responsibility for the welfare of a dog or a cat or some other creature needing regular care and attention.

Even our grandparents knew that it was a good thing to allow children to have pets, and there has been nobody in modern times to gainsay the wisdom of this policy.

The regard for an animal may be something small and unimportant in itself, but it is the seed of that goodwill or fellow-feeling I have spoken about above and, as such, it could be the germ of something more universal and more important. It is worth cultivating for its ultimate fruits, and the advantage of basing a moral training upon it, in part at least, is that one can be sure of engaging the children's continual interest and co-opera-tion. Also, as the appeal of animals among the young is wellnigh uni-versal, the method is one that need take no account of class or creed or colour. This is important in a world where community of interest is apt to be overlooked by reason of too many distinctions between man and man —not all of them very significant distinctions.

Closeness to animals is felt by children more strongly than by adults and, eventually, the growing human being undoubtedly leaves the simpler creatures far behind. This does not mean that the human being has nothing to learn from animals. In childhood, when we are nearest to other creatures in our simplicity, we can profit by observing their successes and their failures. Æsop, the writer of fables, drew many a moral from animal adventures and, to this day, small children will more readily identify themselves with animal characters in a story than with human characters.

Taking all these things into consideration, we might perhaps do worse than people the story of the past with animal characters rather than with human ones and make history into a story of dinosaurs and mammoths and giraffes rather than one of nations and soldier-statesmen and kings. I believe that it is easier for children to learn something definite and useful from what is generally called natural history than from the other sort of history, and this is my excuse for the chapters which follow. These chapters tell, in the main, of what is past, but their lesson for the present is just this, that, in the long run, kindness pays better than brute strength.

The kindness of the creatures is a very limited kindness, as we know from the way a sheep will butt away a lamb that is not her own. It is in the human heart to overflow with a less partial sort of kindness. The grown man or woman wants to be kind to all children and not merely to those within the family.   This sort of goodness does not often find a parallel in the jungle life of the creatures, and so we come, after all, in Chapters 5, 6, 7 and 8, to stories about human beings.   The story in Chapter 5 is about kindness to a child from an unhappy home.

Whether or not the kindness of a total stranger to children can be accepted at its face value is a question dealt with in Chapters 6, 7 and 8. All too many children are led astray by strangers with bad intentions, but it is a pity to scare the natural friendliness out of our children by teaching them that all strangers are potential kidnappers or worse. The situations in which children might or might not safely encourage the advances of a stranger are described in the chapters already mentioned.

Among the many distinctions between human beings and animals is the " self-consciousness " of the human being.   Naturalists believe that animals are unconscious of what they are.   They can be seen walking into traps that are already littered with dead or injured creatures of their own kind.   Would they do this if they recognised themselves as being the same and liable to suffer the same fate?   Sooner or later every human child becomes aware of the self in a way that animals never seem to do. This awareness includes a consciousness of sex and of physical mortality.

The questioning mind of the child demands some explanation for sex differences and also a rational justification for the natural process of growing old and dying.   Chapters 9 and 10 supply in story form some brief answers to what are popularly regarded as difficult questions.

The much larger question of broad social relations in the present-day world calls for some notice in a book such as this.   From what angle should it be approached?   Shall I liken the complex society of human beings to the society of bees or ants or termites?   I do not really think there is a close parallel, so I shall not suggest that as regards the organisation of our community life we have much to learn from the creatures.   In family life some of them set us a pattern worthy of emulation, but the herd and the hive are not for us.   Nevertheless, our great and increasing numbers require that we should share the good things of the earth according to some plan which meets with more or less general agreement.

In human societies of long ago the rules were all made by some tribal chief or other absolute and all-powerful ruler. Out of this arrangement there grew the rule of kings and the principle of hereditary succession.

Kingly rule has not always proved acceptable and most societies eventually revolted against it. The tendency has been for peoples to take into their own hands, or give into the hands of elected representatives, the offices of government. The result has been our modern democracy and its several variants. An important chapter in the section which follows, called "Living Together," deals with the organisation of human society in the present day, with special reference to Britain and the British Commonwealth of Nations.

The future is to be described only by a prophet, and prophecy is seldom wise. However, most of us would think it possible to discern something of what lies ahead. In many respects the daily round is becoming easier and easier because machinery is doing the heavier work formerly done by horses and men and doing it faster. In the last 60 years the working day has been shortened from 12 or more hours to 8, with gains rather than losses in pay. The housewife must still work 7 days a week, but she has been relieved of much drudgery and strain by such aids as the sewing machine, the vacuum cleaner, the clothes washer and the spin drier. Everyone has more leisure than formerly—more time in which to please himself or herself. How to spend the extra spare time has become quite a problem for some people, and so there has been a great increase in facilities for sports and entertainments. Of opportunities for doing kind deeds like the one described in the story on page 432 there has, however, been a steady shrinkage, because the Welfare State is rebuilding the slums and providing more help for those in need. This may at first seem a sensible idea, but it leaves ordinary people free to forget everyone except themselves and that could be bad. Already there are signs that many young people are growing up to be utterly self-centred and bored, more inclined to be rude and violent than courteous and kind. In a country where everything is automatically taken care of by the state it is difficult to be good because there are few good things that need doing and Satan finds mischief not only for idle hands to do but for idle hearts and idle souls as well. This is a problem the politicians have not yet started to think about.

Chapter 2
AUNT AGATHA AND THE ANIMALS

JAQUELINE and Michael were very excited, as they were going to stay for a short holiday in the country with their Uncle Arthur and Auntie Agatha. Both of them were very fond of Uncle Arthur, because he told them wonderful stories, always about real things, and made them understand real things better. They liked Auntie Agatha too, as she was kind; but Auntie Agatha was rather strict and she had old-fashioned ideas that she thought better than Uncle Arthur's. She always said that Uncle Arthur spoiled Jaqueline and Michael, and that if it were not for her strictness they would soon be "little limbs of Satan." Uncle Arthur just used to smile at this and go on being kind to the two children.

The day after the two children arrived for their visit, Uncle Arthur said that he wanted to go up to town and see someone at the Natural History Museum there. "You two children can come with me," he added; "the Museum is full of interesting things."

"Stuffed animals and bones were all I saw there," grumbled Aunt Agatha; "we've got enough live animals here in our garden, I should have thought, without you wanting to go and look at a lot of old dead ones."

"The live ones are best, I admit," said Uncle Arthur; "and the children love old Henry the horse, and Towser the dog, not to mention Fluffy the cat and Archibald the duck. But there is something to be learnt from studying the way animals are made. I would like them to see how very closely we resemble the animals inside our skins. It might save them from growing too vain and superior later on in their lives."

"Oh, fiddlesticks," said Aunt Agatha; "you can tell me till you are blue in the face that my bones are like those of an old horse, but I won't believe I'm a horse for all that."

"I didn't ever say you were," protested Uncle Arthur; "you and the horse have grown up on different lines, but in some ways you and the horse are alike."

"Thanks very much," said Aunt Agatha; "you have told me that before, and I do not consider it the sort of compliment a gentleman should pay a lady. You did not speak to me like that when you were courting me. If you really think I look like an old horse now, you might at least keep your thoughts to yourself, especially before the children."

By this time Jaqueline and Michael were nearly bursting with suppressed laughter. They knew quite well that their uncle meant no harm by his remarks, but Aunt Agatha always misunderstood him and, to the children, she seemed to do it on purpose.

Uncle Arthur was still scratching his head and looking miserable when the three of them set out for the station. "All I meant to say was that living things are alike," he grumbled; "your aunt has four limbs; so has the horse. She has two eyes, a nose and a mouth; so has the horse. She has a backbone and ribs; so has the horse. I could go on with the comparison indefinitely."

"Perhaps Auntie thinks she is prettier than a horse," said Jaqueline, opening her eyes very wide.

"So she is," agreed Uncle Arthur, "and much better than a

horse in lots of ways. But she cannot get away from the fact that she is structurally very like a horse, just as I am and just as you children are. It is as though Nature had had a store of parts, something like a box of Meccano, and had made different creatures out of these parts, using the same ones in all sorts of different designs. The horse is one kind of creature and the human being another."

"Poor Auntie," said Jaqueline; "you will only make her feel worse if you tell her she is made up of bits like a Meccano model. You will have to take her a box of chocolates and a bunch of flowers when the time comes to go home. Then she will forget how rude you were."

"Was I rude?" asked Uncle Arthur rather pathetically.

"Not really," answered Jaqueline, "but ladies do like to be admired." Jaqueline tossed her curls as she said this, whereat Uncle Arthur and Michael both burst out laughing.

"Such vanity I never did see," Michael managed to say at last; " the horse is tossing its mane! "

"Be quiet!" Jaqueline retorted fiercely; "or I'll twist those monkeys' ears of yours."

"Tut-tut," muttered Uncle Arthur; "I never meant to start all this."

Just then there was the loud rumbling of a train, for the station was in sight.

"Is that our train?" Michael asked, becoming serious in a moment.

"I think it is," Uncle Arthur replied, and all three began to run. They just had time to buy their tickets and scramble into the train.

"Oughtn't we to have got into a horse-box?" giggled Michael.

"Now, now," warned Uncle Arthur, "that is enough of joking; but when we get to the Museum I will show you the skeletons of horse and man, and you will see then that for each bone of the horse there is a rather similar one in man. The bones are longer or shorter or fatter or thinner, but there they all are. Man even has tail bones, but they are so short that nothing shows from the outside. His hind-limbs are long and strong, so as to take his whole weight, whereas his fore-limbs are short and more delicate, so that they can be used for an altogether different purpose from walking. We call these limbs arms, but that does not prevent them from having some like-ness to the legs of four-footed animals.

"As you might expect, the bones of the foot of the horse are rather different from those in man. The horse goes on one toe, as it were, and the others are so small as not to be of any use for walking. Also by standing on tiptoe the horse has for the lower part of his leg a bone corresponding to one that, with us, is a part of the foot. The first backward bending joint going up the back leg is really the same as our ankle joint, and the heel is there too. What we call the knees of the horse in his front legs are really the same as our wrist joints.

"In the skeleton of a dog you will see that, in spite of the tiptoe attitude, it has the equivalent of all our toes and fingers quite clearly distinguishable.

"Monkey skeletons are absurdly like ours, even though they may be curved over for going on all-fours. The skeleton of the gorilla is not even curved over, but it is very solidly and heavily made, because the gorilla is a large and powerful animal.

"The oddest of the skeletons are those belonging to the birds and bats. If you look carefully at a bird skeleton you will see that it is basically the same as our own, but the hind-limbs are short and weak, whereas the fore-limbs are enormously long and strong. Bones equivalent to those in our arms and hands serve as spreaders for feathers, and we say that a bird has wings without always realising

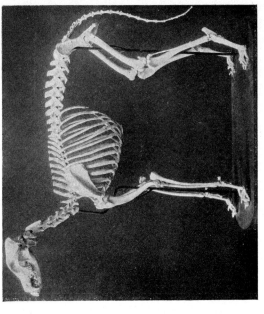

Dog. (Notice the tip-toe position of the hind feet, bringing the bone like our heel bone well up the leg.)

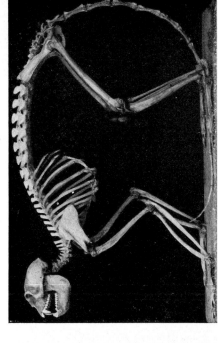

Monkey. (This skeleton would closely resemble a man's if it were upright.)

By courtesy of the British Museum

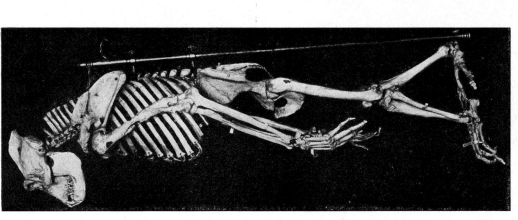

Man. (Notice small tail bones.)

Gorilla.

Generally similar in many respects, these skeletons suggest that different animals may have descended from a common ancestor.

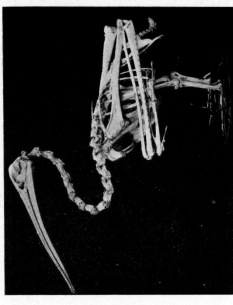

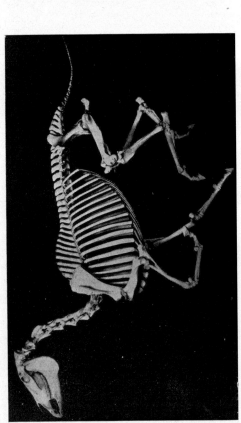

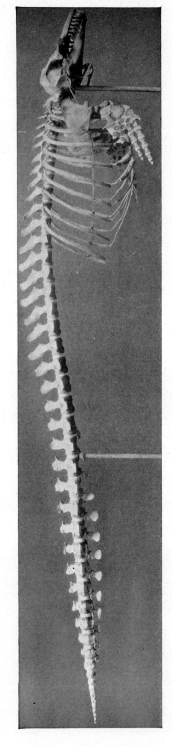

Bird. (Differently proportioned in all its parts, this skeleton is nevertheless recognisably like that of a horse or man.)

Horse at full gallop (in each foot only one toe is really useful so it is greatly enlarged, whereas the others have almost disappeared).

Whale. (Once a land animal, this creature has gradually become adapted to life in the sea. Its fore limbs have turned into paddles and its hind limbs have become scarcely perceptible vestiges, the bones of which are not shown in this example.)

By courtesy of the British Museum

C. IV—411

that wings are really arms or front legs in another guise. In the bat the finger bones are tremendously long, and are used to keep the leathery wings stretched out.

"The neck bones in animals such as the giraffe, and in some birds such as ducks and swans, are very much elongated, so that the head is held high. Also in some creatures, such as birds and crocodiles, the jaw parts of the face are long and narrow. But with all these differences there is still a common resemblance, and that is what I meant when I said to your auntie that we were all made like the animals."

"You haven't said anything about fishes," said Michael.

"You might say whales and dolphins and porpoises were fishes," said Uncle Arthur; "but you would be wrong, because they are animals, and they have to come up every now and then for air. The whale is made like us, with the same set of bones, but the fore-limbs are very stunted except for what compares with our hands, and these are paddles for swimming. The hind-limbs are almost non-existent, but in some of the Museum skeletons you will see very tiny bones hung on with wire, just where the long tail begins. These are vestigial leg bones. If the whale had ever tried to go on living on land, perhaps these bones would have become larger and stronger. As it is, they remain tiny and useless. The great bony girdle called the pelvis that takes the leg sockets in man and many land animals is only a vestige in whales, so that this too may appear to be missing. But in a complete set of whale bones you will find traces of pelvis and hind-legs, just as you find traces of a tail in man."

Uncle Arthur told the children so many interesting things about animals that they reached the end of their journey without noticing their progress. Once in town, they were soon at the Museum, and then Uncle Arthur left Jaqueline and Michael to look at the stuffed animals and skeletons while he went to see his friend. After an hour or so he returned and showed the children some photographs of skeletons. "I have bought these," he said, "to remind us of our talk about bones. We can show them to Aunt Agatha when we get home."

"No," contradicted Jaqueline, shaking her head; "show her some chocolates and a bunch of flowers like I said before. She does not want to be reminded of her bones. Bones make her depressed."

"Very well," said Uncle Arthur; "I will take your advice."

On the way home he bought a very big box of chocolates and a bunch of roses. Aunt Agatha was delighted with her gifts, and she prepared a splendid tea for the hungry travellers. Naughty Michael, however, kept on taking the photo showing a skeleton of a horse at full gallop from his pocket and slyly showing it to Jaqueline. At last Jaqueline could contain her giggles no longer, and she exploded in a cup of tea so violently that it splashed all over her plate.

"Oh dear," she spluttered, "a crumb," and she flew from the room, half choking, half crying.

Uncle Arthur looked rather serious. "We've had enough of that joke," he said when Aunt Agatha had gone out of the room to get a cloth to wipe up the spilled tea. "You will get your little sister into trouble if you persist in behaving like that."

"Sorry, Uncle," murmured Michael.

"Apology accepted," replied Uncle Arthur; "but remember in future that jokes at other people's expense are not nice. Your little sister did the handsome thing when she said I ought to bring home chocolates and flowers for your auntie, and you see how right she was. It made Auntie happy. You have been trying to make fresh mischief with that photo. Pack it up, lad, pack it up."

Aunt Agatha returned at this moment and mopped up the mess

Jaqueline had made. Michael ran out to look for Jaqueline. "Come back and finish your tea," he said.

"It's no use," Jaqueline answered; "I shall never manage to keep a straight face after that. If anyone looks at me I shall burst, I know I shall."

"But bones are solemn things," protested Michael.

"Not the ones of that ghost Derby winner," retorted Jaqueline, and she went off again into such peals of laughter that the tears rolled down her face. Michael was forced to join in, and when Uncle Arthur came to look for them a few moments later he found them both quite helpless.

"Here," he said, "I've brought some buns for you. You had better go and sit outside with the duck and finish your tea there. I'll go in now before I catch the giggles myself."

Chapter 3

THE LAW OF THE JUNGLE

UNCLE ARTHUR and the two children Jaqueline and Michael had been for a long tramp over the hills, and they were all very hungry when they came in. Aunt Agatha had prepared a big meal of stew and dumplings, followed by gooseberry tart.

"What shall we do this afternoon?" asked Michael.

"Sleep off our wholesome meal, I should think," laughed Uncle Arthur; "I shall not be in a fit state to go for another long walk to-day."

"Will you tell us a story, then?" Jaqueline said in her most pleading manner.

"What about?" countered Uncle Arthur.

"About animals," answered Jaqueline promptly; "we both love to hear about animals—don't we, Michael?"

Michael nodded.

"Very well," said Uncle Arthur, "I will tell you the story of how animals are supposed to change through the ages and become better fitted for the lives they have to lead. As you know, people can breed dogs or horses or even plants to bring out their finer points and, in Nature, the same sort of refinement is supposed to be always going on. If the process goes on continuously in the same direction it may, after many thousands of years, produce such a tremendous

414

By courtesy of South African Railways

Giraffes taking a walk.

The present-day descendants of the creatures Long Spot and Lanky Spot mentioned in the text.

By courtesy of the East African Office

Jungle camouflage

The striped zebra escapes the notice of his enemies if he stands still among the bars of light and shade that form the jungle scene.

change in a particular creature as to make it virtually a new one. For instance, legs could turn to arms or wings or flippers if the creature were really better fitted by its surroundings to have arms, wings or flippers than forelegs.

"Some naturalists think that by a process of change animal shapes have altered so much through the ages that all the ones we know now may once have come from an entirely different ancestor that was common to all. I have already told you how alike are the bones of horse, dog, monkey, bird, whale and so on. This theory of change is one possible explanation of the similarity.

"Another word for natural change is 'evolution,' and the theories about it are not new. About 150 years ago many naturalists supposed that creatures could improve themselves in life (as an athlete does) by so exercising one set of muscles as to make them more useful, and then pass the improvement on to their offspring. However, this is no longer recognised to be possible. Charles Darwin, the famous naturalist of about 100 years ago, supposed that it was the naturally occurring differences, usually small, between the young of any one generation that gave the advantage to one individual over another, and that it was these small natural differences which, in favourable conditions, would be passed on and made more and more exaggerated with each new generation. Natural differences, like big ears, or a long nose, or brown-coloured hair can, as you know, be passed on by parents to offspring.

"Present-day naturalists think that the process of change may sometimes be much more rapid than Darwin thought possible. Occasionally some very large and important variation appears suddenly, as for instance when a beech tree suddenly appeared with copper-coloured leaves instead of green ones. Such extreme and unaccountable variations are called 'sports' and a sport may become the forerunner of a new multitude of living things as, indeed, the original copper beech did.

"Naturalists do not pretend to know how or why variations occur, but they feel sure that variations in any one direction over a long period of time can make a great difference in the end. They have skeletons of animals going back many millions of years ago which seem to show that the horse was once only a little creature, like a dog in size."

"How about a story?" Michael asked.

"I am coming to that," said Uncle Arthur. "I will tell you the story of how the giraffe is supposed to have got its long neck.

"Once upon a time, tens of thousands of years ago, there lived a family of spotted animals with stumpy legs and short necks. It was before there were any people in the world to call everything names, and so I cannot tell you what these spotted animals with stumpy legs and short necks were. But there was Father Spot, Mother Spot and lots of Little Spots. They all lived in the stripy and spotty jungle, and when they played hide-and-seek they did not need to go behind things, because they were perfectly hidden if only they would stand still amidst all the other spots and stripes in the jungle. If Old Man Tiger came stalking their way they all stood still, so that he should mistake them for bits of jungle, and then he passed them by. If one of the Little Spots had fidgeted, Old Man Tiger would have noticed Master Fidget at once and gobbled him up. For life was like that in the jungle before people came into the world to pull up all the trees and build houses in their place.

"Now as the years went by all the Little Spots began to grow up, and one of them had rather longer legs and a rather longer neck than the others, so that he was much taller. We will call him the Long Spot, because that is what boys would probably have called

IT IS NOT NICE TO BE SO TALL THAT
EVERYBODY LAUGHS AT YOU

him if there had been any boys in those far-off days to see him. Well, all the other Little Spots teased Long Spot. I cannot tell you if they disliked him, or if they were jealous, but anyway, they teased him and Long Spot was very unhappy except at blackberry time, when his long legs and long neck enabled him to reach juicy blackberries that none of the other Little Spots could get near.

"Poor Long Spot played a good deal by himself, as his brothers and sisters always pushed him away if he came near them. There were other families of Spots living in the jungle round about, and sometimes Long Spot tried to make friends with the children of these other Spot families. All of them snorted at him rudely, however, and pushed him away because they had stumpy legs and short necks, whereas he had long legs and a long neck. They thought he was a freak, and they did not like him at all. You will understand, then, that Long Spot was very lonely and sad, often having to go for long walks all by himself to pass the dreary time away.

" One day Long Spot was rambling by himself, far from his own bit of jungle, when he met another lonely Spot with long legs and long neck just like his own, but somehow this creature was different. In some ways the strange creature was like Long Spot's sisters, so he knew that he must be extra polite because it was a girl Spot.

"Now the strange girl Spot was lonely for exactly the same reason as Long Spot: nobody would play with her on account of her long legs and long neck. If her brothers and sisters could have spoken to her, they would have called her Lanky Spot, and that is what I shall call her.

" When Lanky Spot saw Long Spot she nearly jumped for joy, and Long Spot was no less delighted. They walked towards each other, and as they met they rubbed noses. After this they wandered through the jungle side by side, and they did not feel lonely any more. Every day after this Long Spot met Lanky Spot in the jungle, and together they rambled among the thickets, eating the the tender green shoots that grew on the trees and anything else that was nice. Their dumpy-legged brothers and sisters with short necks herded together in other parts of the jungle and celebrated marriages and christenings among themselves, but Long Spot and Lanky Spot were never invited, and although, as the years went by, many more Little Spots were born into the jungle, there did not ever appear another Spot with such long legs and long neck as were possessed by Long Spot and Lanky Spot. These two were freaks, and they were alone in their freakishness. But having one another for company they did not mind. They grew up together, side by side, and were happy.

"Then a terrible thing happened. A very severe winter in the jungle was followed by a treacherous spring. Some warm weather in the months of March and April caused all the trees to show green buds, but in May the wind changed and became blustery and cold, bringing snow by day and bitter frosts by night. Nearly all the green buds and leaves on the trees became withered and black. The ones that were still left green were not nearly enough to feed all the hungry Spots looking for their daily food. All the hundreds and hundreds of dumpy-legged short-necked Spots were running frantically round searching for food, and soon all the green buds and leaves close to the ground were eaten up, because there were so many dumpy-legged short-necked Spots to fight over them. Long Spot and Lanky Spot did not fight with the others because they were able to reach green leaves and buds high up in the trees, where there was none to compete with them. Although the high buds and leaves were few in number, they proved to be quite sufficient for these two creatures, just because they were only two and not any more. Long Spot and Lanky Spot wandered about together far away from the others, as they always did, and they did not know what a bad time the others were having. They did not know that brothers were fighting each other, and even fighting their sisters, in order to get a share of the insufficient food on the trees. Eventually the Spots were killing each other in their mad hunger, but Long Spot and Lanky Spot knew nothing about all this.

"By the middle of June all the thousands of Spots with dumpy legs and short necks had either killed each other or died of starvation, so that the whole jungle belonged to Long Spot and Lanky Spot, who continued to keep together and who eventually became quite grown up.

"Many years later Long Spot and Lanky Spot had some little Spot babies of their own, and what do you think? The babies grew to be like Mother and Father, with long necks and long legs. There was not one with dumpy legs and short neck like the Ancestor Spots. However, the children of Long Spot and Lanky Spot were not all the same, some being taller than others, and even taller than their parents.

"After many hundreds and hundreds of years the jungle became full of Spots once more, but they were all long-legged long-necked Spots, much more handsome than their stunted ancestors of past centuries. When a bad spring season came, all the Spots fought for food, and the ones that were tallest in the leg and longest in the neck got most, so that they lived while the others died. When these survivors had children the children were like themselves, but some were even taller. So as generation succeeded generation the Spots became enormously tall animals, and by the time men appeared in the jungle the Spots were simply huge.

"'What shall we call this great animal with the long legs and the long neck?' said Adam to Eve.

"'Let us call it the Giraffe,' replied Eve, and so this is the name the Spots have been known by ever since."

"Is that the end of the story?" Jaqueline asked, sitting up very straight.

"That is the end," said Uncle Arthur.

"Is it a true story?" asked Michael.

"Yes and no," answered Uncle Arthur; "the giraffe really did get his long neck in some such gradual way as I have described, but

I am not too sure about the Adam and Eve bit. It may have been someone else who first thought of calling the giraffe by that name."

"How did the giraffe get his spots?" Jaqueline asked.

"You could make that story up for yourself, my dear," Uncle Arthur replied. "In the beginning I daresay the ancestors of the giraffe did not have spots. They were unable to keep hidden from Old Man Tiger and were often eaten up. Then, perhaps, a few freaks were born with spots on them, and these managed to escape the eye of Old Man Tiger better than the others, so that eventually there came to be more and more spotted creatures and fewer and fewer unspotted ones. This process of sifting out creatures with advantages from those without is called 'NATURAL SELECTION' by the scientists who study such things. The way in which Long Spot and Lanky Spot managed to live when the others died is called the 'SURVIVAL OF THE FITTEST,' for it happened that they were really fitter to live under jungle conditions than their dumpy-legged, short-necked relations. The fighting and jostling that goes on among living creatures in their efforts to get a living is called the 'STRUGGLE FOR EXISTENCE.' You can understand now that when any peculiarity of a living creature turns out to be an advantage to it in the struggle for existence, it may survive because of its special fitness while others die. Its babies will be like itself, and may show this special fitness to an even greater extent, so that once again there is survival and, with the next generation, an increase of fitness.

"We can say that butterflies have become prettier and prettier because it made them safer and ever safer from birds to become pretty like the flowers. Nowadays, because of their colouring, they can hide among the flowers so well as to escape the sharp eyes of birds looking for juicy morsels to eat."

"But how did flowers get their lovely colours?" asked Michael.

MOTHS, BUTTERFLIES
AND OTHER INSECTS
ARE OFTEN SO MUCH
LIKE FLOWERS, OR
OTHER PARTS OF PLANTS,
THAT BIRDS LOOKING
FOR FOOD PASS THEM BY.

"From the same sort of cause," answered Uncle Arthur; "flowers need insects to carry their pollen to one another. They are like people who stay in one place, but are always sending messages to each other, and they use insects as we use the postman. They cannot tell the insect postman what to do, however, so they just have to look as bright as they can in order to attract his notice. The flowers that have succeeded in doing this are able to survive, but those that were unsuccessful could not make enough seeds, so they have died out and become extinct. Besides looking gay and pretty, flowers have learnt other tricks. They have learnt to smell nice and to be generous and pay the insect postman with tiny drops of sweet nectar—the stuff bees collect and make into honey."

"Are there any dull flowers that insects are beginning not to notice?" asked Jaqueline.

"Some flowers are dull," answered Uncle Arthur; "they have found that they can get the wind to do their work for them. This blows the pollen from one to another. As a consequence, these flowers have managed to survive without acquiring any special charms. They neither look pretty nor smell nice nor offer honey. Some of the flowers of trees are like this—flowers of oak, hazel and so

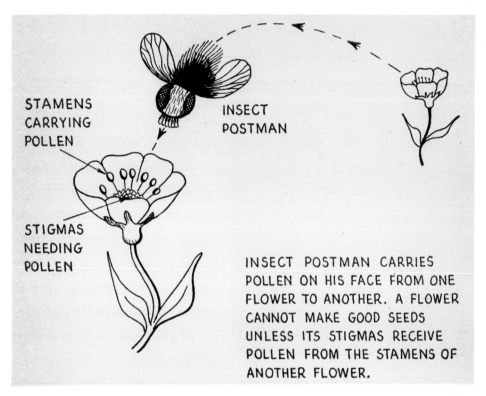

STAMENS
CARRYING
POLLEN

INSECT
POSTMAN

STIGMAS
NEEDING
POLLEN

INSECT POSTMAN CARRIES
POLLEN ON HIS FACE FROM ONE
FLOWER TO ANOTHER. A FLOWER
CANNOT MAKE GOOD SEEDS
UNLESS ITS STIGMAS RECEIVE
POLLEN FROM THE STAMENS OF
ANOTHER FLOWER.

on. Such flowers are just dull catkins *making* pollen, and dull little clumps of stigmas *collecting* pollen. A few trees, the lime for instance, and the pussy willow or sallow, make more attractive flowers, and insects do pay some attention to these; and then, of course, there are the trees with rose-like flowers—apple, plum, pear and so on, which do definitely rely on insects to be their postmen. Because they must attract insects these fruit trees have the most heavenly blossom."

"Flowers are made nice just to please insects, then," said Jaqueline sadly; "they were not meant to please us at all."

"They were meant to please children," Uncle Arthur contradicted; "you see, children have inquisitive little noses and heaps of time. They often go round smelling flowers and then they do the work of flower postmen too. If it were not for school and lessons, I

HAVE I GOT ANY POLLEN ON MY NOSE?

dare say children would help the flowers and trees quite a lot by sniffing the goodness from different blossoms and shaking boughs to send pollen scattering on the breeze."

"Did the stick insects grow like sticks and the leaf insects grow like leaves, and some caterpillars grow like twigs because that made them safe from the prying eyes of enemies?" asked Jaqueline.

"Precisely so," answered Uncle Arthur. "Very gradually these creatures acquired these resemblances, and because each improvement helped to increase the chance of survival, the resemblances have become more and more perfect. I can tell you of other resemblances that also have to do with this game of hide-and-seek. Some insects taste horrid to birds, or have stings, and so they are left alone. Many quite nice-tasting insects faintly resembled the nasty-tasting or stinging ones, so they too were often avoided. Gradually, as a result of natural selection, this resemblance has become more and more perfect until to-day we have different kinds of insect that are almost indistinguishable from one another, yet one kind tastes sweet and is harmless, whereas the other kind tastes horrid or has a nasty sting. Birds have to be very clever in these days if they are to choose the right insects for their food."

"Goodness gracious!" exclaimed Michael. "Look at the clock. It is nearly time to eat again!"

IS NATURE CRUEL?

The same evening Aunt Agatha was tucking up Jaqueline in her bed when Jaqueline said, "Auntie, can you ask Uncle to come up and say good-night?"

"But I thought you kissed him good-night before you came up to bed," protested Aunt Agatha.

"I did," answered Jaqueline; "but I want to do it again."

"Oh, very well," grumbled Aunt Agatha; "I will ask him to come up."

"Yes, my dear, what is the matter?" Uncle Arthur said as he entered Jaqueline's room.

"Oh, Uncle," cried Jaqueline, "I've been thinking."

"That was a dangerous thing to do, wasn't it?" laughed Uncle Arthur.

"About what you told us to-day," Jaqueline went on. "Don't you think Nature is very cruel? I mean, those Spot creatures could not help having short legs and short necks. Why did they all have to die? It doesn't seem fair to me that some should live and others die, just because some have long necks and others not."

"Oho," laughed Uncle Arthur again, "you've started finding fault with God's world already, have you? Well, folk have always been finding fault, only they do not usually start like you, at nine years of age. So you think Nature is unfair, do you? Well, now, I will tell you this. The Spot creatures with short legs and short necks were very satisfied with themselves, so much so that they dared to tease their tall relative. They were what we should call smug, and it just happened that smugness went with short legs and a short neck. If the creatures had been proud of their tall relative he might have stayed with them and reached down some juicy bits of food for them, but they chose to be beastly to him, so he went away and was not there to help them when hard times came. Among human beings thousands suffer poverty and worse because they are

PORTRAIT OF A BOY WHO THINKS HE HAS BEEN TREATED UNFAIRLY.

so pleased with themselves that they never look ahead. Common folk tease and persecute any who differ from themselves, and then, when the freaks get on and make their fortunes, these people say, 'It's not fair — they should share with us.'"

"I wouldn't share," said Jaqueline.

"No, indeed," went on Uncle Arthur; "you must not pity the people who are always grumbling about things not being fair. They grumble because they have a high opinion of their own deserts, yet they never do anything to better their fortunes. I know that it just seems to be a matter of luck whether we are clever or beautiful, but we can all be good, and if we are good we are less likely to suffer, because we shall be surrounded by friends who will come to our aid if we get into difficulties. Besides, goodness makes us more clever."

"Thank you, Uncle," said Jaqueline, reaching up to kiss him; "I feel better about it now. I thought it all seemed rather unfair, but I see that I was wrong."

Chapter 4

HOW KINDNESS CAME INTO THE WORLD

You have heard Uncle Arthur tell Jaqueline and Michael how the giraffe may have become long in the legs and neck, and now you know the way in which naturalists believe the creatures to have been fashioned, one out of another. Any small change in the shape or character of a creature tends to become accentuated as generation succeeds generation *if the effect of that change proves to be an advantage in the struggle for existence.*

Extra strength or extra ferocity was a help to some animals in the beginning, just as extra height was to others; and at first naturalists supposed that the struggle for existence favoured only the selfish and cruel tendencies in creatures. They were so insistent on the cruel side of the process that their theory was considered to be exaggerated and wrong. It seemed as though the gentle and kind creature must always be beaten in its attempts to compete with the rough and the ruthless. However, since the days when Charles Darwin first started the great argument about evolution, naturalists have had time to think again, and now they are agreed that gentleness and kindness may have had their uses too. No matter how strong and fierce a creature may be it does not live for ever. After a certain number of years it dies, and if it has not devoted part of its life to rearing baby creatures like itself its race may become extinct.

To lay eggs which the warmth of the sun or of rotting vegetation will hatch out is one way of making sure that there will be successors, but it is a lazy way.   When the world became more crowded with ever-hungry animals in search of food the egg left to itself was liable to be discovered and eaten.   Creatures that could not (or would not)

CREATURES THAT DID NOT STAY TO PROTECT THEIR EGGS HAD THEM EATEN BY ENEMIES, AND SO THEY COULD NOT LEAVE ANY DESCENDANTS. THEIR RACE BECAME EXTINCT.

learn to guard their eggs often failed to leave successors, and it is possible that many antediluvian monsters became extinct for this very reason.   They had all the strength and ferocity needed to take care of themselves, but they lacked interest in their eggs and in the frail baby creatures that hatched out of those eggs.   Such an interest became necessary to their survival, but because they never acquired it their race became extinct.

We can see clearly that Nature had a use for kindness at this stage in the world's history, and many creatures must have owed their survival to its emergence as part of their characters. The remote reptile-like ancestor of the present-day bird must have learnt to hide its eggs from its enemies. Then it must have learnt to care for them enough to stand guard over them and over the fledglings. Any creature not showing enough care was bound to decrease in numbers as generation succeeded generation, ultimately becoming extinct. Our birds are a glorious proof that this did not happen in every case. The bird mother is quite perfect in her way, and now she has the help of the bird father, for such were the difficulties encountered in the struggle for existence that he too had to learn to play a kindly part.

Throughout Nature you can see creatures that have acquired an instinctive kindness causing them to feed and protect their little ones. Most human beings possess the same instinct.

You may say that Nature could have ensured the survival of negligent creatures by enabling them to lay an ever-increasing number of eggs so that no matter how many were eaten by enemies there would always be enough left to produce a fresh generation. As a matter of fact many negligent creatures did learn to succeed in this very way, and we can see them around us to-day. The housefly, the fish and the frog all lay hundreds or thousands of eggs, only to forget them after the deed has been done. Most of these eggs come to nothing for the reason that they are gobbled up by other creatures, but enough are left to generate a host of new flies, fish or frogs. This is a very wasteful process involving great loss of life, and only creatures without feeling could permit themselves to breed in this way. More highly developed creatures produce fewer offspring and tend them with loving care. The creatures that have learnt to be kind are bringing joy into the world instead of suffering.

Their little ones are not too numerous to be cared for properly, so all survive and grow to maturity.

Selfishness and carelessness succeed in Nature to a limited extent, but we know now that the greatest triumphs are reserved for kindness and love. The kindly bird triumphs over the thoughtless fly, and man seems destined to triumph over the whole animal kingdom because of his determination to see that little human children receive every possible care.

Is the ultimate victory of kindness over cruelty an absolute certainty? Some people think it is not. There are times when human beings seem to put aside their better instincts to become fierce and destructive again. At such times they wage war among themselves and use all their wonderful knowledge of science to encompass the killing of their fellows. Aircraft and nuclear weapons can undo in a few hours all that the labour of patience and love has taken centuries to perform. The wicked use of such things cannot destroy everybody, however, and neither can it destroy the accumulated wisdom of mankind. The people who remain alive after a great and terrible war can go on practising the saving grace of kindness; also they can draw upon the great fund of knowledge that is stored up in good books to rebuild a new and better world.

The instinct of kindness is never wholly uprooted and killed. It was put into our hearts by necessity in the remote past and strengthened through countless millions of years so that we can count on finding it there to-day if we will look within ourselves. This powerful instinct gives each one of us a conscience, so that we feel shame if we go against it and injure someone younger and weaker than ourselves. It gives us a sense of duty too, so that if we neglect to do good when the chance occurs we are sure to feel regret afterwards.

The old instinct to fight and to grab everything for ourselves is in our hearts too, and bad people may try to foster it at the expense of our newer and better instincts, but we must hold fast to what God has given us and not let ourselves be corrupted into savages again.

Chapter 5

A KIND DEED

JAQUELINE and Michael had had a lovely day in the big city with Uncle Arthur. They had been up and down the river in a little steamer, admiring all the wonderful bridges. Then they had been

A MEAN STREET

up to the top of a tall tower and admired the wonderful view from there. The day had been very hot, and after tea in a nice teashop they looked forward to the train journey back to the cool green country where they were staying with their uncle and aunt.

"We will walk part of the way to our station," said Uncle Arthur; "it will not take us long from here."

The children admired the view as they went along, but after crossing one of the bridges over the river Jaqueline became rather solemn.

"What an awful place this is," she said; "the houses look so dirty, and they haven't even the tiniest scrap of a garden. I should just *hate* to live here." She shuddered as she spoke.

"Lots of children do live here, though," Uncle Arthur said; "shall we go and have a peep at them?"

They turned down a mean-looking side street, where many children were running about. In every doorway there were groups of children. Some were playing happily, others were quarrelling, but all looked very dirty and unkempt.

At the end of the street there was a house so broken and dirty that nobody lived there at all. Sitting on the front step, however, was a little girl with a big doll. She

IN NEED OF A HOLIDAY

was cuddling her baby and rocking from side to side as though trying to make it sleep. She was all by herself, and Uncle Arthur could see by the look in her wide blue eyes that she was not seeing anything of what was before her, but thinking of something inside herself. He pointed her out to Jaqueline.

"Look," he said, "that little girl has gone to get a bit of peace all by herself, and now she is in the fairyland of her own dreams."

"Oh," exclaimed Jaqueline, horrified, "isn't she dreadfully thin, and what awful rags of clothes she's got."

"Jaqueline, dear," Uncle Arthur said gently, "would you feel awfully jealous if I asked that little girl to come home with us for a holiday in the country, away from these dreadful surroundings?"

"Oh, Uncle!" exclaimed Jaqueline joyfully; "would you really do it?"

"I wouldn't dare to if you said I mustn't," Uncle Arthur replied.

"Oh, do, do!" urged Jaqueline, "I should love it."

Uncle Arthur looked at Michael. "Well, old chap?" he queried. "What do you think of the idea?"

"Jolly good wheeze of yours," answered Michael heartily.

Uncle Arthur went up to a big fat woman standing in one of the open doorways and pointed out the little girl to her. "Excuse me," he said, raising his hat, "but can you tell me where that little girl over there lives. My kiddies want to ask if she can come to the country with us for a holiday."

"Bless you, sir, for your kind thought," said the big fat woman; "it'll do her the world of good, poor little soul. She's that thin I could cry every time I look at her; but it's not food that she wants. She gets plenty given to her, but it doesn't agree with her. It's my belief that she isn't very well and needs a change. Her Mum would give her own life to get her taken away for a bit. The father's a bad lot and spends all he gets on the drink, or the dogs, or his dirty old pipe. It's nothing but blows and foul words she gets out of him. And she, poor soul, scratting and scraping all day to make ends meet! I doubt if you'll find her at home yet, though you can try. Number 23 it is, down on the other side."

Uncle Arthur thanked the big lady for her information, and then he led Jaqueline and Michael down the street to Number 23.

"Look at the step, Jaqueline dear," said Uncle Arthur, "and the curtains. They are kept nice and clean. If the little girl is dirty it's not that the mother doesn't try. But how can a child keep clean in such a playground as she's got, and going among such little raga-muffins as come from some of these other houses?"

Uncle Arthur knocked, and Jaqueline thought with glee of the lovely surprise that was coming to the people living at Number 23. "Almost as if God Himself had come to pay a visit," she said to herself, looking proudly at her kind old uncle.

The door of Number 23 opened, and a terribly old woman, like a witch, peeped out. Jaqueline stepped back in horror, not expecting to see such an apparition. Uncle Arthur, however, lifted his hat again and asked if he could see the lady of the house. "It is about her little girl," he said; "I'd like to give her a holiday in the country."

"I'm her Grannie," piped the very old woman, "and I'd be real grateful to see her get a treat. It's not much fun for her here, and it's my belief she won't live long if she doesn't get more flesh on her poor little bones. Her mother will be back directly. Perhaps you would like to come in and wait?"

Uncle Arthur bared his head and went in after the old Grannie. Jaqueline and Michael followed, feeling that they were entering a witch's cave. It seemed terribly dark and stuffy in the mean little house after the glaring sunshine of the street.

"You'd like a country holiday yourself, I expect," Uncle Arthur said to the old woman kindly.

"Yes, indeed," the old woman replied; "but it's Maggie needs it most. She has all her life before her, and I'm only an old woman. It'll be holiday enough for me thinking of her away from this dump of a place and away from her brute of a father, who doesn't care two pins for her." As the old woman said these words her eyes blazed with hate, looking like two coals of fire. Jaqueline and Michael both saw the look, and they shuddered.

"Uncle," said Jaqueline in a whisper, when the old woman left them for a moment, "I don't know how you dare to talk to such people. I think you are awfully brave."

"Oh, come," laughed Uncle Arthur, "even the lions would receive you kindly if you could let them know that you were about to give them their heart's desire. The old Grannie is all right really, but hard work has bent her and shrivelled her up, and she's never managed to save enough money to buy herself some false teeth. You could turn her into a dear kind old fairy godmother if you had the money to spend on making her look nice again."

Jaqueline squeezed her uncle's hand hard, but she said nothing. She was thinking how right he always was.

Presently the old woman came hobbling into the room again. "My daughter's coming down the road now," she said; "it's the dearest wish of her heart that you are going to give her, and I thank you most kindly. An angel of the Lord you must be, and no mistake."

"Only your very humble servant," answered Uncle Arthur, bowing politely.

Maggie's mother was nearly speechless with joy when she heard of Uncle Arthur's plan. She ran about looking for clean things in which to dress Maggie, and then she went down the road screaming, "Maggie, Maggie!—it's your bit of Paradise come for you at last!"

All the people in their doorways stared, and word flew up and down the street that Maggie was going to get the holiday she so badly needed. Faces that had been dreadful and scowling a few minutes before became wreathed in kindly smiles. Everyone wished Maggie joy, and not one person felt jealous or meanly

READY TO START

envious. Looking out through the doorway of Maggie's house, Jaqueline saw all the excited, happy people, so shabbily dressed and so toilworn, yet with love lighting up their faces. Several ran indoors to look for an odd sixpence or some other little gift for Maggie.

When, eventually, Maggie was dressed and ready, Uncle Arthur said "good-bye" to the smiling mother and Grannie and set out down the street for the station. Maggie put her bony little hand confidingly in one of his, and Jaqueline hung on to his other arm, peeping round every now and then to have another look at Maggie, who had not yet come out of her dream. Hats waved as they went along the street, and loud praises were sung from every door. Even the little boys stopped fighting one another to gape at the remarkable change in the usual sullen scene.

C. IV—16*

"There," said Uncle Arthur to Jaqueline, "some spend ten shillings or more on a theatre ticket to get a change of scene, and even then it is only a false change. You and I haven't spent a penny yet, but we've changed a whole street in the twinkling of an eye; and it is a real change too. There'll be some shillings spent before it is all over, I don't deny that; but it will be a pitifully small sum compared with the good that it will do."

Very soon Uncle Arthur and the children were in the train speeding homewards. Maggie was still in a daze, but every now and then she met Uncle Arthur's eye and she seemed to come to herself. A great toothless smile spread over her face, for she was at the age when baby teeth were coming out and new ones taking their place. The smile was full of confidence and happiness. After looking at Uncle Arthur she turned to look out of the carriage window again. So far, she showed no sign of wanting to talk to Jaqueline and Michael.

"Uncle," said Jaqueline suddenly, "Aunt Agatha! Whatever will *she* say?"

"Your aunt may not like our little friend at first," Uncle Arthur replied, "but I am sure she will when we explain everything."

At this moment Maggie saw some cows in a field near the railway, and she so far forgot her reserve as to grab Jaqueline by the arm and point to the wondrous sight. After this, Jaqueline stayed by her side and chatted with her about all the things that could be seen from the train. For Maggie it was wonderful to be seeing so many new things. For Jaqueline it was wonderful to have this new sister who needed so much and to feel that it was in her power to give all.

It was in the evening when the train finally arrived at the little country place where Jaqueline and Michael were staying.

Aunt Agatha was rather cross when she saw Maggie, and at first she did not like her very much. Still, she said nothing in front of the children, who soon ran off to show Maggie the drake Archibald, and all the things in the garden.

"It was rather rash of you to bring that child here, Arthur," Aunt Agatha said at last, when the children were unable to hear her views; "Maggie does not look very clean and she may have something catching. She looks

AUNT AGATHA DOES NOT LIKE MAGGIE—

very thin to me. Don't you think you ought to let the District Nurse have a look at her before we decide to keep her here with Jaqueline and Michael? You would never forgive yourself if anything happened to them."

"What things are you thinking about?" Uncle Arthur asked.

"For one thing," Aunt Agatha answered, "her hair ought to be examined. Sometimes children have insects in their hair. It isn't their fault: they just catch things from others who are careless about washing and combing their hair. And Maggie might have other things the matter such as skin troubles. I am sure the Nurse ought to see her."

Uncle Arthur agreed with Aunt Agatha, and later that day he took Maggie to see the District Nurse.

"Well now, Mr. Purser," said the Nurse, when she heard Uncle Arthur's tale; "that's a real nice idea of yours. I am sure we can make the little girl all right. Come here, my dear."

The Nurse looked at Maggie's hair and nodded. "We shall have to do something about this," she said; "but we shall have it put right in a brace of shakes. It's funny how people fuss over a little thing like this. It's nothing really, and so easy to put right." The Nurse attended to Maggie's needs and looked her over for anything else that might be wrong. At last she said Maggie was fit to go home with Uncle Arthur.

"Why is she so small?" Uncle Arthur ventured to ask before leaving.

"All the wrong sort of food, very likely," answered the Nurse; "too much bread and jam, too much starch altogether. Give her plenty of good meat and fresh vegetables and fruit, especially orange juice. And when you send her back, give her a big bottle of that cod-liver oil and malt to eat on her bread instead of jam. If you get a good make it tastes as nice as honey, and children love it. There, Mr. Purser, the little lady is all sweet and clean and ready for you now, and I wish you the joy of her company in your house. She looks a dear little soul. What does your good lady think about it?"

Uncle Arthur smiled rather sadly as he watched Maggie run out to look at the neat and pretty garden in front of the Nurse's house. "Maggie isn't everyone's idea of a lovable child," he said at last.

"Never mind, Mr. Purser," the Nurse said heartily; "Mrs. Purser will come round in a day or two, I dare say. Some folk are born to have their minds made up for them. They could never begin to do a good deed on their own initiative; it has to be started for them by someone else, someone who is not discouraged by the awkward and difficult steps that have to be taken first of all. If you will excuse me saying so, Mr. Purser, your good wife is like that. Good as gold really, but no 'go.' She couldn't have married a better man than you to keep her up to the mark. Never a kind thing would she ever have done if it hadn't been for you starting it, and you've started many."

Aunt Agatha looked rather cross in the evening, but she felt

DON'T FORGET TO BRUSH YOUR TEETH

BATH MAT

— SO UNCLE ARTHUR IS KEPT BUSY LOOKING AFTER HER

reassured by the Nurse's verdict, and so she made up a bed for Maggie.

"It's you who will have to see that she cleans her teeth and washes herself, Arthur," she said; "I could not bring myself to touch her yet, after what I saw of her when you first brought her."

"It suits me," said Uncle Arthur; "poor little creature, I'd do anything to make her happy, and I like her right well."

So Uncle Arthur acted as lady's-maid to Maggie for the next few days, washing and dressing her and combing her hair. In less than a week she had a fresh colour in her cheeks, and she became really pretty. Uncle Arthur was very proud of his handiwork.

"She does you credit, Arthur, my dear," Aunt Agatha said on the eighth day after Maggie's arrival; "I should never have believed it possible to work such a change in her. Now that she is nice I should like to manage her myself, but I suppose you would be too jealous to let me."

"No indeed," answered Uncle Arthur; "I should be glad for you to take her under your wing."

That very evening Aunt Agatha ordered

AUNT AGATHA LIKES MAGGIE AT LAST

Maggie to follow her to the bathroom for the nightly ceremony of preparing for bed, but Maggie became scared and looked imploringly at Uncle Arthur.

"It isn't any use, Arthur," said Aunt Agatha; "she's your child, and rightly so. Her loveliness is your doing, and I do not deserve her confidence after the way I received her in the beginning. It is the same with the animals: they all love you and have no use for me. Archibald only flies for me and pecks me when I go outside."

"Oh, Auntie," cried Jaqueline, aghast, "I believe you are crying!"

"Hush, child," answered Aunt Agatha; "it is nothing, and I am very happy."

Jaqueline rushed to her auntie and put her arms round her. "Oh, Auntie!" she said, "you must not be so upset. You are ever so kind to us all really, and Maggie doesn't understand."

"It is nice of you to say so, dear," Aunt Agatha said, wiping her eyes; "but if it were not for your uncle I should have passed for a wicked and selfish old woman."

Sounds of merry laughter and splashing water came from the bathroom.

"Listen, my child," Aunt Agatha went on; "it might have been the clinking of beer glasses and the rude mirth of a man hearing nasty stories. I am lucky to have a husband who rejoices in such simple homely things. He spends less money than anyone I know, and yet it is all spent on giving pleasure to others. I am jealous of him often and often, which is why I am so prickly, but I am not really unmindful of my blessings, God be praised."

Chapter 6

WE HAVE TO DECIDE WHETHER A STRANGER IS NICE OR NASTY

MOST children are ready enough to make friends with people who go out of their way to be agreeable to them. Parents naturally feel a little anxious about this; yet, while wishing to make their children cautious, they hesitate to make young folk fearful or suspicious of everybody who approaches them with a smile. A narrow-minded person may easily deprive a child of some friendship that might prove of inestimable worth. A classic instance of this was when a schoolmistress kept back from one of her pupils a letter written by Lewis Carroll, the author of *Alice in Wonderland*. The child was quite grown up before she received that letter to remind her of the kind old man who had once amused her in a train. It was found among the effects of the schoolmistress, after that lady had died, and alas, by that time Lewis Carroll had died also.

Opportunity knocks at the child's door just as it knocks at our own, and it rarely knocks twice, so that we must open the child's eyes to life's great possibilities, and beware of letting our own ill-considered fears and prejudices become a blight across the youthful prospect.

Because I believe the subject to be worthy of thought, I have included two short stories, following this chapter, to show the line of reasoning any child might be expected to employ in weighing up the character of a friendly stranger. The situations which can tax the judgment of the normal child are far too numerous to be dealt with at length in this book, but I have singled out two fairly typical ones to exemplify what might be regarded as right parental guidance in this difficult matter. I have conceded so far to popular feeling as to make the stranger a man and the children girls in each of my two stories, but this does not mean to say that I am unaware of the existence of unpleasant female characters.

There is an etiquette which all would-be friends of children should observe most scrupulously if they are desirous of learning to play their part properly; and children can be made acquainted with the rules. The first consideration of any really nice and thoughtful stranger is to avoid confronting a child with the need for making a difficult decision. He can address any child in the presence of the parents, because the decision to be friendly or otherwise then rests with the parents, and puts no strain on the child. He can also speak to an unaccompanied child in a train, if there are several other pleasant-looking passengers observing him, because the child feels quite safe in such goodly company. He should, however, seek to become more distant as the end of the journey approaches, in case the child wishes to beat a hasty retreat when deprived of the moral support of the other passengers. He should not speak to a strange child in a park or playground unless he has first given unequivocal proof of his high standing among the child's friends or co-equals. He should refrain, therefore, from going straight up to a strange child in a public playground and offering, for instance, to help her start her swing. But he might excusably do this in half an hour's time, after he has given her a chance to watch him playing on terms of easy intimacy with several little friends of long standing. By this time she herself may very well be on the point of asking if she too can join in the fun.

In case of accident or other emergency, it may be necessary to set formality aside, and trust to making a favourable impression on a child immediately, but in the ordinary way, direct approach, either by a man or woman, is in bad taste, because to children, more than to anyone else in the world, we owe a clear and transparent account of ourselves before we approach them, asking to be favourably received.

I believe that most uninhibited children are naturally gifted at reading character, and that their intuition often makes a short approach possible. But this intuition must not be taken for granted. A measure of shyness and diffidence, matching the child's own, is the principal characteristic of the person who means well but has to leave out some of the preliminaries of the politer form of approach. True refinement gives a person a manner that is quite distinctive in many other little ways, and children can sense its presence or absence very quickly.   For, behind all natural graciousness, there lies the talent of being able to love patiently and unselfishly and universally—a talent that shines forth in the face and cannot be hidden. The light of this great love may go out to children of any age, anywhere, at any time, from the face of man or woman, youth or maiden; and when it beckons, there will be no holding them back.   They are wiser with their age-old instincts than all the lessons in prudence could ever make them. "Mummy," they say, " we saw such a nice person to-day," and no amount of questioning will elicit anything more tangible by way of information than the added explanation, " Well, he was just *nice*, in the nicest sort of way."

How indeed is it possible for the child to be more explicit than this? What grown-up person would care to try to satisfy another as to his reasons for loving some third person?   Outside the invisible bond of understanding and sympathy that links people together, there can be no reason for love. But such reason as there is is all-sufficient, for it makes people in effect nice to one another—" Just nice, in the nicest sort of way."

Section Nine: Past, Present and Future

Chapter 7

THE NICE STRANGER

JENNIFER and Jacqueline burst into the house in great excitement and threw down their hats; "Oh, Mummy," they shouted, in chorus, "we've seen such a nice man at the swings. He gave us catches, and he pretended we were clocks and wound us up."

Both the little girls giggled at their recollections of the friendly stranger. Then they remembered something else. "He said he would be there again next Saturday."

Mummy went on slicing the beetroot in her hand as if nothing could disturb her. Then she looked at her little girls with a twinkle in her eye. "I thought I told you not to talk to strangers," she said at last.

"Oh, but *Mummy*," protested Jacqueline, "he was ever so nice, *really* he was."

"How did you know he was nice?" Mummy asked. "Come, you are big girls now—nearly ten—and you ought to be able to tell me *why* you thought the stranger was nice."

"Well," said Jennifer slowly, "for one thing, there were two other children there who called him Daddy."

"Bravo!" said Mummy. "That's a good sign. A man out with his own children is usually quite a safe person—but go on."

"Another thing," said Jacqueline, "was that several children seemed to have played with him before, because they knew his name. They kept calling, 'Catch me, Mr. Green,' or, 'It's my turn now, Mr. Green.'"

"Do you think he was a teacher?" asked Mummy.

"I don't know," replied Jacqueline; "but lots of children seemed to be very familiar with him, and there didn't seem to be any harm in us joining in the fun."

"Well, girlies," said Mummy, "I am proud of you both, because you seem to have kept your wits about you and made sure of the stranger before trusting him. But tell me, did *all* the other children that were with you like being caught?"

"There were one or two rather shy ones," replied Jennifer. "When they said they didn't want to be wound up, the man said, 'Oh, I forgot—you are 400-day clocks, aren't you? You only need winding once a year.' And when we all pretended to be juicy ripe pears and bananas on the roundabout and invited the man to pick us off and eat us, there was one big girl who didn't seem to like being picked, so the man just gave her one tug and said she couldn't be ripe enough, because ripe fruit came away from the tree easily with the least touch."

"He didn't tease anybody, then?" said Mummy.

"Oh *no*," interposed Jacqueline, "he was a real gentleman. I was a bit shy of him at first, wasn't I, Jenny? But he was really sweet about it, and he didn't make me feel silly at all. In the end I *had* to give in."

"Did he play with boys too?" asked Mummy.

"Oh yes," cried the little girls together; "he played with everybody; and the boys tried to see if they could knock him down. They threw themselves off the swings at him with all their force, but he stood up to them all right."

"He sounds a real good sort," said Mummy.

"Can we go and play with him next Saturday?" pleaded Jacqueline.

"I should think so," replied Mummy, "if it is a nice day. I might come along myself just to see if it is really all right, but from what you say I am sure I can trust you, and him."

"Oh, Mummy, you're a dear!" exclaimed Jacqueline, squeezing her mother's hand joyfully.

"Run along, now, both of you," said Mummy; "it is time you washed for dinner. Daddy will be home in a minute."

Chapter 8

THE DOUBTFUL STRANGER

THE bus was full one rainy day;
It had no room for little May;
"Now I'll be late for school," she cried;
But then a car stopped by her side.

"Jump in, my dear," the driver said,
But May drew back and shook her head.

450

She'd never seen the man before;
His car was not of those she saw
Go by to work each day, while she
Stood waiting for bus Number Three.
"I cannot come with you," said May;
"Please shut your door and go away,
Your business here I do not know,
You really mustn't tempt me so.

My Mummy gave me this advice
To tell if folk were bad or nice:
'The nice,' she said, 'will never speak
To-day, to-morrow or next week

Until they know a girl has seen
Clear signs of all the good they mean;
Perhaps they'll let her see them do

Some kindness to a child or two;
Perhaps they'll wait until they've shown
That friend of hers they've always known;
But wait they will, if they are nice,
Before they try to break the ice.'
Your offer may be very kind;
To take it I feel most inclined:
But no," cried May, "I'll stand and wait,
Even if it makes me late."

The man, in anger, drove away.
"I'm glad he's gone," said little May.
Just then she heard a welcome sound.
"Hooray!" she cried, on looking round,
"At last here comes a Number Three
With room inside for little me."

Chapter 9

MARJORIE AND JACK

THE Easter holidays were getting very near, and Marjorie was very excited at the thought of not having to go to school for two whole weeks. Her cousin Jack was coming to stay at her house so that she should not miss her school friends and feel lonely. Jack, like Marjorie, was an only child, and his mummy was very pleased when Marjorie's mummy wrote to ask if he could come for a visit. In her answer she wrote, " Jack will be very pleased to come. He never knows what to do with himself after he has been at home for a day or two, and he will enjoy having Marjorie to play with."

" When will Jack come, Mummy? " Marjorie asked at breakfast on the Wednesday before Good Friday.

" He will come on the first coach on Saturday morning," answered Mummy, " it stops at the bottom of our lane, and you can go down all by yourself, if you like, to meet him. He should arrive at half-past eleven."

" Perhaps he will have a heavy bag to carry," Marjorie said doubtfully.

" Oh no, he won't," said Mummy; " your Auntie wrote to say that he would be carrying only one small case with his pyjamas and a change of underclothes and one or two other things inside. She said she would have the other things sent by carrier." Marjorie still did not look satisfied. "Why, I believe you are shy of going to meet your cousin," laughed Mummy.

"I am a bit," admitted Marjorie.

"Oh, well," went on Mummy, "perhaps if I am not too busy I will come with you and meet him too."

On Saturday morning Marjorie could hardly wait. Directly after breakfast she put on her coat and hat, but Mummy said it would be two hours before Jack arrived. At last the clock said a quarter-past eleven, and Mummy said, "Off you go, then, darling."

Marjorie darted off. She had made up her mind to go by herself after all. It was more grand, and she wanted to impress Jack.

At the bottom of the lane was the busy main road. Cars were rushing past in both directions. Marjorie knew that the coach had to come from the road on her right. Jack would step out on the same side as her lane, so that he would not have to cross the busy road.

Several coaches went past without stopping, and Marjorie began to think that Jack was *never* coming. At last a lovely blue coach came in sight and, as it drew near, it began to move over to Marjorie's side of the road and slow down.

The blue coach stopped right where Marjorie was waiting, and out of it stepped a boy of her own size, carrying a small case. He looked up and down the road without seeming to see Marjorie, so the conductor pointed her out. "Perhaps that young lady has been sent to meet you," he said.

Marjorie stepped forward. "Are you Jack Brown?" she asked shyly.

"Yes," answered the boy, "are you Marjorie Duke?"

"Yes," said the little girl, holding out her hand. "How do you do."

The coach conductor saw for himself that Jack had found a friend, so he rang the bell and the coach glided away. It was soon out of sight and out of earshot.

Neither Marjorie nor Jack remembered having seen one another before, but as they walked along the lane, back to Marjorie's home, they found plenty to say to one another. They were like old friends by the time Marjorie was able to take her cousin by the arm and point out the chimneys of her house peeping over the tree tops.

"Race you there!" cried Jack, and both children broke into a run.

Going up the garden path, breathless from their race, the children met Mummy.

"Ah, there you are!" exclaimed Mummy; "I was just coming to look down the lane and see if you were anywhere in sight. Well, Jack, have you had a good journey?"

"Oh yes," cried Jack, "it was a topping coach. We did fifty miles an hour most of the way down."

"Come and have lunch now," said Mummy. "I had it laid early because I felt sure you would be hungry after your early start."

After Marjorie and Jack had washed their hands they went into the dining-room for lunch. It was lovely Irish stew and dumplings, with treacle pudding to follow.

In the afternoon Marjorie showed Jack all over her big old country house, not forgetting the mysterious attics and all the sheds and barns and stables outside. When the light began to grow dim they went into the dining-room again, where there was a blazing fire. Mummy had cut a whole loaf of bread into slices, and she gave the children a toasting-fork each.

"You can do some work while you are warming yourselves," she said.

So Marjorie and Jack toasted the bread for their tea, and they must have toasted their cheeks too, for it was two very rosy-faced children who, a quarter of an hour later, went to sit up at the tea-table.

When tea was finished and cleared away, Marjorie said to Jack, " Now I'll show you all my toys."

She went out of the room and came back with armfuls of treasures. She went out again several times, returning each time with a load of toys or books. Girl and boy were very happy for an hour or two, playing with all these things, until at last Mummy looked at the clock and said, " Bed-time."

So that was the end of Jack's first day with Marjorie. He had had a lovely time.

The weather was not good during Jack's stay with Marjorie. At first it was too cold; then, although it became much warmer, it was too wet. The two children played indoors, but, in the end, there was nothing fresh for them to do, so Mummy read one or two books aloud to them. One of the books she read to them was *The Water Babies*, by Charles Kingsley. It was all about a poor little half-starved boy, only ten years old, who used to help an unkind man to sweep chimneys. The man made him go right up inside the biggest chimneys to brush them clean and, of course, the poor little boy got black from head to foot. At last he escaped from the unkind man by running away. One of the first things he did was to take off all his clothes and get into a nice clean stream of water to wash off all the soot. Then something magic must have happened, because he found himself living under the water like a fish with lots of other little naked children. He had many adventures under the water with the water babies, so that Marjorie and Jack thought his story a very exciting one.

The day before Jack had to go home the rain cleared up and the sun came out. The air was very clear and calm, and towards the middle of the day the sun was really hot, just like summer. The children were glad to race about the garden after their long stuffy days indoors, but presently Marjorie said, "Phew! I'm hot. I'd like to be a water baby."

Mummy was sitting nearby in the sun, and she said, "Well, why not? There's the rain-water tank round by the stable. It is quite clean. You can both of you undress and get into it if you like. I'll come round presently with my camera and take a photo of you both."

Marjorie jumped with joy, but Jack looked worried. "I'm not used to cold baths," he said.

Mummy burst out laughing. "No boy ever liked cold water yet," she exclaimed, and her teasing helped Jack to pluck up courage.

So Jack and Marjorie scrambled out of their clothes, and they felt the warm spring sunshine kissing their bodies. Together they ran to the rain-water tank and jumped in. It seemed rather chilly at first, but after they had been splashing about for a few seconds they were used to the cold water.

Presently Mummy came over to the water tank with her camera. "You are shivering," she said. "Have a quick race round the lawn to get warm and dry, then I'll take a picture of you both."

The children darted off and very soon the bright sun had dried their skins. They came back and sat on the edge of the tank, resting their feet on the other edge.

"Now then, water babies," said Mummy, "it's lunch-time, and I hope you have caught me some fish in that old tank."

Marjorie and Jack both laughed at what Mummy said, and, at that instant, the camera went "click."

"Oh, can we see the picture?" cried both children, jumping down from their perch.

"No," answered Mummy. "The film has to be developed first, and I shall not get the picture back from the shop for about a week. Jack will be gone by then, but I will send him one. Now go and put your clothes on again."

Jack had gone home over a week before, but still the film from Mummy's camera had not been sent back from the shop. Every day when Marjorie came home from school she asked if it had come.

At last the day came when Mummy answered her question with a "yes" instead of a "no."

"Do let me see, Mummy," cried Marjorie.

Mummy pulled the photos out of their envelope and gave Marjorie the one of herself and her cousin Jack sitting like water babies on the edge of the old rain-water tank.

Marjorie looked first at the picture of herself, then at the picture of Jack.

"Jack's funny," she said at last; "he's not made like me, is he, Mummy?"

"Not quite like you, darling," answered Mummy. "It wouldn't do for little boys to be made exactly the same as little girls, or how should we know the difference? Boys have to have their hair cut short and be brought up differently from girls, and their bodies are made a little different, so that Mummies and Daddies know that they must be brought up as boys and not as girls."

"Must there *always* be two sorts of people?" asked Marjorie. "Couldn't everyone be brought up to be the same?"

"Oh no," replied Mummy, "that wouldn't be possible, and it wouldn't be nice. Boys grow up big and strong, usually much stronger than girls, and often much bigger. You see, they have to grow into daddies who are able to work hard and earn lots of money. Sometimes daddies have to fight. It would never do to bring up a boy so that he could not look after his family properly."

"And how shall I grow up?" asked Marjorie. "Won't I be big and strong too?"

"You will grow up as big and strong as you need to be," answered Mother, "but, you know, a mummy has to be soft and cuddlesome, and so girls grow up that way. I was a little girl once; you wouldn't have liked it if I had grown up exactly like Daddy, with a whiskery face and a great strong hard body, would you now?"

"Oh *no*," cried Marjorie. "I should want a mummy as well as a daddy. I wouldn't want you both to be the same."

"Well, dear," went on Mummy, "it is just as I said. There have to be two sorts of people, and that is why you and Jack are made differently. He will grow into the Man sort of person, and you will grow into the Woman sort of person. Are you pleased to think that you will be a woman one day?"

"Boys have a better time than girls," Marjorie answered slowly.

"Don't you believe it!" Mummy laughed. "A girl often gets everything she wants, just by having a pretty face. A boy has to work and fight if he is to have the things a man must have."

"That isn't fair," went on Marjorie.

"Oh yes, it all evens out nicely," said Mother; "the big strong man enjoys being a big strong man, and the pretty girl who has won a husband and a home and lots of babies finds that there is plenty of work to do to keep all her treasures sweet and nice. God is very fair, darling.

"You can keep that picture to remind you of all I have said, and now I will send a copy of it to Jack."